Epworth

Genera.
Ivor H. *J.*

The Gospel of Mark

Epworth Commentaries
Already published

Genesis
Clare Amos

The Book of Exodus
Richard Coggins

The Book of Deuteronomy
Ronald Clements

The Book of Job
C.S. Rodd

Psalms
Adrian Curtis

Isaiah 1–39
David Stacey

Isaiah 40–66
Michael Thompson

The Book of Jeremiah
Henry McKeating

The Book of Ezekiel
Charles Biggs

The Books of Amos and Hosea
Harry Mowvley

The Apocrypha
Ivor H. Jones

The Gospel of Matthew
Ivor H. Jones

The Gospel of Luke
Judith Lieu

The Gospel of John
Kenneth Grayston

The Acts of the Apostles
James D.G. Dunn

The Epistle to the Romans
Kenneth Grayston

The First Epistle to the Corinthians
Nigel Watson

The Second Epistle to the Corinthians
Nigel Watson

The Epistle to the Galatians
John Ziesler

The Epistle to the Ephesians
Larry J. Kreitzer

The Epistle to the Philippians
Howard Marshall

The Epistle to the Colossians
Roy Yates

The Pastoral Epistles
Margaret Davies

The Epistle to the Hebrews
Paul Ellingworth

The Epistle of James
Michael J. Townsend

The Epistles of Peter and Jude
David C. Horrell

The Johannine Epistles
William Loader

Revelation
Christopher Rowland

The Gospel of
MARK

C. S. RODD

EPWORTH

Copyright © C. S. Rodd 2005

British Library Cataloguing in Publication data

A catalogue record for this book is available
from the British Library

0 7162 0561 0

First published in 2005
by Epworth Press
4 John Wesley Road
Werrington
Peterborough PE4 6ZP

Typeset by regent Typesetting, London
Printed and bound in Great Britain by
William Clowes Ltd, Beccles, Suffolk

CONTENTS

General Introduction   ix
Bibliography   xi
Abbreviations   xiii

In Place of an Introduction   xv

   Note on 'literal' and 'literally'   xvii

Mark's Narrative   1

Mark's Portrait of Jesus   189

   Jesus Himself   195
   Christianity Today   197

To Christopher Evans
The best of supervisors

and in memory of
Leslie Mitton
The best of principals and a true friend

GENERAL INTRODUCTION

The *Epworth Preacher's Commentaries* that Greville P. Lewis edited so successfully in the 1950s and 1960s having now served their turn, the Epworth Press has commissioned a team of distinguished academics who are also preachers and teachers to create a new series of commentaries that will serve readers into the twenty-first century. We have taken the opportunity offered by the publication in 1989 of the Revised English Bible to use this very readable and scholarly version as the basis of our commentaries, and we are grateful to the Oxford and Cambridge University Presses for the requisite licence and for granting our authors generous access. They will nevertheless be free to cite and discuss other translations wherever they think that these will illuminate the original text.

Just as the books that make up the Bible differ in their provenance and purpose, so our authors will necessarily differ in the structure and bearing of their commentaries. But they will all strive to get as close as possible to the intention of the original writers, expounding their texts in the light of the place, time, circumstance and culture that gave them birth, and showing why each work was received by Jews and Christians into their respective Canons of Holy Scripture. They will seek to make full use of the dramatic advance in biblical scholarship worldwide but at the same time to explain technical terms in the language of the common reader, and to suggest ways in which Scripture can help towards the living of a Christian life today. They will endeavour to produce commentaries that can be used with confidence in ecumenical, multiracial and multifaith situations, and not by scholars only but by preachers, teachers, students, church members and anyone who wants to improve his or her understanding of the Bible.

Ivor H. Jones

BIBLIOGRAPHY

By far the best commentary for general purposes is:
  Hooker, Morna D., *The Gospel According to St Mark*, Black's New Testament Commentaries, A. & C. Black, 1991.

A larger commentary that I found valuable is:
  Marcus, J., *Mark 1–8*, Anchor Bible, Doubleday, 2000.

Other recent commentaries are:
  Evans, C.A., *Mark 8:27–16.20*, Word Biblical Commentary, Thomas Nelson, 2001.
  Guelich, Robert A., *Mark 1–8:26*, Word Biblical Commentary, Word Books, 1989.
  Gundry, Robert H., *Mark: A Commentary on His Apology for the Cross*, Eerdmans, 1993.*
  Keenan, John P., *The Gospel of Mark: A Mahayana Reading*, Orbis Books, 1995.
  Moloney, Francis J., *The Gospel of Mark: A Commentary*, Hendrickson, 2002.
  Tuckett, C.M., *Mark* in John Barton and John Muddiman (eds), *The Oxford Bible Commentary*, Oxford University Press, 2001.
  Van Iersel, Bas, *Reading Mark*, T&T Clark, 1989.

Several older commentaries still repay study:
  Cranfield, C.E.B., *The Gospel according to St Mark*, The Cambridge Greek Testament Commentary, Cambridge University Press, 4th edition, 1972.*
  Nineham, D.E., *Saint Mark*, The Pelican Gospel Commentaries, Penguin Books, 1963.
  Rawlinson, A.E.J., *St Mark with Introduction, Commentary and Additional Notes*, Westminster Commentaries, Methuen, 1925.
  Schweizer, Eduard, *The Good News according to Mark: A Commentary on the Gospel*, SPCK, 1971.
  Taylor, V., *The Gospel according to St Mark*, Macmillan, 1952.*
* On the Greek text

Studies of central issues relating to Mark include:

Best, Ernest, *Disciples and Discipleship: Studies in the Gospel according to Mark*, T&T Clark, 1986.

Best, Ernest, *Following Jesus: Discipleship in the Gospel of Mark*, JSNTSup 4, Sheffield University Press, 1981.

Best, Ernest, *Mark: The Gospel as Story*, T&T Clark, 1983.

Casey, Maurice, *Aramaic Sources of Mark's Gospel*, SNTSM 102, Cambridge University Press, 1998.

Hooker, Morna D., *The Message of Mark*, Epworth Press, 1983/1993.

Kingsbury, Jack Dean, *The Christology of Mark's Gospel*, Fortress Press, 1983.

Martin, Ralph P., *Mark: Evangelist and Theologian*, Paternoster Press, 1972.

Riches, John K., *Conflicting Mythologies: Identity Formation in the Gospels of Mark and Matthew*, Studies of the New Testament and Its World, T&T Clark, 2000.

Robinson, James M., *The Problem of History in Mark and other Marcan Studies*, Fortress Press, 1982.

Rodd, C.S., *The Teaching of Jesus in the Gospel according to St Mark* (unpublished University of London PhD thesis, 1976).

Santos, Narry F., *Slave of All. The Paradox of Authority and Servanthood in the Gospel of Mark*, JSNTSup 237, Sheffield Academic Press, 2003.

Telford, William R., *Mark*, New Testament Guides, Sheffield Academic Press, 1995.

Telford, William R., *The Theology of the Gospel of Mark*, New Testament Theology series, Cambridge University Press, 1999.

Telford, William R. (ed.), *The Interpretation of Mark*, Issues in Religion and Theology 7, SPCK, 1985, revised and enlarged edition, T&T Clark, 1995.

Tuckett, Christopher, *The Messianic Secret*, Issues in Religion and Theology 1, SPCK, 1983.

Weeden, T.J., *Mark: Traditions in Conflict*, Fortress Press, 1971.

For the development of Christology in the New Testament see:

Casey, Maurice, *From Jewish Prophet to Gentile God*, James Clarke, 1991.

Dunn, James D.G., *Christology in the Making: An Inquiry into the Origins of the Doctrine of the Incarnation*, SCM Press, 1980, 2nd edition, 1989.

ABBREVIATIONS

ad Magnes.	Ignatius of Antioch, *Letter to the Magnesians*
Antiquities	Josephus, *Antiquities of the Jews*
AV	Authorized Version, also known as the King James Version
CD	Damascus Document, Qumran community
CEV	Contemporary English Version
GNB	Good News Bible, also known as Today's English Version
m. Ber.	Mishnah, Tractate Berakhoth (all references to the Mishnah are taken from Danby, Herbert, *The Mishnah. Translated from the Hebrew with Introduction and Brief Explanatory Notes*, Oxford University Press, 1933)
m. Sanh.	Mishnah, Tractate Sanhedrin
m. Shab.	Mishnah, Tractate Shabbath
m. Shek.	Mishnah, Tractate Shekalim
m. Yad.	Mishnah, Tractate Yadaim
m. Yom.	Mishnah, Tractate Yoma
NAB	New American Bible
NEB	New English Bible
NIV	New International Version
NJB	New Jerusalem Bible
NRSV	New Revised Standard Version
REB	Revised English Bible
RSV	Revised Standard Version
Test. Naphtali	*Testament of Naphtali*
Vita	Josephus, *Life of Flavius Josephus*
War	Josephus, *War of the Jews*

IN PLACE OF AN INTRODUCTION

We come to the Gospel we call Mark through clouds of ignorance. We do not know who wrote it. We do not know when. We do not know why he wrote it, or for whom. We do not know whether it ends as he intended. We cannot be certain that it even begins as he originally wrote it. It is true that tradition has passed some information down to us, though whether it is correct information or not we cannot tell, and scholars have made their learned guesses, but the fact remains that we do not *know*.

This ignorance suggests that the most profitable way to approach the Gospel is simply to read it. For what we have is the written text. Yet even this is not without its difficulties. For one thing it was written in Greek, the everyday Greek that was spoken all over the Mediterranean world of the first Christian century. We read it in translation, and every translation is an interpretation. Every translator has had to decide which English word comes closest in meaning to the Greek. They have to resolve ambiguities in the meaning, for no phrase in one language will exactly represent the breadth of meaning in another. They have to decide how a sentence is to be interpreted, for the new language will state things differently. They have to select the style to be adopted in the translation. Is it to be as close to the original as possible or is it to be a virtual paraphrase in order to convey the underlying sense? Is the language to be 'high level' or colloquial? This commentary is based on REB, a good translation but not without its faults, as we shall see from time to time.

There is more. Once written, a book is on its own. The living voice is lost. The author has tossed his child upon the waters. All that we possess are symbols on a sheet of papyrus or vellum. As we read we put our own interpretation upon the words. We may even decide not to read the book at all, so that the poor orphan is totally bereft. We all know how easily what we write in a letter can be misunderstood. All down the centuries since Mark was first written readers have placed their own interpretations upon the words. Recently great interest has been shown in the 'afterlife' of biblical books and a whole series of commentaries is being prepared to examine and record this history of interpretation. Yet being aware of the extent to which the meanings we give to the words of the Bible are *our* meanings should make us more sensitive to what the writers originally intended. And if we wonder whether the original meaning is so much more important than the ways it has been understood in Christian worship and devotion, we might ask ourselves which is the 'true' meaning of a letter, what the writer intended or what the recipient read into it.

We approach Mark in this commentary simply as a text, but we shall also be very conscious that it comes from a society vastly different from our own. The scrolls and fragments that were discovered in the caves at Qumran by the Dead Sea give us glimpses of the ideas held by one group of Jews living at about the time of Jesus. We should not suppose that all the Jews in Palestine thought as this group did, but their ideas are much closer to the thought we find in the Gospels than our ways of thinking in the twenty-first century. Mark's book needs to be set within its own society.

Yet it is in this twenty-first century that we are living, and as we read Mark questions come into our minds that would never have been remotely imagined by those who listened to Mark's book being read for the first time. In this commentary we shall keep sensitively alert to the kind of questions that the society in which we live forces upon us.

One last point: Mark wrote a narrative. In narratives events are related in a sequence. What comes after is not known by the readers as they read. Although readers of a book can look back, and can even take a peep at the end to see how it worked out, the narrative itself moves only forward. In this commentary we shall give full weight to narrative and allow it to unfold.

This, then, is not a conventional, verse-by-verse commentary. We shall ignore the chapter divisions, and only refer to the verses as a convenient way of indicating the point we have reached. We shall refuse to be tied down to any particular method that has been devised by scholars. We shall not attempt to conceal our ignorance, and we shall not flinch from facing up to issues that are forced upon us by life in today's world. Although the gospel story is so well known to us, we shall try to read Mark as if it were the first account of Jesus that we have met. The commentary, therefore, mirrors Mark's narrative and is intended to be read straight through, like a novel, from the beginning to the end. Only when we have read the whole narrative shall we look at the portrait of Jesus that he has painted.

For this reason no list of 'sections' is included in the Table of Contents. I cannot, of course, prevent readers from turning to particular passages to see what I have said about them, and should they choose to do so the marginal references will quickly guide them to the place they are seeking. They must be warned, however, that they may well not find everything about the topic at that place, and only very rarely will they encounter a forward reference to later discussions.

Note on 'literal' and 'literally'

From time to time in this commentary I offer 'literal' translations of the Greek. Literal translation, however, is tricky. Strictly, I suppose, it should mean translating each word in its dictionary definition and retaining the word order. This can produce nonsense. I simply attempt to keep closer to the Greek than REB does, so that my 'literally' should strictly have been 'more literally' and must be understood in this sense.

MARK'S NARRATIVE

1.1   *The beginning of the gospel of Jesus Christ the Son of God.*
Immediately we are faced with five problems.

First, 'the Son of God' is omitted in some good manuscripts. Did Mark simply write 'the gospel of Jesus Christ'? Possibly, but since the title, the Son of God, was important to him and he uses it several times in his book, it is probably original.

Second, more than 1,900 years of Christian dogma stand between us and Mark. It is difficult for us to read Mark without the lumber of later doctrinal debates and the beliefs that we have learnt to regard as the foundation of the Christian religion. The words, 'the son of God', would have had a very different meaning from what they have to us who live on the other side of the Nicene Creed.

Third, by the time that Mark wrote, Christ had almost become a proper name. The Greek word literally means 'anointed' but Mark may not have consciously thought of this when he wrote 'Jesus Christ'. We shall have to wait for the narrative to unfold before we can decide whether he thought of Jesus as the Jewish messiah, the 'anointed one'.

Fourth, what place does the sentence have in the book? Is it a kind of title? If Mark was the first of the four books that we call Gospels, as it probably was, then it is extremely unlikely that he was referring to his own book, for there were no 'Gospels' yet. More probably he seems to be saying that 'the gospel of Jesus' is his account of the life and death of Jesus and this began with the work of John.

Fifth, the word translated 'gospel' means literally 'good news', but despite its popularity in Christian circles 'good news' sounds extremely odd in these days when news is out of date as soon as it is broadcast on radio or television. Perhaps REB is wise in retaining 'gospel'. If we wish to adopt a different term, we could say that Mark's narrative is the 'joyful message' about Jesus.

1.2–13   Imagine that we are the little group of Christians listening to Mark's narrative being read. He begins with a quotation from Isaiah, which he interprets as a prediction of John the Baptist. Then John appears, calling on his Jewish listeners to repent and receive baptism. Crowds flock to him and are baptized. Mark reports that John declares that someone is about to come who is mightier than he is. This mighty one will baptize them with the Holy Spirit. Jesus is among the crowds and John baptizes him. Mark then tells us that, as he came up out of the water, Jesus saw the Spirit coming down on him like a dove. There is a voice from heaven: 'You are my beloved Son; in you I take delight'. At once the Spirit drives Jesus into the desert, where he remains for 40 days and is tempted by Satan. It is a vivid story, filled with action. The whole account takes only a dozen verses.

Mark sees the appearance of John the Baptist on the banks of the Jordan as marking the beginning of the joyful message about Jesus. He recounts no stories about the birth of Jesus. There is no stable, no manger, no shepherds, no angels, no wise men, no star, no Herod. Mary is not mentioned. Instead John suddenly appears in the desert as a grown man. *We* construct Christmas by picking bits and pieces from Matthew and Luke and stitching them together. The *Revised Common Lectionary* does the same. After making a start on Mark's narrative, it plunders the other Gospels to give us the traditional story. Mark may not have known any legends such as these. If he did, they seem to have had no spiritual or theological meaning for him. What he regards as important is the coming of John.

1.2–3   *In the prophet Isaiah it stands written*. But it doesn't. At least not all of it. Although Mark ascribes his quotation to Isaiah, in fact it is pieced together from Exodus 23.20, Malachi 3.1 and Isaiah 40.3. And there are other oddities. *I am sending my herald ahead of you* and *A voice cries in the wilderness, 'Prepare the way for the Lord; clear a straight path for him'* appear to be quoted from the Greek translation of the Old Testament (usually called the Septuagint on account of the legend of the way it was made), while *he will prepare your way* is close to the Hebrew of Malachi 3.1 (the Greek has 'he will look attentively at a way before my face'). The mistake was noticed very early, for some manuscripts have 'in the prophets' instead of 'in the prophet Isaiah'. Obviously someone tried to correct the error. Perhaps Mark relied on an early Christian collection of texts, put together as evidence for the truth of the new faith, and did not realize that the phrases came from different places. Perhaps he said Isaiah because most of the quotation came from there. We do not know. But three important things come out of this strange feature.

First, the Bible of the early Christians was the Greek Septuagint. Although several of the New Testament writers translate directly from the Hebrew, Mark quotes from the Septuagint, which differs from the Hebrew in linking 'in the wilderness' with where the 'voice' is crying instead of where the way of the Lord is to be made. This points more directly to John, preaching in the desert, than the Hebrew does, though one would hardly describe the banks of the Jordan as the desert. The quotation from Isaiah also ends slightly differently from the Septuagint's 'Make the paths of our God straight' (the Hebrew has 'Make straight in the desert (or steppe) a highway for our God'). Mark's words are literally 'Make his paths straight'. Mark himself may have made the alteration, though he may have found it in his collection of texts, if that was where he obtained the quotations, or have quoted from memory, or remembered a text that was often mentioned in his church. Whatever it was, the effect is to fit the prophecy and his account of John closely together.

This leads to the second point. This is the only place in Mark's book where he himself introduces biblical prophecies with 'it stands written', although he includes several quotations of Scripture by Jesus. His use of the Bible here is not so very different from that of the men at Qumran. Among the scrolls found in the caves are a number that have been called 'commentaries'. They are not commentaries in our sense, however, for the writers take the biblical text, phrase by phrase, and point out events in their own times that it predicted. It seems that the early Christians mined the Old Testament in a similar way, looking for predictions of Jesus.

Third, in rabbinic Judaism the messenger in Malachi 3 was interpreted as Elijah. It may be that this is how the verse was understood at the time Mark was writing, and he accepted the Elijah tradition as a prediction of the appearance of John the Baptist. By linking the words of Malachi and Isaiah 40, however, and taking 'the Lord' to mean Jesus instead of God, as in the original, Mark declares that John was preparing the way for Jesus.

These three features raise an important issue regarding the meaning of the Old Testament for Christians. We have been taught by several generations of biblical scholars that the prophets were 'forthtellers not foretellers', addressing the men and women of their own days, not speaking of events in the distant future. This is in stark contrast to the way the Old Testament was read by the early Christians. They believed that Jesus was the messiah. They then searched the Old Testament for statements that they interpreted as predictions of Jesus. The belief came first, the collecting of prophecies second. The procedure is not so very different from that of liberal-minded Christians with a social concern who select a few verses from the Bible to support ethical stances that they have adopted on quite other grounds than the authority of Scripture, and who extend the meaning of the quotations to include the present moral issue.

This set of quotations, then, is offered by Mark as confirmation of his understanding of John the Baptist as the forerunner who proclaims the coming of the mighty one.

1.4–8   *John the Baptist appeared*. One of the difficulties in understanding any writing is knowing how much the writer assumes that his readers know. Even when he is writing directly to us the writer may think we know things that we do not know or have forgotten. It is particularly difficult when the writer is not addressing us. Mark introduces John without any explanation apart from the title, 'the Baptist' (not the noun found in 6.25 and 8.28 but literally 'the baptizer'). Mark assumes that his readers know who John was. But how much knowledge did he take for granted? We cannot be sure, but the question should make us look with extra care at what he actually does tell his readers about John.

He was *in the wilderness*. In the Exodus traditions the desert was where the Israelites sinned against Yahweh, but later it came to be thought of as the place where Israel's religion was pure and Israel was obedient to Yahweh. The Qumran community withdrew to the desert and supported this by quoting the same verse from Isaiah 40 that Mark does. By the time of Jesus there seems to have been a widespread belief that the messiah would appear

in the desert, and several leaders of revolutionary move-
ments collected their following there (Acts 21.38 and
Josephus, *War* II.13.4–5 [258–63]; VII.11.1 [437–41]). That
the banks of the Jordan would not normally be described
as the wilderness shows that to Mark the phrase was not
so much a historical description as an indication that the
appearance of John fulfilled the prediction of Isaiah 40.3.

The way John was dressed is significant. The *rough cloak
of camel's hair* marked him out as a prophet. In 2 Kings 1.8,
Elijah is described by King Ahaziah's messengers as 'a
hairy man with a leather belt round his waist'. His food of
locusts and wild honey has less obvious significance. It
seems that Mark is presenting John as Elijah, predicted as
coming to prepare for the messiah, though we cannot be
absolutely sure, since he quoted Malachi 3.1, but not 4.5,
where Elijah is named.

Ought it not to strike us as odd that Mark says that John
was *proclaiming a baptism*? One normally practises or performs baptism, or simply 'baptizes'; why 'proclaim'?
Probably it is to maintain and emphasize the link between
John and the quotations in vv. 2–3. John is the 'herald', the
'voice' predicted by the prophets.

The most characteristic thing about John was that he
baptized people in the river Jordan. The Jewish historian
Josephus, writing at the end of the first century, agrees,
although he places rather more emphasis on John's call to
the Jews 'to lead righteous lives, to practise justice
towards their fellows and piety towards God, and so
doing join in baptism. In his [John's] view this was a
necessary preliminary if baptism was to be acceptable to
God. They must not employ it to gain pardon for whatever sins they committed, but as a consecration of the
body implying that the soul was already thoroughly
cleansed by right behaviour' (*Antiquities* XVIII.5.2 [117]).

Mark describes the baptism that John proclaimed as
'of repentance to forgiveness of sins' (in a literal translation of the Greek). REB translates this with *in token of
repentance, for the forgiveness of sins*. This suggests to us
today that it was an outward indication that they had
repented and that by confessing their sins in this public
way they secured forgiveness. Mark meant something
rather different.

Washings are frequent in the Old Testament, usually as

a means of removing uncleanness (e.g. Lev. 15.5, 8, 13, 16), and when a prophet tells his hearers to 'wash and be clean' (Isa. 1.16) we are wrong in supposing that he is referring to the removal of sin or guilt. It is the impurity (the 'blood on their hands') that is removed by the washing; the sins are to be 'put away' and a new life of goodness and justice to be lived. Uncleanness and sin (and guilt) belong to two different spheres of thought. It is true that sin makes a person unclean, but what washing and sacrifice remove is the uncleanness, not the guilt, for which forgiveness must be sought. By the time of Jesus it seems to have been normal for all converts to Judaism to take a ritual bath, presumably to remove the uncleanness of being a Gentile. Mark would also have known Christian baptism, although he does not mention it in his book. If his intended readers were also Christians (as seems probable, though we do not know for certain) they too would have been baptized.

Given this background, how did Mark understand John's baptism? Before we can answer this question we need to look at the words that Mark quotes. John foretells the coming of a mighty one and declares: *I have baptized you with water; he will baptize you with the Holy Spirit* (more literally 'in holy spirit' – expressed differently from 'with water' in most manuscripts, although some omit 'in' and so have 'with holy spirit', exactly parallel to 'with water'). With our knowledge of Acts, we tend to interpret the baptism with the Holy Spirit as a reference to the coming of the Spirit at Pentecost. What Mark thought John's words meant, however, is impossible to say. Possibly he knew some such account of the coming of the Spirit as Luke describes in Acts 2, but there is no evidence of this, and we must not interpret Mark on the basis of Luke–Acts. Perhaps he assumes that his readers will connect their own Christian receiving of the Spirit with this prophecy, but again this is a mere guess. If we read on we shall discover that Mark never describes Jesus 'baptizing' anyone with the Spirit. Indeed, apart from these words by John and the coming of the Spirit on Jesus at his baptism (1.10, 12), he mentions the Holy Spirit only three other times (3.29; 12.36; 13.11). Our present purpose is to try to discover what the words that Mark wrote meant, so that we shall not rush, as many do, to compare the Gospels with each other and wonder whether John actually said: 'he will baptize you in holy spirit and fire' (or even 'in wind and fire'), symbols of judgement.

Mark emphasizes that John was the 'voice' predicted by Isaiah, the messenger, who probably was thought of as Elijah. It seems likely, therefore, that his understanding of John and Jesus was determined by the idea that the 'messianic' age was dawning. I have placed 'messianic' in inverted commas to distinguish it from our use of the word. In the two centuries before the turn of the eras, there were many hopes of a change of fortunes for Israel and the arrival of a golden age. These hopes were expressed in several different ways, sometimes with a messianic figure, human or heavenly, sometimes as brought about by the direct intervention of God. The idea of the beginning of a new age, sharply different from the miseries of the present is found in all of them.

If Mark believed that a new age was dawning, that the prophecies about its coming were being fulfilled in John, that John foretold the coming of one far greater than he was and that this greater one would baptize 'in holy spirit', the baptism that John proclaimed was more than just a token that individuals were sorry for their wrong-doing and wanted forgiveness from God. In the first place, he was calling on Jews, not Gentiles, to be baptized. Even if it was similar to the washing that Gentiles undertook when they converted to Judaism, it could not be the same when demanded of Jews who were already God's people. It is true that the members of the Qumran community accepted many washings, but that was to ensure their complete ritual purity as they sought to keep the Law. John's call to baptism was different. It seems to have been once for all. Most importantly, it was part of the events that the prophets had foretold. By repenting of the past, confessing their sins, and being baptized, those who flocked to John were preparing themselves for that new age that God was about to bring in. To Mark, writing about 'the gospel of Jesus Christ, the son of God', the new age arrived with Jesus.

We still need to try to understand what this baptism in 'holy spirit' is. Mark depicts John as believing that, in order to make them partakers of that new age, the 'mightier one' would baptize his followers in a new way – with 'holy spirit'. John could only have thought of the 'spirit' in Old Testament terms. There the spirit is one way among several that express Yahweh's power and activity, and it stands alongside such other symbols as his 'mighty arm'. John probably believed that the coming one would empower his followers in much the same way that Yahweh empowered Gideon or Saul, the great difference being that he would empower all of them, not just chosen leaders. Because Mark never describes Jesus as baptizing his followers with the spirit, it is impossible to know what his precise beliefs were.

1.9–11   Mark links almost all his stories by 'and'. This is a common Hebrew practice, where even books can begin with 'And' (e.g. Jonah, Esther, omitted by all the English translations), and one scholar who attempts to reconstruct the Aramaic behind Mark's narratives begins most sentences with 'and'. The Greek papyri discovered in Egypt, however, show that it was also a feature of the ordinary Greek spoken at the time. Matthew and Luke often change Mark's 'and' to 'but' or 'then', especially at the beginning of a story. To provide a more idiomatic English style REB omits most of these 'and's, and in common with several modern translations (and even the Bible Society Greek text) it inserts headings that split up the continuous narrative which Mark wrote. Chopping up the Gospels into tiny fragments is partly the result of form criticism, and looking at the individual stories separately has its place. But Mark's narrative flows on.

Jesus joins the crowds flocking from the countryside of Judaea and the city of Jerusalem to be baptized. Mark mentions Jesus as suddenly as he mentioned John, and equally without any explanation. Again our attention is directed to what Mark tells his readers. He says that he came from *Nazareth in Galilee*, but makes no comment on the place. Nazareth is not mentioned in the Old Testament or the Jewish traditions preserved in the Talmud, and Josephus never refers to it. Perhaps Mark mentions it simply as a fact. Perhaps it is Galilee that is important to him, for he seems to make a contrast later in his book between Galilee and Jerusalem. Just possibly the coming of the messiah from an obscure village is part of the picture of Jesus as a hidden messiah that Mark impresses on his whole account.

Jesus is simply one of the many people who came and were *baptized in the Jordan*. The messenger does not recognize the greater one when he arrives. Mark does not say that Jesus confessed his sins like the others, but since he has stressed that repentance and the forgiveness of sins were involved in John's baptism, he presumably expected his readers to assume that there was no difference between Jesus and the rest of the crowds. It presented problems for the other Gospel writers. Mark has no difficulty with it at all, and it is very unlikely that he thought that Jesus was merely identifying himself with sinners, as some commentators suggest. But Mark has no interest in the psychological or moral state of Jesus, and he would not expect his readers to have any such interest either. His concern is with what happened immediately after Jesus had been baptized.

As he was coming up out of the water, he saw the heavens break open and the Spirit descend on him, like a dove. And a voice came from heaven: 'You are my beloved son; in you I take delight.' John predicted that the greater one would baptize with the Holy Spirit, but Jesus receives the Spirit. Again some questions are too hasty. What actually happened? Was it a visionary experience? Did John and the others who were there hear the voice, or only Jesus? And what about the dove? We must stick firmly to what Mark wrote. 'To see' can mean 'to understand', 'to grasp a truth', but we should not adopt this too quickly here and talk theology, saying that the breaking open of the heavens was simply an image for revelation or even that it is linked with such Old Testament passages as Isaiah 64.1 and points to a fresh activity by God in saving his people. The Old Testament prophets 'saw' things, and there is no reason to question that Mark means precisely what he says. Jesus 'saw' a cleft in the sky and 'saw' the Spirit coming down. At that time earth and sky were thought to be exactly as they look. It was recognized that some natural events were normal and others unusual, but there was no conception of an independent physical universe. The picture that Mark draws would have nothing of the impossible about it that it has for us. Jesus saw the divine power that Mark calls 'spirit' coming down upon him from the break in the sky.

What precisely 'like a dove' means is not clear, but it

9

seems difficult to picture anything else than that the spirit was in the form of a pigeon. It must have had some shape to be seen, so that to suggest that the phrase merely points to the way the spirit descended seems an unnecessary attempt to make the story conform to our conception of the universe. So far as we know, God's spirit was not linked to the image of a dove in the first century, although later rabbinic writings regard the voice of the turtle-dove in the Song of Songs 2.12 as the voice of the spirit and speak of the spirit hovering over the waters in Genesis 1.2 as like a dove. It is more important to remember that Mark did not think of the spirit as the Third Person of the Trinity. In the Old Testament, as we have seen, the spirit is simply one way of expressing God's presence and power among others. Prophets were clothed with the spirit, and the coming of the spirit on Jesus need be no more than marking him out as a prophet. There were, after all, other charismatics in Palestine at about this time. Mark, however, probably regarded the descent of the spirit as indicating that Jesus was the 'son of God' (in his sense of the term).

This is confirmed by the voice. God spoke directly to prophets and kings in the Old Testament, and the words of the voice are similar to Psalm 2.7 and Isaiah 42.1, and echo several other passages, although they are not an exact quotation, either of the Septuagint or the Hebrew. The king was regarded as a son of God. Some have seen in the phrase 'my beloved son' an indication of unique sonship, since 'beloved' was used in the Septuagint of an only child in Genesis 22.2 and elsewhere, but 'son of God' certainly did not carry credal overtones in the time of Mark and the term did not indicate a pre-existent 'Son' who became incarnate. For this reason it will be better to write 'son of God' with a small letter. The title 'son of God' was of great importance for Mark, whether he wrote it at the very beginning of his book or not.

It is difficult to avoid talking theology here and asking if the words spoken by the voice indicate that God 'adopted' Jesus as his son at his baptism. Psalm 2 is quoted several times in the New Testament. It is often claimed that in this psalm God 'adopts' the king as his 'son'. There is no evidence of the practice of adoption in the Old Testament, however, although it is found elsewhere in the ancient

Middle East, and it may be that modern ideas are being imported into the psalm. Whether the psalm was interpreted in the first century as a prophecy of the messiah is also doubtful. Fragments from the Qumran have been found in which the messiah is spoken of as God's son, possibly with reference to this psalm. Some later Christians taught that Jesus was a human being who was adopted by God, and this was condemned as heretical. How far back the idea can be traced is uncertain. Romans 1.3–4 and Acts 13.33 may indicate that one of the earliest views was that Jesus became God's 'son' on the day of the resurrection. That Mark believed that God 'adopted' Jesus as his 'son' at his baptism, that he *became* the 'son of God' by receiving the spirit and through the words spoken by the voice, cannot be ruled out.

If we interpret the incident as a mystical vision that Jesus experienced, we need to be clear that this is *our* interpretation. The text cannot forbid us from describing it in any way we choose, but we should not suppose that it was how Mark understood it, or that this is how his readers would have taken it. They were not interested in the personal psychology of Jesus, or how he became aware that he was the messiah. We are also inclined to ask how Mark knew about the spirit and the voice if it was a personal experience of which the bystanders and John saw and heard nothing, and wonder whether Jesus told his disciples about it. Mark is writing from faith, and tells the story in order to confirm that Jesus is the 'son of God' of the opening of his narrative. We shall never know where he obtained it from.

1.12–13   *At once the Spirit drove him out into the wilderness, and there he remained for forty days tempted by Satan. He was among the wild beasts; and angels attended to his needs.* To understand Mark we must put out of our minds the account of the temptations that we know so well from Matthew and Luke, and look at the bare words that stand here, a single sentence in the Greek.

The power of the spirit is immediately active, forcing Jesus to go into the desert. The idea of the spirit is again closer to that of the Old Testament than to the Holy Spirit of Christian theology. It drives Jesus in just the same way that the spirit drove prophets and others (cf. Judg. 11.29; 14.6, 19; 1 Sam. 10.10; 1 Kgs. 18.12; 2 Kgs. 2.16). This is not

11

later trinitarianism. Indeed, if we take the spirit to be the Third Person of the Trinity, the account of God the Holy Spirit forcing God the Son to go into the desert can be nothing but utterly confusing, if not actually absurd.

Mark has told us that John was already in the desert, so that it is obvious that historical detail is not in the forefront of his mind. The emphasis is upon the dangers and deprivation, as the mention of the 'wild beasts' shows. In some Old Testament and later writings they were thought of as demons, but this does not seem to be so here. To suggest that Mark is thinking of the reversal of the Fall, because a few Old Testament descriptions of the happy future age include the expulsion, if not the annihilation, of all dangerous animals (Ezek. 34.25, 28), or a time of peace with them (Hos. 2.18; Isa. 11.6–9), goes well beyond what is probable. Mark says no more than that Jesus was 'with the wild animals'. As for the angels, perhaps we are to think of them as bringing Jesus food, as ravens and an angel did for Elijah (1 Kgs. 17.6; 19.5–8). It is possible that Mark thought of the wild beasts as hostile to Jesus, while the angels support him. A Jewish work probably written in the second century BC sets together a promise that the devil will flee from you, wild animals will be afraid of you, and angels will stand by you (*Test. Naphtali* 8.4; cf. also Ps. 91.11–13).

Why Mark tells us that Jesus spent 40 days in the wilderness is also not immediately apparent. Moses spent 40 days on the sacred mountain of Sinai (Exod. 24.18; 34.28), and Elijah travelled for 40 days to the same mountain (1 Kgs. 19.8), but both of them were with God and not with Satan. Mark makes no allusion to these stories, and probably the 'forty days' is no more than a conventionally long time.

In the Old Testament 'the satan' (the adversary) is one of Yahweh's servants, a member of his heavenly court (Job 1.6–12; 2.1–7; Zech. 3.1–2), who was a kind of police investigator and public prosecutor, with a suspicious frame of mind. The word only became a proper name in 1 Chronicles 21.1 and in later Jewish writings. Here he is envisaged much as our ideas of 'the Devil', but we must not think of him as a fallen angel. We may wish to treat the entire incident symbolically, but to Mark and his readers Satan, the wild beasts and the angels are equally real. This does not mean that they have no symbolic meaning, as the wilderness had, but the force of the symbolism depends upon the acceptance of the reality.

The account of the temptations in the other two gospels makes it easy for us to interpret them psychologically as the way Jesus thought out what being the messiah was to mean for him. There is nothing of this in Mark. Neither should we piously spiritualize Jesus's temptation, as reflecting the way high moments of emotion are often followed by depression, nor as providing an example of how we should ourselves resist temptation. All this may well be true of religious experience, but it is foreign to Mark's narrative. Some have seen Mark's brief account as the description of a battle with Satan. This also is far from obvious from the sentence that Mark wrote. If he thought of it as a battle, he gives no hint as to its outcome. Perhaps he assumes that it would be obvious that the 'son of God' would defeat Satan. Yet although he says no more here than that Jesus was 'tempted', possibly 'tested', by Satan, later in his book he depicts a struggle between Jesus and various forces of evil. Conflict is never far away.

1.14–15   *After John had been arrested, Jesus came into Galilee.* John the Baptist is important to Mark, and he states that Jesus's work began only after John's work came to an end. 'Arrested' is an inadequate translation of a word that can mean 'to deliver up a prisoner' (as in Matt. 5.25), but has deep theological overtones: John was handed over by God into the power of his enemies. There is a strong sense in which everything has been determined by God in advance. John came as the messenger predicted by Isaiah. Having uttered this message and baptized Jesus his work was complete.

Galilee was not the region of Palestine where many expected the messiah to appear. There is obviously a historical basis to the activity of Jesus here, but Galilee seems to have had a special meaning for Mark. He begins his account of Jesus with his coming from Nazareth and continues with his coming to Galilee. We may wonder whether the Christian community to which he belonged lived in Galilee. Did Galilee (over against Judaea and Jerusalem) have symbolic meaning for Mark? Galilee is mentioned very rarely in the Old Testament, but one of these is Isaiah 9.1, which introduces the prophecy of the 'child' who brings in the new golden age. Mark, however, does not refer to this passage (contrast Matt. 4.15). Or is it simply a historical fact that Galilee was the main area where Jesus worked? We cannot answer any of these questions.

Jesus comes *proclaiming the gospel of God*. The 'gospel of Jesus Christ' in 1.1 has become the 'gospel of God'. It may be that now it means 'the message *from* God', but given Mark's overall view it seems more likely that it is 'the message *about* God's action', action that controls the activities of all the actors in the drama. This is supported by the opening words of the summary of Jesus's message: *The time has arrived*. The meaning is plainer if we keep to the older translations: 'the time is fulfilled'. Now is the moment when the plan, formed of old and foretold by the prophets, is going to be carried out.

This is made more explicit in the next phrase, *the kingdom of God is upon you*. In Mark's book Jesus never explains what he means by 'the kingdom of God' and Mark seems to have assumed that his readers know. There has been an enormous discussion about the term, and most scholars tell us that the phrase meant the 'kingly rule' of God. The exact phrase does not occur in the Old Testament, although God is referred to as a king and as ruling over the world. In Mark, however, the central meaning is fairly clear. He looked forward to the end of the world, when God would truly be king. This is why he uses the phrase in several different senses, as we shall see as we read on.

The meaning of the Greek verb translated 'is upon you' has also caused much debate. Three possibilities have been proposed: 'has drawn near' (or 'is close at hand'), 'has arrived', and 'is in process of coming'. While the last two interpretations used to be popular, scholarship now seems to be returning to the traditional 'has drawn near'. Mark, however, believed that God would exert his rule over the world fully only at some point in the future. With the coming of Jesus it has drawn near.

By linking Jesus's arrival in Galilee with the arrest of John the Baptist Mark says that the sequence of events that will lead up to God's universal reign has been set in motion with the preaching of John the Baptist. The reign itself will come only in the future, but because the events are predetermined and must run their course now that they have begun, the kingdom has truly 'drawn near' – hence the note of urgency.

The rest of Mark's account of the message of Jesus, *Repent, and believe the gospel*, is similar to that of John, but the repentance is linked with believing in the message rather than with baptism and forgiveness. Like the rest of the summary, it is highly compressed. We today tend to fill out 'the gospel' with our understanding of the justifying faith in Jesus that Paul taught or the Johannine faith in the Son, sent by God out of his love for the world so that men and women might have eternal life. Taken at their face value, however, it is difficult to see what meaning Mark's words could have had for those listening to Jesus for the first time. The content of 'the gospel', what it is all about, is no more explained than the meaning of 'the kingdom of God' was. How can you believe a message if you are not told what it is? It is strange that Mark introduces these words right at the start of his book without explanation.

1.16–18   Mark's narrative runs on. Incident follows incident: Jesus's baptism – his 40 days in the desert – his coming into Galilee – his teaching expressed in a single sentence in the Greek. Now, walking along by the sea of Galilee (Mark stresses Galilee yet again) he sees two fishermen and utters the strange command: *Come, follow me, and I will make you fishers of men*. It is, of course, a pun: the 'fishermen' catching fish will become 'fishermen' catching people. The metaphor is found in Jeremiah, but as a threat: 'I shall send for many fishermen, says the LORD, and they will fish for them. After that I shall send for many hunters, and they will hunt them from every mountain and hill' (Jer. 16.16). Jesus could not have meant that Simon and Andrew were to hunt out evil men and women and bring them to judgement. So it is an odd command, but this is not the main peculiarity. In the time of Jesus teachers collected disciples to accompany them, listen to their teaching, and learn it. The pun makes it clear that Mark saw the work of a disciple as attracting other people to the Christian faith. It seems likely that he wishes to urge his Christian readers to do the same.

With the same rapid pace, Mark tells us: *At once they left their nets and followed him*. To ask whether Simon and Andrew may perhaps have met Jesus before, or to suggest that it was the strength of Jesus's personality that made them drop everything and immediately obey his call, is beside the point. Mark describes the two men responding to Jesus as true disciples should – at once and without any questioning.

1.19–20   Mark repeats the scene, perhaps to emphasize the way the call of Jesus is to be obeyed. This time James and John are mending their nets, but when Jesus calls them they respond equally abruptly, leaving their father in the boat and following him. The mention of *hired men* reveals that the Zebedee family were well-to-do fishermen, but this is not the point that Mark is making. Like Simon and Andrew, James and John immediately drop what they are doing, leave their father and the fishing business, and follow Jesus.

1.21–8   Rushing on with his account, Mark describes the visit by Jesus to the synagogue in Capernaum on the next sabbath. This reveals further characteristics of his narrative. Jesus *began to teach* and drives out a demon from a man *possessed by an unclean spirit*. Mark depicts Jesus as a wandering teacher and exorcist.

Although he includes less teaching than the other Gospels do, Mark stresses that Jesus was a teacher, and that *the people were amazed at his teaching, for unlike the scribes, he taught with a note of authority*. Judging from the evidence of the later rabbinic writings, the scribes would have taught by referring to earlier rabbis and traditions, although some leading rabbis seem to have offered new teaching or their own fresh interpretations of older traditions. Jesus spoke on his own authority. It seems that for Mark the fact that Jesus taught with authority was more important than the content of his teaching. To us this seems strange. The greater the authority, the greater, we might think, the importance of the actual words that were spoken. We wish to know what Jesus taught, because we suppose that this teaching will give answers to our moral problems and show us more about God. Mark, intent on presenting 'Jesus Christ, the son of God', finds part of the answer to this in the authority with which he taught in the synagogue. Who Jesus is was more important to him than what he said.

The exorcisms create considerable problems for us, mainly because we no longer attribute mental illness to being possessed by demons. To understand Mark it is necessary to become clear about the first-century world. Although there are few overt references to demons in the Old Testament, they are frequently mentioned in the writings from the last couple of centuries BC. In the time of Jesus men and women believed that beyond the visible world was the world of spirits and demons, and various kinds of sickness, such as mental illness, epilepsy and even deafness were attributed to them. Jews and others in the time of the Roman Empire practised exorcism, as did the early Christian Church. How people react to something that happens depends upon their view of the world. Mark depicts Jesus as a particularly powerful and effective exorcist. In the battle with the unclean spirits Jesus is victor. The point of this story as Mark tells it is that Jesus's effectiveness as an exorcist is further evidence that he is 'the son of God'.

There is more. The man utters the words, but it is the unclean spirit who is speaking: *I know who you are – the Holy One of God*. So far as is known, the expected messiah was not called 'the Holy One' in Judaism. In the Old Testament the term is applied to Aaron (Ps. 106.16, REB 'consecrated to the LORD') and Elisha (2 Kgs. 4.9) as well as to God himself (Isa. 40.25; 57.15). Precisely what the address implied, therefore, is uncertain. Mark probably took it to mean that the spirit, despite being 'unclean', knows who Jesus is. Jesus responds with the command: *Be silent*. Literally the word means, 'Be muzzled' (as in the Septuagint of Deut. 25.4, quoted in 1 Tim. 5.18, of muzzling oxen), and has been found in magic spells from the period. It seems to have been commonly used in exorcisms. The command, however, has a special meaning for Mark. Jesus is depicted as commanding the spirit to be silent because it has revealed who he is.

After the spirit had thrown the man into *convulsions* and uttered a *loud cry*, it *left him*. Since spirits are invisible, Mark presumably thought that the evidence that the unclean spirit had gone was that the man now acted normally. In some accounts of exorcisms from about this time spirits reveal that they have left a person by performing some action, such as overturning a jar. This is not found here, but we should not suppose that the absence of any such action places Mark's account on a 'higher' spiritual plane. He believed that demons existed and would have found no difficulty with such stories. Again everyone is *amazed*, and now they link the *authority* of Jesus's *new kind of teaching* with his power to make the unclean spirits *obey* him. Instantly Jesus becomes famous everywhere throughout Galilee. This is further evidence that Mark's central concern is with the authority and power of Jesus.

We must not hurriedly rationalize this story by suggesting that Jesus's powerful personality and his obvious concern for the man restored him to health. Nor must we use it to justify practising exorcism today. The mind remains mysterious, but research has helped us to understand more of its hidden workings. What we cannot do is still hold to the world of demons and unclean spirits that Mark knew.

1.29–31   The healing of Peter's mother-in-law follows, showing that Jesus's power extended to other illnesses than mental disorders. While the *fever* is not attributed to an evil spirit, the fact that it 'leaves' the woman, even though it is not the same Greek verb as in the previous story, suggests that Mark thought of the fever as 'personal' in some way and subject to the authority of Jesus. No words are spoken, and the healing is by touch. Neither is there any mention of faith. Mark knows that Jesus has the power to heal her, and the fact that the disciples told Jesus about Peter's mother-in-law probably shows that they expected him to be able to do something about it.

1.32–4   No work is to be done on the sabbath, so that it is only after the sabbath ended (at sunset) that the people of the town *brought to him all who were ill or possessed by demons*. Mark distinguishes between those suffering from *various diseases* and those from whom Jesus *drove out many demons*. Although he has stressed that Jesus *taught* with authority, so far he points the reader to Jesus's authority as a *healer* and *exorcist*. This presents us with a considerable problem today. We look to doctors and hospitals for healing, and do not believe that mental illness is caused by demons. We might wonder whether those liturgies that imply that healing today is identical with healing in the time of Jesus are not misleading.

Again Mark emphasizes that Jesus *would not let the demons speak, because they knew who he was* (literally, 'knew him'). Some manuscripts have 'knew him to be Christ', but REB follows what is probably the correct text. The demons supernaturally know the truth, that Jesus is the 'son of God', and Jesus does not allow them to speak and reveal the fact. This is a further example of the stress that Mark places on the refusal of Jesus to allow who he is to be known. We may wonder why.

1.35–9   *Very early next morning he got up and went out. He went away to a remote spot and remained there in prayer.* Mark emphasizes that it was still night when Jesus got up and that he went to 'a desert place'. The desert may have had symbolic meaning for Mark, but there is no need to suppose that he thought of Jesus going to the desert to rethink his mission – was he to be a healer and exorcist or a preacher and teacher? We must beware of allowing modern susceptibilities to influence our interpretation. With our embarrassment at the prominence that Mark has given to the healings and exorcisms of the day before, it is easy for us to suppose that Jesus left Capernaum in order to escape from the pressure to heal and cast out demons, and free himself to pray and teach. Jesus's words when Peter and his companions catch up with him and tell him that everyone is looking for him are *Let us move on to the neighbouring towns, so that I can proclaim my message there as well*, and might encourage this idea. For Mark, however, the exorcisms were just as important as the teaching. He tells us that Jesus then *went through the whole of Galilee, preaching in their synagogues and driving out demons.* Jesus left Capernaum not to avoid being overwhelmed by people seeking healing, but in order to extend his work into the whole of Galilee. Driving out the demons is part of the message that the kingdom of God will shortly arrive. It is impossible to read Mark attentively and push the demons aside. Only if we are prepared to enter imaginatively into Mark's world shall we be in a position to come to terms with the meaning of his book.

1.40–5   The next incident that Mark records is the healing of a *leper*. REB keeps the word. Indeed, there seems to be no alternative, even though it is well known that what the man was suffering from was not Hansen's disease. To understand this story it is necessary to go back to the Old Testament, with its concern for 'purity' and its fear of the 'uncleanness' produced by such things as menstruation, childbirth, mould on buildings, and skin rashes that led to a piebald appearance. All of the attempts to find another word in translations of the Old Testament are unsatisfactory because they fail to capture this sense of uncleanness – 'a contagious skin-disease' (NJB), 'an infectious skin disease' (NIV), 'a malignant skin-disease' (NEB), 'a virulent skin disease' (REB), 'a dreaded skin disease' (GNB). If 'leprosy' is to be avoided, GNB is perhaps the best, but even it fails to convey the sense of uncleanness and ostracism both from God and from human beings that the patches on the skin involved. In Mark only NJB ('a man suffering from a virulent skin-disease') and GNB ('a dreaded skin disease') avoid the word 'leper', but several add a note that the term can refer to several skin diseases, not necessarily leprosy in the modern sense.

The point of the story is not that the man had an incurable disease ('leprosy' obviously could disappear, as the requirements set out in the Old Testament laws for removing the uncleanness after the skin was again healthy show), nor that his appearance was unpleasant, but that he was ritually unclean. To come into contact with a leper would make one unclean, yet Jesus *stretched out his hand* and *touched him*. Does Mark imply that uncleanness cannot pass to Jesus as 'the son of God'? He then spoke the words *be clean*, and *the leprosy left him immediately*, as if it were a demon. Jesus told the man to do as the Law required, to *show* himself *to the priest*, who would check that the leprosy had disappeared, and then to *make the offering laid down by Moses for your cleansing*. To us this sounds like a thank-offering, but it was not so. The rites in Leviticus 14.2–32 are complex, involving two birds, two male lambs and one ewe-lamb, with the alternative of one lamb and two turtle-doves or pigeons for those too poor to offer three lambs. All this was to remove the uncleanness of the leprosy and shows how seriously uncleanness was regarded. Mark depicts Jesus as fully accepting both the ideas of uncleanness and the need to obey the Law.

The phrase *that will certify the cure* does not exactly represent what Mark wrote, which is literally 'for (or as) a witness to them'. It is uncertain whether these words are to be linked with 'laid down by Moses' (Moses decreed the sacrifices as a witness) or whether the witness is to convince the leper's contemporaries. There is nothing to show to whom 'them' refers. In Leviticus 13 the priests determine whether skin disease is leprosy and if it has disappeared, but the rites in Leviticus 14 are not a symbol that the leprosy has been healed.

There are further difficulties in this apparently straight-forward narrative. REB says that Jesus was *moved to anger* when the leper approached him. This is what a few manuscripts read. The others, including almost all of the early ones, have 'was moved with compassion', and this is what most of the other modern translations adopt. It is difficult to decide which is original. The two Greek words are so different in form and sound that the change must have been deliberate. Presumably the translators of REB found it impossible to believe that anyone would have changed 'being filled with compassion' to 'being angry', but we must avoid being influenced by our own attitudes or by what we imagine Jesus's reaction would have been. A scribe who altered compassion to anger may have thought that Jesus was angry because the leper ought not to have come to him. If the anger goes back to Mark, he probably regarded it as directed against the demons and the forces of evil. A similar problem occurs when Jesus sends the man away. *Then he dismissed him with this stern warning* is REB's translation. The Greek is very harsh and implies that Jesus admonished the man and then sent him away (the verb is the same as when the spirit 'drove' Jesus into the desert (1.12) and when he drove out demons (1.34, 39)). In the strongest terms, Jesus commands the man to tell no one, just as he muzzled the demon in the synagogue (1.25) and would not let the demons speak (1.34).

The man disobeyed Jesus and *made the whole story public, spreading it far and wide*. Mark expresses it in Christian language: 'he began to preach' (proclaim, the word used of Jesus in 1.14 and 1.38) and 'spread the word' (a more general phrase). The man acts like a disciple, in spite of the stern command of Jesus. So great is the popular fervour this arouses that Jesus cannot *show himself in any town*, but stays *outside in remote places* (again Mark has 'desert places').

2.1–12   Jesus does not stay long in the desert, however, and *after some days* we find him back in Capernaum. Crowds gather and Jesus is depicted as *proclaiming the message to them* (literally, 'he spoke the word to them') inside a house, with others pressing round the door. The dramatic scene is vividly described, with the paralysed man carried on a pallet bed, his four friends digging up the brushwood and clay roof to let him down directly to Jesus, the striking words of Jesus, *'My son, your sins are forgiven'*, the thoughts of the scribes, *'How can the fellow talk like that? It is blasphemy! Who but God can forgive sins?'*, Jesus's awareness of what they are thinking, and his questions, *'Why do you harbour such thoughts? Is it easier to say to this paralysed man, "Your sins are forgiven," or to say "Stand up, take your bed, and walk"?'*, followed by *'But to convince you that the Son of Man has authority on earth to forgive sins'* – he turned to the paralysed man – *'I say to you, stand up, take your bed, and go home.'* The story ends with the man immediately taking up his bed and going out *in full view of them all*, and the astonished reaction of the crowds, *'Never before have we seen anything like this.'*

Perhaps our first reaction to the story is to interpret it as the healing of a psychosomatic illness, and so to make it no longer a miracle but the cure of a man whose sense of guilt brought on his paralysis. This may have been so, but Mark certainly regarded it as a miracle. It is not primarily as a miracle, however, that he includes it in his book. In my summary I quoted all the words that were spoken, including the thoughts of the scribes, because this is the main focus of the story. We may pick out five features.

First, the overall theme is the conflict between Jesus and the scribes, the upholders and expounders of the Law. We are beginning to see how prominent conflict is in Mark's book. There has already been the conflict between Jesus and the demons. Now we have the first conflict between Jesus and the religious authorities.

Second, although this is a healing miracle, attention is directed to the authority of Jesus in being able to forgive sins, proof of which is given when the paralysed man picks up his bed and walks away. This is another important theme. Jesus taught with authority (1.22, 27).

Third, here for the first time Mark mentions faith (2.5, though note the verb 'to believe' in 1.15). The exact nature of faith is not explained. Moreover, it is not the faith of the paralysed man but that of the four friends (though the man may have possibly been included in *their* faith). This means that it refers primarily to their confidence that Jesus is able to cure their friend.

Fourth, although Jesus has given some teaching inside

the house, the astonishment of the crowds, which results in their praising God, arises from the healing of the paralysed man. In Mark, as we have seen, the miracles and exorcisms cannot be pushed aside. They form a dominant strand in the book.

Fifth, here, for the first time, Jesus uses the term 'Son of Man'. There is no explanation of its meaning, but it is clear that Mark regards it as a title for Jesus.

Each of these presents problems for the reader in the twenty-first century.

1.   Writers of drama may declare that conflict lies at the heart of all their work, but in real life we all wish that there were less of it. We long for a time without international wars, and a large part of our disillusionment with the politicians is that their main interest seems to be in scoring points over their opponents rather than supporting the best policies. Yet Jesus takes up the challenge of the scribes and the other religious leaders and appears to delight in beating them down with the clever soundbite. Mark was probably writing against a background of persecution. His readers were facing attack and one purpose of his book appears to have been to reassure his readers that their Master had faced similar persecution and had overcome it.

2.   Perhaps we find the stress on Jesus's authority less disturbing, since, even though we have grown suspicious of authority, we are still willing to accord authority to Jesus, and tend to interpret this incident in terms of his eternal sonship. True, only God can forgive sins, but that Jesus can both forgive sins and provide proof that they have been forgiven when the paralysed man gets up and walks away, carrying his bed, can only mean that he is God. Is Jesus, then, God walking on earth? Was this what Mark meant? We should be hesitant. Possibly he accepted that prophets and others were God's representatives who could speak in his name without themselves being divine. In any case, to use the word 'divine' takes us too far beyond Mark's own world. Yet even so, there is no evidence that in his time there was any suggestion that a human being could forgive sins. It has been suggested that besides presenting the authority of Jesus as son of God, the emphasis on his authority to forgive sins gave Mark's readers confidence that he would forgive their own sins. This may be so, but the only other references to

the forgiveness of sins in Mark are in the preaching of John the Baptist (1.4), the statement about the 'unforgivable sin' (3.28–9), and later, Jesus's call to forgive others (11.25 [–26]), none of which speaks of forgiveness given by Jesus himself. In any case, the wording is strange. Why did Jesus ask whether it was easier to tell the man that his sins were forgiven or to tell him to get up and walk? Which would have been easier? Presumably to say that sins were forgiven, since there would be no outward proof of this. Probably the point is what most readers have always taken it to be, that to give the command to walk is the more difficult, since onlookers could see straight away if he was able to effect the cure. As it is, the cure offers proof that the man's sins have indeed been forgiven.

3. To those brought up on the centrality of faith in Paul's writings, and the Reformation stress on the doctrine of justification by faith, the way faith appears in Mark's book presents a problem. Up till this point Mark assumes that those who came to Jesus for healing simply accepted that he was another travelling healer and teacher, and he just as simply heals their diseases and drives out the demons. Perhaps this is the kind of 'faith' that he has in mind here. The four friends are confident that Jesus can cure their friend if only they can reach him, and they go to extreme lengths to bring him to Jesus. Faith, then, is confidence that Jesus is able to heal disease. Troubled theologians, who cannot accept this because they hold that the only saving faith must be that of the one who is saved, speak of vicarious faith. It is difficult to see what this can realistically mean. How can anyone have faith for someone else? Maybe Jesus includes the paralysed man among those with faith. Even if this is so, the faith is still confidence in Jesus's power to heal.

4. In thinking about the healing of the paralysed man it is vital to distinguish three levels of thought: that of Mark, the historical event in the life of Jesus, and present-day interpretations. For Mark there are no problems. Jesus is a travelling teacher and healer and his healings provide evidence of his authority as 'son of God'. They happened precisely as he describes them, and are parallel to the exorcisms. It is impossible to say what occurred in the historical life of Jesus, since all that we possess are the stories that Mark and the other Gospel writers tell. Almost cer-

tainly Mark was not primarily concerned to produce an exact historical record of the life of Jesus. He probably would not have been in a position to check the stories that circulated within his community, and certainly would not have had a sharp eye to distinguish between firm history and hagiographic legend. When we try to go behind Mark and ask what actually happened, we do so with our twenty-first-century beliefs and prejudices, dominated as they are by the discoveries of science. As we have seen, this miracle presents fewer problems for us than many of the others, since we fasten on Jesus's reference to the man's sins and immediately interpret his paralysis as psychosomatic – deal with the underlying psychological problem of guilt and the disease will be cured. It may have been so. But Mark knew nothing of this. What he may well have believed, however, is that illness is punishment for sin (cf. John 9.1–3; 1 Cor. 11.30; sin and punishment are linked in many places in the Old Testament). Forgiveness, therefore, would result in healing, for the two go together. If that is so, it provides a good example of the need, not only to attempt to enter into the first-century world of Mark, but also to avoid making too rapid comparisons with today. We reject the idea that disease is caused by an individual's sin and that it is a punishment imposed by God. So while superficially our interpretation might appear similar to what Mark may have thought, at heart it is very different. To compare the healing of the paralysed man with the modern medical case of a woman who succumbed to paralysis when she felt (wrongly) that she was responsible for a crime and who was immediately and completely cured when she was reassured that she was in no way guilty is to obscure the vast difference between Mark's world and ours.

5.   Much has been written about the 'Son of Man', a phrase that is as odd in the Greek as it is in the English. It is now agreed that it is a literal rendering of an Aramaic phrase that meant no more than 'a man' or 'a human being'. In Daniel 7.13 'one like a son of man' is a human being set against the four 'great beasts' that represent the four world empires depicted in the book, Babylon, Media, Persia and Greece (cf. REB). It is not a title, and is probably a symbol for the people of God, either the whole of Israel or a faithful group within it, though some scholars hold

that it is the one who will bear rule in the coming kingdom. Scholars debate whether Jesus used the phrase as a
title and drew its meaning from Daniel or from other
Jewish writings that he may have known, or whether it
was a way of referring to himself as 'the man' or 'a man',
rather like the use of 'one' in certain social circles. It may
not even have had any special meaning in one or two
places, although it seems impossible to suppose that here
Jesus meant that human beings in general have the
authority to forgive sins. Mark, on the other hand, clearly
regarded it as a descriptive title of Jesus. He may have
attached no particular meaning to it. This means that,
while we may still wonder what Jesus might have meant
by the phrase, for Mark the meaning is controlled by his
understanding of who Jesus was.

2.13–17   A second conflict between Jesus and the religious
authorities follows the call of Levi to become a follower.
Mark appears to depict Levi as employed by Herod
Antipas on the frontier between the region he ruled and
that of Philip. Like the four fishermen, he straight away
rose and followed Jesus. Antipas, like the Romans, farmed
out the collecting of taxes, and tax-collectors were notori-
ous for their dishonesty. Moreover, their frequent contact
with Gentiles and the fact that they were directly
employed by the Romans or by rulers appointed by them
made them outcasts from Jewish society. The fifth disciple
that Jesus called, therefore, was a man with whom pious
Jews would have had nothing to do. It has been suggested
that Mark placed the story of his call here as an example of
the forgiveness that Jesus offered. This is unlikely. It is not
as a story about Pauline saving grace that Mark tells it, but
as the introduction to the accusation by *some scribes who
were Pharisees* that the company Jesus keeps shows that he
is not truly religious.

Meals play an important part in the Gospels, as they did
in the life of people in Palestine. To eat a meal together
implied the closest of friendships. It is not clear if the meal
was in Levi's house. The most natural way of taking the
clause, *When Jesus was having a meal in his house,* is to take
'his' as referring to Jesus, and it is possible that Jesus was
the host. There is no evidence, however, that Jesus possessed any property, and the meal can hardly have been in
his family home. Perhaps Mark did not notice the ambi-

guity, being sure in his own mind where the meal took place. The detail only matters for those who want to stress the welcome that Jesus gave to outcasts. Mark's concern is with the complaint of the religious leaders. The accusers are described by REB as *some scribes who were Pharisees*. The Greek is 'the scribes of the Pharisees'. It is an odd phrase, and several manuscripts read 'the scribes and the Pharisees'. Probably REB gives the correct meaning. The Pharisees were deeply religious men who kept strictly to the Law and later interpretations of its meaning. The name probably means 'separated ones', and one characteristic was their attempt to maintain their own purity by keeping aloof from those they regarded as failing to keep the Law in its entirety. The accusation that Jesus was associating so closely with *tax-collectors and sinners* that he joined them in a meal would come naturally from them. They do not challenge Jesus directly but put their question to the disciples. Jesus overhears and utters the aphorism: *It is not the healthy who need a doctor, but the sick; I did not come to call the virtuous, but sinners.*

We must be careful not to go beyond what the story contains. To suggest that, in the same way that a doctor can venture among sick people and remain healthy, Jesus could mix with sinners without being contaminated by their sin does just that. To wonder whether Jesus believed that there were some people who were 'virtuous' and did not need him does the same. Mark stresses two things: that conflict was building up between Jesus and the Pharisees and other religious leaders, and that Jesus came to call 'sinners'.

2.18–20   A further conflict concerns fasting. We discover that not all of John the Baptist's disciples transferred their allegiance to Jesus. It may be that the relation between those who followed John and those who followed Jesus was still a live issue when Mark wrote. Both *John's disciples* and the *disciples of the Pharisees* were *keeping a fast*. We may wonder why Mark links the two together, given his obvious hostility to the Pharisees. Did he regard John's disciples as equally outside the Christian community and as belonging to the old order? REB says that *some people ask, 'Why is it that John's disciples and the disciples of the Pharisees are fasting, but yours are not?'* Who asked the question is uncertain. Mark has simply 'and they come and say to him'. Possibly

REB is right in suggesting anonymous questioners, but since the story comes in a collection of hostile encounters with the Pharisees, Mark may have intended that it was some from the two groups he has just mentioned who ask the question. This time it is addressed to Jesus directly. Jesus again replies with an aphorism: *Can you expect the bridegroom's friends to fast while the bridegroom is with them? As long as he is with them, there can be no fasting.* To Mark the bridegroom is Jesus, as the next sentence makes plain: *But the time will come when the bridegroom will be taken away from them; that will be the time for them to fast.* There has been much debate as to whether this second sentence goes back to Jesus or comes from Christians who had reintroduced fasting. Mark understood the saying to mean that during Jesus's lifetime the disciples did not engage in fasting, but that after his death, in the period when he was 'absent', that is between the resurrection and the 'second coming', they were right to do so.

How soon fasting was adopted by Christians is unknown. Luke tells of Christians fasting at Antioch and in the churches in Asia Minor (Acts 13.2–3; 14.23). In the Sermon on the Mount Matthew mentions 'when you fast' as if fasting were a normal practice (Matt. 6.16). By the time of the *Didache*, a Christian handbook coming from early in the second century, regular fasting had become established, and the writer decreed that Christian fasts were to be on Wednesdays and Fridays, not on the Mondays and Thursdays of the Jews (*Didache* VIII.1). Mark refers to fasting only here ('and fasting', found in many manuscripts in 9.29, is absent from the two earliest ones and is probably a later addition), but the saying may have provided authority for what very quickly became an accepted Christian practice. There is no evidence that Mark ever thought of fasting as a religious exercise or as a good work (contrast Matt. 6.16–18).

2.21–2   At this point Mark inserts a little piece of direct teaching by Jesus that seems unrelated to anything on either side of it. The teaching is in aphorisms like the saying about calling sinners. The new Christian way cannot be stitched on to Judaism like a patch; the old wineskins of Judaism will burst if the new Christian wine is put in them. There must be a total renewal. Jesus has brought a completely new religion. Mark's emphasis is on the final sentence: *New wine goes into fresh skins,* originally even sharper: 'new wine into new skins' (two different Greek words for 'new' are used). Perhaps there is a difference between the two sayings. The first is concerned with preserving the old garment. A patch from a new piece of cloth will leave a bigger hole. Presumably what is needed is a patch from an old piece of cloth. In the second it is the new wine which is to be preserved and which cannot be contained in old skins. To Mark both express the same truth. Christianity is incompatible with Judaism. If any attempt is made to combine the two, the new religion will cause damage to the old, or both the old and the new will be destroyed.

Many commentators treat the two sayings as completely independent and lacking any background setting in the life of Jesus. They then attempt to determine what their original meaning might have been. This is a fruitless task. The difficulties may indicate that Mark collected as much of Jesus's teaching as he could find and put it where it seemed to him most appropriate in his narrative.

The relation between Christianity and Judaism has been a problem throughout history. Hostility between the two religions developed very early. It may even underlie some of the material that Mark included in his book. By the time that John wrote his Gospel the antagonism had become so acrimonious that he refers to 'the Jews' as if Jesus had not been a Jew, and describes them as children of the devil (John 8.44). Apart from a few individuals who looked for friendship with them, Christians hated the Jews and persecuted them when they were powerful enough to do so. In our day we are unable to forget the Nazi plan to exterminate the Jews from the whole of Europe. We all have a guilty conscience. Recently attempts have been made to find a theology that has a place for Judaism alongside Christianity, while on the Jewish side the Chief Rabbi tried to find a place for other religions alongside Judaism. Some scholars have spoken of two covenants, both of which remain in force. God is God of the Jews as much as he is God of the Christians. The covenant on Sinai has never been revoked. Others claim that this destroys the uniqueness of Christ, through whom alone salvation comes. Mark would have agreed. With Jesus something came into the world that is utterly new. A clean break with Judaism has to be made.

2.23–6   It is easy to regard the incident when the disciples pluck
ears of corn on the sabbath as an example of the pettifog-
ging rules that the Pharisees developed and to see Jesus as
cutting through them to uncover the basic purpose of
God's gift of the sabbath. In fact there are many oddities
about the story. Even the opening description of what the
disciples were doing is strange. *As they went along his disciples began to pluck ears of corn* irons out the sentence which
literally reads: 'and his disciples began to make a path
plucking the ears'. This might mean that the disciples were
trampling through the field ahead of Jesus, making a path
for him to walk along, quite literally making a path for
the king-messiah, but it seem very unlikely. Possibly the
phrase comes from Latin, where 'to make a way' means 'to
go on a journey', and this appears to be how REB and most
English translations reaching back as far as Tyndale take it,
reversing the main verb and the participle. Those who go
behind the Greek to a possible original Aramaic, suggest
that the disciples went along a path and plucked the corn
that was left for the poor, according to the law in Leviticus
19.9. It may also find some support from the law in
Deuteronomy 23.25 where it is permitted to 'break off the
ears with your hands' (translated by the Septuagint, 'you
may gather the ears with your hands') when you go into
your neighbour's standing corn, but not to cut it with a
sickle, a law often regarded as applying to travellers.

The Pharisees challenge Jesus about the disciples'
action, complaining that they are doing *what is forbidden on
the sabbath*. In later Jewish tradition reaping, threshing,
winnowing and grinding are among the main classes of
work forbidden on the sabbath (m. Shab. 7.2). The Pharisees regarded the disciples' action as one of these. This
seems ludicrous to us, but we need to remember that they
were simply intent on making sure that they were keeping
the Law exactly and fully and so not committing an
offence against God.

In reply Jesus turns first to the story of David in
1 Samuel 21.1–6: *Have you never read what David did when he
and his men were hungry and had nothing to eat? He went into
the house of God, in the time of Abiathar the high priest, and ate
the sacred bread, though no one but the priest is allowed to eat it,
and even gave it to his men.* This assumes that the law of
Leviticus 24.5–9, which decreed that the loaves of bread

set out in the sanctuary were 'holy' and were to be eaten only by the priests, was in force at the time, a natural assumption when Mark was writing. The point that Jesus makes is that even David, the model king, broke the Law by doing something that was forbidden, excusing it on the grounds that he and those with him were hungry. Need permits the overriding of the requirements of the Law. Jesus does not challenge the Pharisees on whether the action of the disciples is actually against the Law, and his reply suggests that he accepted that it was. The disciples' hunger justifies their action. It is just possible, however, that Mark found special significance in the mention of David. Jesus, the greater David, is able to dispense with the Law as David had done before.

The priest at the time was Ahimelech not Abiathar (his relationship to Abiathar is confused; 1 Sam. 22.20 says that Abiathar was the son of Ahimelech, but in 2 Sam. 8.17 the relationship seems to be reversed (see REB mg.)). Those anxious to maintain the infallibility of Scripture or the omniscience of Jesus are troubled, and try to evade the obvious sense by saying that the meaning is that the incident occurred in the time of Abiathar who later became high priest or that Jesus referred his critics to the story 'in the passage about Abiathar the high priest', which would not require that he was actually high priest at the time of the incident. It was in fact a simple slip, Abiathar having a more prominent place in the stories about David than Ahimelech. Since the account in Samuel implies that David did not actually enter the sanctuary – Ahimelech brought out the loaves – it may be that Mark or Jesus drew on a popular account of the incident.

2.27   The disciples' action is justified by two further aphorisms. *The sabbath was made for man, not man for the sabbath* (more exactly 'the sabbath came into being for the sake of human beings, not human beings for the sake of the sabbath') is found in later rabbinic teaching in the form: 'The sabbath is delivered unto you and you are not delivered unto the sabbath' (Mekilta on Exod. 31.14). Perhaps Jesus is referring to a saying that was current among some rabbis in his own day, although the teaching has been attributed to rabbis who lived much later. Mark, however, takes it as an authoritative statement by Jesus concerning the sabbath. It was not long before Christians deliberately

31

opposed observing the Jewish sabbath. In about AD 110 Ignatius could write that they no longer 'sabbatized' but lived according to the Lord's Day, for Jesus Christ is their only teacher (*ad Magnes*. ix.1).

2.28   The second aphorism, *so the Son of Man is lord even of the sabbath*, does not fit very neatly with what has gone before. If human need can override the sabbath requirements and human beings are not to be subordinated to it, there is no need to declare that the Son of Man has authority over how it is to be observed. It has been suggested that 'Son of Man' here meant human beings in general, or that the Aramaic 'a man is master even of the sabbath' referred to both Jesus and his disciples. Mark certainly took the Son of Man as referring to Jesus. The same 'Son of Man' who is lord of the sabbath is the one who defends the disciples by referring to David's actions when he was hungry, and who declares that the sabbath was instituted for the benefit of human beings. He taught with authority.

3.1–6   REB attempts to increase the historical realism by using modern Jewish terminology and introducing the next incident with *On another occasion when he went to synagogue*. Mark simply has: 'And he went into the synagogue again', the same phrase that Josephus uses, though he has a different, common word for synagogue ('I . . . entered the Prayer-house', *Vita* 56 [293]). It is not clear whether Mark supposes that the incident is engineered by Jesus's enemies or whether it was by chance that the man *who had a withered arm* happened to be there, but the statement that *they were watching to see whether Jesus would heal him on the sabbath* suggests that he may have supposed that it was deliberately planned. This is perhaps confirmed by the added tension. They were watching *so that they could bring a charge against him*. According to Exodus 31.14 'if anyone profanes it [the sabbath] he must be put to death', and in Numbers 15.32–6 Yahweh gives the express command that a man caught gathering sticks on the sabbath was to be executed. These laws could not have been enforced by the Jews under Roman rule, but they show how serious such a charge would have been. The hostility increases. In the first story that Mark tells, the scribes simply 'think' that Jesus has spoken blasphemy. In the next the 'scribes who were Pharisees' ask his disciples why he has a meal with tax-collectors and sinners. Jesus is directly confronted by the Pharisees about the actions of his disciples in the two stories that follow. Now 'they' (Mark means the Pharisees, continued from the previous incident, although the scene has changed) watch Jesus so that they can formally charge him with breaking the sabbath.

To the Pharisees healing was work and so was forbidden on the sabbath. We may notice that there is no question about the ability of Jesus to heal the man if he chooses to do so. This is not a story about a miracle, but a matter of breaking the sabbath and ultimately of the authority of Jesus and his ability to vanquish his opponents.

Jesus deliberately confronts them by calling the man to *come and stand out here*. Then, as he often does, he meets his opponents with a question: *Is it permitted to do good or to do evil on the sabbath, to save life or to kill?* It is rather like asking, 'Have you stopped beating your wife?', for the stark opposites do not allow doing nothing at all. It is no wonder that they are silent. Because they do not take kindly to the idea that Jesus is scoring a point over his opponents, many commentators attempt to give a positive meaning to the question. Jesus is contrasting his 'doing good' by healing the man with their 'doing evil' by trying to charge him with serious law-breaking. Both are positive actions and so are, in a way, work on the sabbath. Others take the sentence as expressing a general principle: we should do good on the sabbath and not evil, and not to heal the man would be to do evil. But if this were so it is not clear why saving life or killing was added, for the man with the withered arm was not in any danger of dying and the healing could easily have been put off until the next day. Others suppose Jesus was intent on showing the true intention of the Law, which was to secure the full well-being of human beings. By opposing the healing the Pharisees are destroying life rather than saving it. This goes too far in taking the Old Testament Law in a modern, moralizing sense, and in any case it is not the point here. Others again suggest that Jesus is only defending the occasional breaking of the sabbath in the face of some special human need.

There is considerable uncertainty as to what the religious leaders in the time of Jesus actually taught. The Qumran community refused to allow anyone to assist an animal to give birth or to lift an animal out of a pit on the sabbath, although it was permitted to pull out anyone who had fallen into water or fire (*CD* XI.13–14, 16–17). A later rabbi said: 'If a man has a pain in his throat they may drop medicine into his mouth on the Sabbath, since there is doubt whether life is in danger, and whenever there is doubt whether life is in danger this overrides the Sabbath' (m. Yom. 8.6). All this is irrelevant. Mark is not interested in rabbinic disputes. For him it is sufficient that the 'son of God' has arrived, teaching and acting with authority. To suggest, as some do, that Jesus felt the need to heal the man immediately because he was engaged in the final battle with evil, and that his opponents did not accept that the new age had dawned, tries too quickly to determine what was in the mind of Jesus.

Met by silence, Jesus looks round the synagogue *with anger and sorrow at their obstinate stupidity*. The last two words represent 'the hardness of their hearts'. To us 'hardness of heart' has the sense of lack of sympathy for the sufferer, and it is possible that Jesus's anger was roused by the Pharisees' lack of concern for the man. Some think that Mark interpreted it as referring to their failure to accept Jesus as the messiah.

Then, having set the man in a prominent position in the synagogue, he heals him with a word: *Stretch out your arm* (the Greek has 'hand'). The cure is instantaneous. It is a mistake to wonder whether the medical condition was paralysis and to suggest that simply by stretching out his hand the man showed his faith in Jesus. His opponents accepted that Jesus could cure the man if he wished to do so. It is possible that some rabbis held that healing by speaking a word and performing no physical actions such as touching the man was permitted, so that Jesus was in fact innocent of breaking the sabbath. Even if Mark knew of this distinction, that is not the point. Instead of describing the surprise and wonder of those who were present, Mark adds the ominous sentence: *Then the Pharisees, on leaving the synagogue, at once began plotting with the men of Herod's party to bring about Jesus's death.* The shadow of the cross already appears near the beginning of Mark's narrative.

Once more we have to avoid rushing into history, by asking whether the Pharisees and Herod's men began plotting so early, and even if there was a definite Herodian party at the time. To fasten on Mark's 'at once' and accuse the Pharisees of plotting to kill Jesus on the sabbath also goes beyond what he intended. What is significant is that the themes of conflict, persecution and the cross run through the whole of Mark's narrative.

3.7–12   After the group of stories about conflicts between Jesus and the religious leaders, Mark returns to Jesus the exorcist and healer. He emphasizes the great numbers of people coming to Jesus: they came *from Galilee, Judaea and Jerusalem, Idumaea and Transjordan, and the neighbourhood of Tyre and Sidon*. Only Samaria and the Decapolis have been excluded, whether purposely or not it is impossible to say. It may be that the list is intended to be comprised of all the areas with large Jewish populations and to emphasize that ordinary Jews from the whole area were coming to Jesus, in contrast to the leaders who had rejected him.

The reason they have come, however, is to obtain healing. So great is their confidence in his power as a healer that they believe that they will be cured if they simply manage to touch him, and Mark implies that they were healed. 'The sick' are more literally 'those who had scourges', but it need not imply that Mark believed that the suffering was inflicted by God as a punishment. To avoid being crushed, Jesus *told his disciples to have a boat ready*, though he does not appear to have used it. For Mark it emphasizes the size and eagerness of the crowds. The demons know who Jesus is and shout out, *'You are the Son of God'*, but Jesus orders them sternly not to let it be known.

Most commentators see most of this section as a summary compiled by Mark, and, because their main interest lies in recovering what Jesus actually did and said, pay relatively little attention to it. Yet it is very important for understanding Mark's meaning. Having given some examples of Jesus's authoritative teaching, he now presents his authority as healer and exorcist. Having shown the plotting of the leaders, he now sets out in contrast the enthusiasm of the crowds. Most significant of all, he declares that whenever demons meet Jesus they instantly recognize him for who he is, the 'son of God'. And whenever they shout this out Jesus orders them not to reveal it. In 1.25 Jesus simply commanded the unclean spirit to be silent. Here Mark says that he insisted that they should not make it known that he is the 'son of God'. Why?

Possibly the demand for silence is part of the exorcism. To know a person's name is to have authority over them. Jesus has the greater authority and so can silence the demons, even though they know who he is. This would fit the story in chapter 1, but does not explain Mark's phrasing here. Up to this point seven different features can be distinguished. (1) At the beginning of his narrative Mark tells his readers that Jesus Christ is 'the son of God' (1.1). (2) The voice immediately after his baptism tells Jesus that he is God's son (1.11). (3) The demons know who Jesus is, one of them shouts out that he is the 'Holy One of God' and others declare that he is the son of God (1.24; 3.11). (4) Jesus applies the title 'the Son of Man' to himself on two different occasions (2.10, 28). (5) Mark intends his readers to understand the 'bridegroom' as meaning Jesus, who at present is with his friends but at some future time will be taken away from them (2.19–20). (6) The Pharisees and the men of Herod's party know that Jesus is claiming to be the messiah and plot his death (3.6). And yet (7) Jesus orders one demon to be silent, will not let others speak, and insists that they should not make him known (1.25, 34; 3.12).

The only interpretation that makes sense of this apparent contradiction is that Mark was unwilling to allow the demons, the unclean spirits, to reveal who Jesus was. His readers know. God has told Jesus that he is his 'son'. Jesus himself sets up his own authority against the religious leaders and openly declares that he is the Son of Man. The unclean spirits, however, must be silenced, partly because this reveals Jesus's power over them, partly because those who belong to the powers of evil must not be the ones who announce his identity.

It is important not to confuse attempting to understand Mark's narrative and recovering the historical events. Rushing too hastily to the life of Jesus will divert our attention from what Mark actually wrote. Moreover scholarly theories can put us in blinkers in just the same way that Church dogma can. The present purpose is to examine the story that Mark tells in his narrative.

3.13–19a   REB has smoothed out a rather awkward passage. More literally the Greek reads:

And he went up into the mountain and called those whom he wished and they came to him. And he made

twelve [whom he also named apostles] that they might
be with him and that he might send them to preach and
to have authority to cast out the demons. [And he made
the twelve,] and he gave Simon the name Peter, and
James the son of Zebedee and John the brother of James,
and he gave them the name [*or* names] Boanerges,
which is Sons of Thunder; and Andrew and Philip and
Bartholomew and Matthew and Thomas and James the
son of Alphaeus and Thaddaeus and Simon the Zealot
and Judas Iscariot, who also delivered him up.

Some of the problems come from doubts about the original text (the words in brackets are missing from some
manuscripts and may well have been added from
Matthew or Luke), others are caused by the very inelegant
style. How Mark pictured the scene is far from clear.

The mountain is not named. Some commentators think
that to Mark it was symbolic. Jesus goes up a mountain to
select the Twelve in the same way that Yahweh met Moses
on Sinai-Horeb. With its *he went up into the hill-country* REB
obscures this by moving too quickly to a historical recon-
struction. On the other hand, Mark makes no direct reference to Moses or Sinai and we should be cautious about
asserting his supposed intention.

It is not clear whether Mark supposed that Jesus took
a large number of disciples up the mountain and then
selected 12 of them to have a special role, or only the
Twelve accompanied him. The literal translation of the
Greek shows that Mark does not give just a list of names.
'And he gave Simon the name Peter' continues the narrative, which then switches to the list, interrupted by the
statement that Jesus gave James and John the name
Boanerges, which Mark interprets as 'Sons of Thunder'.
The name Peter persisted in the Church – apart from 14.37
Mark uses it consistently in his narrative from this point
onward – but James and John are referred to as Boanerges
nowhere else.

There are some surprises in the list. Andrew was one of
the first two disciples to be called from their fishing by
Jesus, yet he is now placed after James and John and separated from them by the account of the nickname that
Jesus gives them. Moreover although Mark has given an
account of the call of Levi, who, exactly like the first four

disciples, immediately dropped what he was doing and followed Jesus straight away, as a good disciple should, he does not appear in the list. It is usual to identify him with Matthew, but there is absolutely no evidence for this and Mark plainly did not regard Matthew as a second or alternative name for Levi. We must assume that by the time that Mark was writing his book memories had become hazy. It rather looks as if Mark is using a list that was traditional in his community, although it did not precisely match the story he was telling. By his time only four disciples stood out, Peter, James, John and Judas Iscariot, because the first three were leaders in the early Church and Judas had the notoriety of betraying Jesus.

Mark does not explain why the number of disciples was 12. Perhaps he assumed that his readers would relate it to current Jewish hopes that God would restore Israel in its complete original form of 12 tribes. Perhaps he expected them to think of the way Moses appointed 12 'princes' (Num. 1.4–16) who play a major part in some biblical traditions. Yet, as we shall see, he needed to explain Aramaic words and Jewish customs, which suggests that he was writing primarily to Gentiles. Moreover, where he openly refers to the Old Testament he gives quotations, though only once in his own narrative (1.2–3). It is unlikely that he was interested in any special position of authority possessed by the Twelve, in contrast to Matthew and Luke (cf. Matt. 19.28; Luke 22.28–30).

He assigns two tasks to the Twelve: they are to remain close to Jesus, and he is to send them out preaching and performing exorcisms. (REB has *to proclaim the gospel*: taking the verb to have this meaning although the noun is absent. It is possible that Mark understood the verb to refer to Christian preaching as he knew it.) They are to share Jesus's own work of preaching and driving out demons, though it is not specifically stated that they are to heal ordinary diseases, unless it is assumed that all illness is due to unclean spirits.

Does this mean, then, that the churches today should perform exorcisms? Exorcism is a problem for many modern readers. Although some Christians still believe in the existence of evil spirits, and some main-line churches have even appointed official exorcists, most hold that such a belief belongs to the first-century culture. We need to be clear in our own minds. Mark portrays Jesus as a powerful exorcist. He regards exorcism as one of the main tasks of the Church of his own day, for Jesus gave the Twelve authority to drive out demons. It seems probable that official church exorcists today have some success with those who believe themselves to be the victims of evil spirits or think that their homes are haunted. Many would say that what has happened is that those deluded by false beliefs are helped because someone takes them seriously, and shows understanding and compassion. Any exorcism rites that may be performed provide psychological reassurance because those who are suffering are able to interpret them as driving out the imagined ghosts and demons. Others argue that the fact that people today believe that they are afflicted by demons shows that faith is not dead, even in our highly secular and materialistic world, though it seems more reasonable to say that, with the collapse of organized religion and a suspicion of science, people are ready to believe anything, however outlandish.

A commentator on Mark is in a difficult position. Simply to clarify what Mark wrote is to act as if the differences in the cultures of Mark's time and today do not exist, and that is both false and deceitful. But any other discussion must inevitably depend upon the position that the commentator holds. I write from my own viewpoint. I do not believe that evil spirits, demons or the devil exist. I regard the appointment of exorcists by many of the churches as a retrograde step, and a retreat into beliefs that cannot be credibly held in the present day. What was once interpreted as demon possession is now described in medical terms, as epilepsy or mental illness, and treated accordingly. Exorcism, therefore, belongs to the ways of thought in the time of Jesus, and he took it for granted as everyone else did. There is no reason to doubt that he carried out exorcisms and intended his disciples to do the same. But this does not mean that Christians today have to believe in demons and practise exorcism.

3.19b–21   The question of the authority that Jesus possesses remains central for Mark. He has presented Jesus as the son of God, the Son of Man, who preaches with authority, drives out evil spirits, heals with a touch or a word those who are sick, and confutes his opponents with unanswerable aphorisms. Now, although vast crowds still flock to him, *his family heard about it and set out to take charge of him. 'He is out of his mind,' they said.* REB takes the imprecise Greek phrase to mean members of his family. This is probably right, although it might equally well mean his friends. It is not clear where Mark supposed that Jesus was, and geographical details may not have concerned him greatly. He writes simply *He entered a house,* and this might have been anywhere in Galilee. The phrase could mean, 'he went home', but this does not help, since we do not know whether he had a house from which he carried out his work. The family or friends set out, presumably from Nazareth, in order to seize and restrain him because they thought he had lost his senses. GNB, with 'because people were saying, "He's gone mad!"', is blunter but at the same time is unwilling to admit that it was Jesus's family and friends who thought he had lost his senses. Since at the time, mental illness was usually regarded as due to demonic possession, Mark may have supposed that the members of his family thought that he was possessed by a demon. This would prepare for his next story.

3.22–6   *The scribes . . . who had come down from Jerusalem* are the official representatives of the national religion. Up till now the Jewish opponents have been local Galilean scribes and Pharisees. These Jerusalem officials declare *'He is possessed by Beel-zebul,'* and, *'He drives out demons by the prince of demons'.* The name Beel-zebul is obscure. In 2 Kings 1.2, 3, 16, as Beelzebub (possibly 'Lord of flies'), he is the local god of Ekron, but the true name appears to have been Beelzebul (perhaps 'Lord of the lofty residence', or more probably 'Baal the prince'). What the name meant does not matter much. The accusation by the scribes suggests that Mark understood it as a name for Satan. We notice that the scribes accept that Jesus possesses the power to drive out the evil spirits, but explain this by asserting that he is in league with the devil. The local religious leaders condemned the lax religious practice of Jesus and his disciples. The Jerusalem scribes attack his authority. Mark does not say anything about the grounds on which the charge was based. What he does not say is as important as what he does. He is not interested in the details of the accusation but is chiefly concerned with the fact of the conflict, and the way Jesus is able to vanquish his opponents.

On hearing their accusations, Jesus immediately exerts his authority: *He summoned them,* or with a less peremptory verb that is closer to the Greek, 'called them to him' and *spoke to them in parables.* 'Parables' may strike us as an odd word to use for a direct question and then three short similes. We think of parables as stories such as the Prodigal Son. In the Septuagint, however, it represents a Hebrew word that is used for a wide range of sayings including aphorisms, proverbs and riddles, and occasionally longer stories, and it was used in the same way in the New Testament.

The logic of Jesus's answer seems obvious to us. If it was Satan who was driving out the demons, it means civil war. No authority so rent with division could survive. Satan could not possibly be destroying his own power to rule. *If Satan is divided and rebels against himself* (literally, 'if Satan rises up against himself and is divided') gives the sense of divided purpose. As with 'the kingdom of God' in 1.15, the primary meaning of Satan's 'kingdom' is his authority, but it includes the idea of the body of his followers who would be at war among themselves.

3.27   *No one can break into a strong man's house and make off with his goods unless he has first tied up the strong man; then he can ransack the house.* Mark interprets the parable allegorically. The 'strong man' is Satan, whom Jesus has 'tied up' and whose kingdom he is now ransacking. Jesus's power is reaffirmed. Whether Mark had in mind a specific moment when Jesus had bound the 'strong man' is uncertain. Some suggest that it was at the temptations, but this is to read Mark in the light of Matthew and Luke. Mark says nothing about the nature of Satan's tempting or testing, or what its outcome was. Probably he did not have any specific time in mind. He concentrates on the fact that by driving out the demons, Jesus has shown that he has tied up Satan.

3.28–30   Jesus then turns directly on the scribes with a statement that has troubled many tender consciences ever since the Bible was accepted as a sacred book. *Truly I tell you: every sin and every slander can be forgiven; but whoever slanders the Holy Spirit can never be forgiven; he is guilty of an eternal sin.* REB moves towards paraphrase, but represents the meaning correctly. 'Truly' ('Amen' in the Greek) emphasizes the solemn seriousness of the words. Those eager to identify 'authentic' words of Jesus point out that he seems to have

41

been unique in using the word at the beginning of a sentence rather than at the end. Even though the Greek word translated 'slander' can be applied to the defamation of other people as well as blasphemy in a religious sense, here it should probably be taken in the narrower sense of speaking evil of God and divine things, for it is set alongside 'sin' against God. Mark's comment, *He said this because they had declared that he was possessed by an unclean spirit* reveals the meaning he attached to Jesus's words. Jesus was in fact driving out the evil spirits by the power (or 'spirit') of God. The scribes say that this power ('spirit') is evil. We might explain it in our own terms by saying that the scribes were treating goodness as evil, and such wilful inversion of values makes forgiveness impossible, but Mark has a much more vivid sense of the spirit world. We might also be tempted to explain the reason why such an attitude is beyond forgiveness psychologically: to persist with an inverted sense of right and wrong and to regard God as evil are the marks of an irreformable character. This is not Mark's thought. Jesus, the 'son of God', the 'Son of Man', the 'greater one' who will baptize with 'holy spirit', has been accused by the scribes of being possessed by the prince of the demons. This is the first place where Mark writes 'the Holy Spirit'. The actual term 'holy spirit' is found only twice in the Old Testament: in Psalm 51.11, 'Do not take your holy spirit from me' and Isaiah 63.10–11, the prophet's statement, 'they rebelled and grieved his holy spirit', and the people's question, 'where is he who put within him his holy spirit'. In both of these places the phrase is a term for the personal presence and power of God. The capital letters of REB here imply a later trinitarian doctrine that would have been alien to Mark. To count God as evil is indeed to put oneself beyond the bounds of forgiveness. But even to express it in this way probably misrepresents Mark's thought. The battle is between God and the unclean spirits. To say that Jesus is possessed by an unclean spirit, indeed, by the leader of the unclean spirits, is to range oneself on the side of the opponents of God.

3.31–5   Mark now seems to pick up the account of the family that he began in v. 21 (if indeed his family was meant there), focusing on Jesus's *mother* and *brothers*. His interest again lies in the aphorism that Jesus speaks rather than in the historical incident: *Whoever does the will of God is my brother and sister and mother.* Jesus is estranged from his family – they *stayed outside*, separated from his disciples and the crowd. It is important to notice that Jesus does not say, 'Those who do what I teach'. His message is centred on God, even though Mark stresses that he is the son of God. Possibly Mark saw these words as encouragement to his own community of disciples who believed that they were doing God's will and so were members of Jesus's family.

Much is said about the value of the family and its Christian basis, and many Church reports attempt to find biblical authority for their teaching on the family. But they always struggle to find biblical support in the face of the way Jesus distances himself from his family. This is absolutely clear in Mark. For Mark there is no 'earthly home in Nazareth'. He does not mention Joseph, and depicts Mary and the brothers and sisters of Jesus as hostile to his activities, regarding him as being 'out of his mind', and trying to restrain him.

4.1–2 At last Mark records some of the teaching that Jesus gave to the crowds. Up to this point all the words of Jesus have been short aphorisms embedded in stories, apart from the summary of his message in 1.11 and a couple of metaphors in 2.21–2. The crowd was large, and Jesus spoke to them from *a boat out on the lake.* Sound carries better over water, and his voice would have rung out. He taught *by parables.* We shall discover the meaning Mark gave to the word as we read the rest of this chapter.

4.3–9 The familiar story of the *sower* who *went out to sow* is told with great vividness and economy of words, and REB does not deviate greatly from the AV, which itself is close to the translation that Tyndale made in 1534. Tyndale may have seen the peasant farmers of his own time sowing seed by hand in just this way. To us it seems extremely wasteful of seed, and we may wonder why the sower was not more careful. Scattering the seed broadcast does not make it easy to be sure where the seed will fall, but not a great deal may actually have been lost.

Scholars have argued that the point of the parable lies in the rich harvest – *thirtyfold, sixtyfold, even a hundredfold* – as an encouragement to his followers and confidence in the power of God. Mark sees it differently. While we imagine that the parables were ways in which Jesus presented his teaching so that ordinary people could understand it immediately, Mark regards them as secret teaching that only the disciples can understand, and even they need interpretations. He seems to have taken *'If you have ears to hear, then hear'* to mean that not everyone is able to receive Jesus's message, but only those who have been granted open ears. In much the same way the writer of one of the Qumran hymns declares:

> These things I know
>   by the wisdom which comes from Thee,
> for Thou hast unstopped my ears
>   to marvellous mysteries (1QH 1.21).

4.10–12   Later, when *the Twelve* and other *companions* are alone with Jesus, they ask him the meaning of *the parables*. The word is in the plural, and Mark intends Jesus's reply to refer to all the parables and not only the one that has just been given. Although 'the Twelve' has now become a term for the group of men who Jesus selected 'to be his companions and to be sent out to proclaim the gospel' (3.14), here a larger group of *companions* (the Greek is different; in 3.14 it is literally 'that they might be with him' and here 'those round him') are included with the Twelve. Mark affirms that the *secret of the kingdom of God* (God's royal authority, probably with the implication that it will soon be exerted) is given to a wider group than just the Church leaders, but Christians are distinguished from the general crowd, who are deliberately left in ignorance.

The meaning of the secret is granted to the insiders only; *to those who are outside, everything comes by way of parables, so that (as scripture says) they may look and look, but see nothing; they may listen and listen, but understand nothing; otherwise they might turn to God and be forgiven*. The quotation from Isaiah 6.9–10 agrees with neither the Hebrew nor the Greek and is closer to the Jewish Targum, which has third-person verbs and ends with forgiveness rather than healing. Mark, however, does not introduce the words as a quotation from Scripture – '(as scripture says)' has been gratuitously added by REB – so that we do not know whether he regarded it as a quotation or not.

To us it seems incredible that Jesus would have deliberately given his teaching in cryptic parables in order to pre-

vent the crowds understanding his teaching. We see the
parables as a way of presenting the message clearly, simply and attractively, so that ordinary people can grasp it.
We also suppose that Jesus came to win converts and to
offer forgiveness to everyone. Mark sees things quite differently. Parables are obscure sayings. They can be understood only by those to whom God has given special
insight. The secret about the imminent coming of God's
reign is revealed only to them. The message is given in
parables in order that the rest, the outsiders, will not be
able to understand, however long they keep on looking,
however long they keep on listening. This was Jesus's
deliberate purpose (and God's purpose as well). REB's 'so
that', implying that this is a consequence rather than the
purpose of speaking in parables, and 'otherwise' instead
of 'lest' is an attempt to soften the harshness, and most of
the other modern translations do the same in different
ways. There is no question, however, about the meaning
of Mark's words, and to try to evade this by supposing
that it is a mistranslation of Jesus's Aramaic is to rush too
quickly to the picture of Jesus we have formed in our own
minds.

Mark believes that Jesus's hearers fell into two groups.
Those close to Jesus (primarily the Twelve, but also on
occasion a wider group of disciples) and 'those outside'
(those like the scribes who accused Jesus of driving out
demons by Beelzebul, 3.22–6, 28–9). He also believes that
God deliberately intended these 'outsiders' should fail to
understand and that this was Jesus's purpose in speaking
in parables. The idea is similar to that found in Exodus,
where God hardened Pharaoh's heart (Exod. 4.21; 7.3;
9.16; 10.1, 20, 27), and in 1 Kings, where God sent a lying
spirit into the prophets in order to deceive Ahab (1 Kgs.
22.19–23). It may be that Mark's readers applied the words
to those outside their community (cf. Paul's references
to 'those outside' in 1 Cor. 5.12–13; 2 Cor. 4.16; Col. 4.5;
1 Thess. 4.12).

In any case, we must assume that Mark meant what he
wrote, as his reference to 'the mystery of the kingdom of
God' and his distinction between the disciples and the
outsiders show.

This is the only place where Mark uses the word 'mystery', a word that is fairly common in Paul's letters and is

found also in the Revelation of John. Although 'mysteries' (in the plural) was the name given in classical Greek to the secrets imparted to initiates in the mystery-religions, there is no reason to suppose that Mark understood Christianity as one of these religions. Rather he uses 'mystery' in the sense of a secret that is revealed only to the inside group of disciples.

4.13–20   Yet although knowledge of 'the mystery' is granted to the Twelve and the other companions, Jesus expresses surprise: *Do you not understand this parable? How then are you to understand any parable?* There is tension here. Even these insiders do not understand, and Jesus has to explain the meaning of the parable to them. It is not that those who have left everything to follow Jesus have special insight. They have as little understanding as 'those who are outside'. The 'mystery', then, is a secret that has to be specially revealed by Jesus, and this points to a further distinction that Mark makes. Some teaching was given in plain aphorisms that everyone, including those opposed to Jesus understood, some was given in parables that the crowds could not understand and were not meant to grasp, and some was given only to the inner circle of disciples. The heart of Mark's understanding of the meaning of the life, message and death of Jesus, therefore, is to be found in the teaching given to the disciples alone.

4.14   Jesus's interpretation of the parable may well strike us as banal, for it treats it entirely as an allegory in which each feature has a corresponding 'spiritual' meaning. Yet even now some features are not identified. *The sower sows the word* – but who is the sower and what is the word? Mark does not explain. He appears to assume that his readers will make the identifications, and since he has depicted Jesus earlier in his narrative as teaching the crowds and wrote in 2.2 that he 'spoke the word' (REB 'proclaiming the message'), he probably intends them to realize that the sower is Jesus and the word is the message he proclaims. In some later New Testament writings 'the word' is the gospel (Acts 6.4; 10.36; 1 Thess. 1.6), but we cannot be sure that this meaning was held generally among Christians. Perhaps Mark includes Christian preachers among those who 'sow the word' and this accounts for his failure to identify the sower more directly.

4.15   By a rather awkward switch, attention turns from the sower and the seed to the different types of ground on which the seed falls, as the change in REB's paraphrase shows: *With some the seed falls along the footpath* – the Greek literally reads: 'And these are those beside the path where the word is sown'. The seed may be the gospel, but the emphasis is on the activity of the birds, who represent Satan, and the effect that this has on those who heard the word. *No sooner have they heard it than Satan comes and carries off the word which has been sown in them.* We may be surprised that Satan is still active, for in 3.27 the 'strong man' has been 'tied up'. If Mark has in mind his own church community as well as those who were members of the crowd in the lifetime of Jesus, this may imply that he believed that Satan had still not been finally overthrown.

4.16–17   *With others the seed falls on rocky ground; as soon as they hear the word, they accept it with joy, but it strikes no root in them; they have no staying power, and when there is trouble or persecution on account of the word, they quickly lose faith.* Again to ease the sense REB paraphrases the Greek, which more literally might be translated 'And [similarly] these are those sown on the rocky ground . . . they do not have any root in themselves but are shortlived . . . [then] they immediately fall away' (there is no specific word for faith, and the verb, which is traditionally translated 'stumble', has developed this metaphorical sense from the idea of a trap). Now the seed represents those who have had the gospel preached to them and accept it at first. Mark is very aware of the pressures of persecution. It is probable that Christians were being persecuted at the time he was writing because they were members of this new religion.

4.18–19   *With others again the seed falls among thistles; they hear the word, but worldly cares and the false glamour of wealth and evil desires of all kinds come in and choke the word, and it proves barren.* Yet again REB's paraphrase presents a more consistent picture than the Greek displays: 'And others are those sown among the thorns; these are those who hear the word . . .' The things that choke the gospel so that it does not bear fruit are concerns about what we might term 'secular' affairs, the pursuit of wealth, and desires for other things. None of these are evil in themselves, and REB is falsely slanted with its *evil desires*. The point seems to be that adherence to the gospel must be wholehearted. If it is not then it will fail to be fruitful because these other interests

47

will crowd it out. Following Christ is all or nothing for Mark.

4.20   *But there are some with whom the seed is sown on good soil; they accept the word when they hear it, and they bear fruit thirtyfold, sixtyfold, or a hundredfold.* REB's 'some' suggests that these fruitful seeds are not many! The more literal Greek has: 'And there are those who are sown on the good ground', an extremely awkward phrase which REB tries to sort out. The crop is immense, even up to a hundred-fold. Mark seems here to be thinking of the committed Christians in his community who are living out the gospel as he understands it.

4.21–2   At this point difficulties appear in Mark's narrative. He continues the account as if Jesus is still speaking to the inner circle of followers: [And] *he said to them,* but he may be reverting to the crowd. The figurative saying: *Is a lamp brought in to be put under the measuring bowl or under the bed? No, it is put on the lampstand,* is immediately followed by what seems to be an explanation: *Nothing is hidden except to be disclosed, and nothing concealed except to be brought into the open.* In the light of the way Mark understands Jesus's teaching (4.11–12) and the fact that Jesus has to explain the parable of the sower even to the Twelve, we should see this as a 'parable' that the disciples can understand only when it is explained to them, even though Mark does not designate it as such. On the face of it, the parable and the explanation do not fit easily together. The parable suggests that Jesus has come to bring an open revelation that it would be foolish to hide. As a lamp is put on a lamp-stand, so the message of Jesus is to be set out plainly. It implies that Jesus came to enlighten the crowds. The explanation declares that something has been hidden, but that now it is to be disclosed, and corresponds to the Markan view of parables: they are enigmatic and need to be explained. Yet God's purpose is that they should be made plain. There is a certain tension between this and Mark's theory of parables in 4.11–12.

4.23   *If you have ears to hear, then hear* is similar to the sentence at the end of the parable of the sower (4.9) though not identical. Literally the Greek reads: 'If anyone has ears . . . ' Perhaps the difference is intentional. The warning that only those receptive to the message will grasp its meaning is now made still more definite. Placed after the interpre-

tation of the parable of the sower, where those seized by
Satan, those who abandon the Christian way because of
persecution, and those who do not follow Christ whole-
heartedly fail to produce a crop, each individual is now
challenged.

4.24 *He also said to them.* Mark continues his narrative, and
the emphasis remains on hearing. Notice that he does not
say, 'Take care (REB, *'take note of'*) how you hear' but *'what
you hear'* – listen to God's message (and mine), not that of
false teachers.

It is difficult to see exactly how the next sentence fits
in: *the measure you give is the measure you will receive, with
something more besides.* If we were not trying to read Mark
without any reference to Matthew and Luke, we might
suppose that he has misunderstood its meaning, for the
other two Gospel writers apply it to judging other people
(Matt. 7.1–2; Luke 6.37–8). But Mark must have made
sense of what he wrote and we should try to do so. The
literal Greek may help: 'you will be measured by that
measure with which you measure and it shall be added to
you'. If Mark thought that each individual's ability to
understand the gospel depended on the way he received
('heard') it, then this is reinforcing that assertion. How
you take the teaching of Jesus will determine whether you
are granted understanding, but if you do place yourself in
a position to receive it you will be granted more than just
the beginnings of knowledge of the revelation.

4.25 *For those who have will be given more, and those who have
not will forfeit even what they have.* REB's attempt to avoid
masculine pronouns conceals a change in the form of the
next sentence, which reads baldly: 'For he who has, it shall
be given to him, and he who does not have, even (literally,
'and') what he has will be taken from him'. If the saying is
interpreted in the light of 4.11–12, it may be that Mark
took these words to mean that those who have been given
understanding by God will have it enlarged by grasping
the meaning of the parables, while the parables will
bring those not granted this understanding into greater
ignorance.

The sequence of thought is still obscure, and we may
wonder whether this is due to Mark's attempt to include
every scrap of Jesus's teaching that he knew.

4.26–9 It is difficult to decide whether Mark supposed that

Jesus now returned to address the crowd. The narrative continues 'And he said' (without 'to them'), and Jesus now recounts a full story-parable. This would fit Mark's scheme more neatly if it were given to the crowd, but there is no indication of a change of audience. Perhaps this supports the view that Mark reverted to the crowd in v. 21.

The parable is introduced by *The kingdom of God is like this*. Up till now Mark has mentioned the kingdom of God twice, in the summary of Jesus's preaching (1.15) and in the explanation of the purpose of speaking in parables (4.11), but has not explained what it means. Given his understanding of parables as messages deliberately concealed from the outsiders but revealed to the disciples, the parable must be seen as the beginning of an explanation – but it is still cryptic.

REB represents the sense accurately and clearly. At the end *as soon as the crop is ripe, he starts reaping* is literally 'when the fruit permits, immediately he sends forth the sickle'. The meaning is the same, if less picturesque. The problem is to decide how Mark understood the parable. Commentators rarely face up to this question, because they ask what it meant on the lips of Jesus, and assuming that each parable has a single point they suggest that it teaches that there is a long period between sowing and harvest, or that it gives assurance that the kingdom of God will certainly arrive, or that the kingdom will come when God's purpose is complete, with the implication that it cannot be hastened by human effort, still less by political violence. One commentator, however, argues that for Mark the kingdom of God is displayed in the life of Jesus, but hidden, like the seed. You do not know it is there unless you are let into the secret. But God is at work and finally it will be fully revealed. For Mark's community, living between the 'sowing' of the kingdom and the 'harvest', it offers hope and reassurance.

This may be correct, but perhaps we can guess at a more precise sense. If, as seems probable, Mark intended the interpretation of the parable of the sower to be an example of the way all the parables should be decoded, he would have treated it allegorically. The man may be the Son of Man, Jesus himself, who scatters the seed, the word, if we follow the parable of the sower. He is unable to do any more, and it is up to the ground 'automatically' (our term comes from the Greek word used here) to produce the crop, as it was in the earlier parable. This time, however, the emphasis is placed upon the crop. A time for harvest will come 'when the crop permits it', when it has become sufficiently ripe. Is this a suggestion that sufficient time must elapse to allow the number of disciples to increase? Perhaps *the blade, the ear* and the *full grain* are also to be treated allegorically, pointing to the unfolding of God's predetermined plan leading up to the End and the (second) coming of the Son of Man. Putting in the sickle might seem to imply judgement, but the general sense of joy that pervades this parable suggests that if there is judgement, this seed, which has produced a good crop, will be harvested and brought within the sphere of God's dominion.

4.30–2   It is often thought that this and the previous parable form a pair and that they had the same meaning for Mark. This may be so, although care should be taken not to jump too hastily to conclusions. The two parables are not introduced in the same way. REB presents the sense, although it removes some duplications and makes the narrative flow more smoothly. This time the seed represents the kingdom of God, and a contrast is made between the size of the seed and the large bush that grows from it. We need not worry because mustard seed is not in fact the smallest seed on earth. This was probably how it was regarded at the time. Christian writers later than Mark allegorized the parable and found meanings in the branches and the birds, but Mark may not have gone this far. He appears to have taken the parable as expressing the contrast between the beginnings of the proclaiming of the kingdom of God and its later growth, which offered a further reassurance to the members of his community. It is less easy to understand 'kingdom' as 'kingship' here. It verges towards meaning the people over whom God reigns.

4.33–4   *With many such parables he used to give them his message, so far as they were able to receive it. He never spoke to them except in parables; but privately to his disciples he explained everything.* The first sentence appears to contradict the second, and, indeed, to be at variance with the way Mark understood Jesus's use of parables. 'So far as they were able to receive it', however, is literally, 'as they were able to hear' and this recalls Jesus's words: 'If you have ears to hear, then hear' (4.9, cf. 4.23). This must raise doubts as to whether Mark took the meaning to be that Jesus gave his teaching in parables because this made it easier for the crowds to understand it. Moreover, 'he used to give them his message' is literally 'he spoke to them the word', the identical phrase to that in 2.2. It also recalls the way the sower 'sows the word'. This sentence, therefore, is most probably to be understood in the light of Mark's view that only those granted special insight by God were able to understand the parables, and that Jesus taught in parables deliberately to separate this group from the outsiders.

The second sentence reflects the way in which Jesus had to interpret the parable of the sower to the disciples. Mark believes that even the disciples failed to understand the meaning of the parables and needed to have them explained to them. He certainly does not believe that understanding lies within the power of the hearers. Even when they leave everything and follow Jesus, they still cannot understand the parables, but by being with Jesus and asking him for explanations they receive enlightenment.

4.35–41   *That day, in the evening,* and *in the boat in which he had been sitting* link the story of the stilling of the storm with the beginning of the chapter. Mark has inserted the private teaching given to the disciples into a narrative about Jesus teaching the crowd, and now he continues, 'And he said to them that day in the evening, "Let us go across to the other side"'. As we have seen, exactly which parts of the chapter belong to the private teaching is not clear. It might be simply the interpretation of the parable of the sower; it might include vv. 21–5; the parables in vv. 26–32 were probably spoken to the crowd in accordance with the policy stated in vv. 33–4. 'Them' in v. 35 are certainly the Twelve. REB gives a vigorous translation, occasionally resorting to paraphrase and changes in the constructions, such as rendering the literal 'as he was' by *in which he had been sitting*, and increasing the vividness of 'Teacher, do you not care that we are drowning (or 'about to die')?' with *'Teacher, we are sinking! Do you not care?'*

This is the first time that the disciples address Jesus as *Teacher*. The Aramaic underlying the Greek would be rabbi, but since Mark lays considerable emphasis on the impressive way in which Jesus taught 'with authority', the term will have suited the way he presents him. Jesus addresses the wind and the sea as if they were living beings. He *rebuked* the wind and commanded it *'Be still!'* (literally 'be muzzled') – the same words that Mark used when he described Jesus rebuking the evil spirit in the synagogue (1.25). When *the wind dropped and there was a dead calm* the disciples *were awestruck and said to one another, 'Who can this be? Even the wind and the sea obey him'*, showing that they also regard the wind and the sea as animate, if not actually demonic. The distance from our attitude toward the natural world is obvious. The Greek translated 'awestruck' is literally, 'they feared [with] great fear', a Semitic idiom indicating their utter terror. Elsewhere in Mark the verb mostly expresses ordinary fear (6.20 is less certain), but here it is religious awe in the face of the supernatural wonder.

The first question that comes into our minds as we read this story is, what actually happened? It has been suggested that Jesus's words were really addressed to the disciples, seeking to calm their panic, but that they wrongly supposed that he was addressing the storm. When the wind suddenly died down, they thought that it was his command which had quelled it. When Jesus accused them of being cowards who had no faith, he meant that they should have trusted in God to protect them in the storm. This assumes that Jesus possessed our secular understanding of nature and at the same time accepted that God would actively intervene to prevent his servants from drowning.

Others think that the story is so improbable – seasoned fishermen being frightened by the sudden storm, the like of which they must have been familiar with – that it is impossible to suggest any event that could underlie Mark's account, and they turn to its symbolic meaning, finding its background in the account of the sailors in Psalm 107.23–32 where God is in control of the sea. This is too hasty, for it evades trying to discover what Mark thought had happened.

In a somewhat similar way, it is sometimes suggested that instead of asking whether the miracles were actually performed, we should direct our attention to the way they awaken awe and faith. The logic of this is not clear. In

Mark's story the experience produces terror because everything actually happens as he describes. It cannot do the same for us, because we live in a different world. Similarly, whatever symbolic meaning the events possess arises because they were believed to have happened. It is not simply that Mark knew nothing of the regularities in nature that today are often called 'natural laws', and so accepted a legend without a qualm. He knew what were normal, everyday happenings and what was extraordinary. But because he also accepted that evil spirits existed and did not make any sharp distinction between the natural and spirit worlds, his whole approach to life was different from ours. Given his world, he would have had no difficulty in accepting that the events he describes actually happened as he describes them, and that this was not an everyday occurrence. Commentators cite similar miraculous rescues in Jewish and classical writers.

It is better to try to understand the story as Mark fits it into his narrative about Jesus. For Mark the key question is *Who can this be?* We have seen that in several different ways he has emphasized Jesus's authority. He teaches 'with authority' (1.27). Unclean spirits obey him (1.26, 27, 34; cf. 3.22). He heals diseases (1.31, 34, 40–4; 2.3–12). Now the wind and sea obey him. It is building up a powerful picture of the one whom Mark has presented as the son of God and the Son of Man. This miracle is a further way of revealing the authority that Jesus possessed. But it reveals that authority only within Mark's world. What is not permissible is to suppose that even if the event did not happen it still proves that Jesus possessed the authority of the son of God.

5.1–20 The voyage across the lake is completed and Jesus and his disciples arrive in *the country of the Gerasenes*. The Greek manuscripts differ in the name of the place, some having Gergasenes and others Gadarenes. Whatever the precise location, it was in the predominantly Gentile territory known as Decapolis.

With a certain amount of paraphrase, partly to smooth out some awkward phrasing in the Greek, REB produces a lively story that accurately reflects the spirit in which it was told. There is no need to summarize it, and only a few features need explanation. It was believed that demons inhabited tombs, so that this was a natural place for the demoniac to live. The REB's *flung himself down* correctly states the action but misses the overtones of worship that the verb always possesses in the New Testament. *Legion* was the largest section of the Roman army and comprised some 6,000 men. Pigs were ritually unclean according to the Law (Lev. 11.7), and it was fitting that the unclean spirits should ask to be allowed to go into them.

We have problems with the story, but Mark has none. Several of the features that we have already noted in his narrative recur here. The demoniac puts the same question to Jesus as the man with the unclean spirit in the synagogue: *'What do you want with me?'* (1.24, 'with us'). The demons know who Jesus is, *son of the Most High God*. Indeed, the fact that the man calls him Jesus, although he has not been in that part of the country before, is part of the supernatural knowledge the demons possess. Evidence that they have been driven out is seen in the restoration of the man, who is now found *sitting there clothed and in his right mind*, and the behaviour of the pigs, and the effect on the eyewitnesses and those who come from the surrounding area is depicted as being *afraid* and *amazed*.

But new features appear. The immense strength of the demoniac is emphasized. Jesus asks him his name. The demons *implored Jesus not to send them out of the district* and he agrees to this request by allowing them to enter the pigs. We might feel that this is rather self-defeating, for the pigs immediately *rushed over the edge into the lake and were drowned*. Mark might have regarded the death of the pigs as implying the death of the demons as well, although in theory they would survive as spirits, though they are homeless again. Most striking of all, instead of forbidding the demoniac to say anything about his cure, Jesus does not allow the man to join him as a disciple but sends him home with the charge: *'tell them what the Lord in his mercy has done for you'*. The man then becomes the first preacher, [he] *went off and made known throughout Decapolis what Jesus had done for him*. The words Mark uses are striking. The man *begged to go with him* is literally 'that he might be with him', the exact phrase (though here, of course, in the singular) that marked out the Twelve in 3.14 (REB 'to be his companions' conceals this). And *made known* is 'proclaimed', the word for the proclamation by John the

Baptist and Jesus, and the intended work of the Twelve (cf. 1.4, 7, 14, 38, 39; 3.14). Moreover, Jesus orders the man to tell what *the Lord* had done for him, and he then proclaimed what *Jesus* had done. It is more natural to take 'the Lord' in the Old Testament sense of God, but Mark may either have meant it to refer to Jesus, or by setting the two phrases side by side have wished to emphasize that Jesus was again acting as the representative of God.

As with the account of the storm on the lake, our question is, what actually happened? As with that miracle some resort to rationalizing. Perhaps Jesus, a master psychiatrist, was able to restore the man's troubled mind. Perhaps the man's shouts frightened the pigs so that they ran down a steep bank or over a precipice in panic, and the bystanders interpreted this as the demons leaving the man and entering the pigs. To do this, however, is to make nonsense of Mark's narrative. For Mark the events unfolded exactly as he describes them. The man was possessed by many demons. Jesus was more powerful than the demons, and, after expelling them from the man, was so completely their master that he was able to give them permission to enter the pigs. Only if this were so could the story serve its purpose as revealing the authority of Jesus as the son of God. We have to take Mark's account on its face value or reject it altogether. As we have already seen with the account of the storm on the lake, it is impossible to accept the story as a demonstration of Jesus's power and at the same time interpret it using our own scientific categories.

But the story presents further difficulties and we need to distinguish problems that are intrinsic to Mark's narrative from problems which that narrative causes us.

Up to this point in Mark's narrative Jesus has refused to allow the demons to declare who he is. Now, even though the demoniac has addressed Jesus as *son of the Most High God*, just as the other demoniacs did, Jesus makes no attempt to silence him. Indeed, instead of insisting that nothing should be said, Jesus specifically orders the man to tell his own people about the way God has cured him in words that echo the reasons for selecting the Twelve. Yet he refuses to allow him to join his band of disciples. The inconsistency might be resolved by fastening on the place where the exorcism took place – the other side of the lake, in Gentile territory – and the fact that the man was possibly a Gentile himself and so unsuitable for inclusion in the closer band of disciples. It may be that he is told to tell his own people because this will be in an area where Jesus himself is not going to preach. If this is offered as an explanation, however, it means that Jesus's messiahship is made known to the Gentiles before it is revealed to the Jews, or even to the disciples, which is strange. To alleviate the difficulty by suggesting that revealing the identity of Jesus only mattered in Jewish Galilee, where it was important not to stir up political and military unrest against the Romans, is to confuse what may have been actual events in the life of Jesus with Mark's narrative. Mark has given no hint that this motive had any place in the action of Jesus.

For us, the story contains a moral problem. Jesus shows no concern for the pigs or their owners. He is not troubled when they rush down the hill and are drowned in the lake, and shows no sympathy with their owners who will have suffered a considerable financial loss. We feel that it is no wonder that those living in the area *begged Jesus to leave the district*, though to Mark the reason was that they were afraid of his supernatural powers. There is no ethical way out of this moral problem. Only a firm historical sense is of any help. What we are attempting to do is to read Mark's narrative in sequence, and to discover the picture of Jesus that Mark paints. To Mark the destruction of the pigs and the loss to their owners was not a problem. It did not even come into his mind, for his purpose in telling the story is to present another example of the authority that Jesus possessed and the fact that he was 'the son of the Most High God'. Even if he did not regard pigs as unclean animals, he certainly saw them as possessing little intrinsic value. There was no RSPCA in his day and little awareness of animal rights. We may remember that Paul could not credit God with having any concern for oxen (1 Cor. 9.9). Mark's attitude appears to be the same, and he does not think that Jesus was interested in the welfare of animals. Morality changes in the same way that our attitudes to exorcism change, and a sensitivity to history enables us to accept this.

5.21–43   Jesus, and presumably those with him, return to the other side of the lake and immediately a crowd collects.

Mark now describes two healing miracles linked together. Again REB provides a vivid account, but some significant features, mainly in the middle section, are obscured, inevitably, in a translation into English.

Jesus's fame as a healer has become well known and both a leading figure in the Jewish community and a woman who has been made unclean by her illness (see Lev. 15.25–30) come to him. As we read Mark we see that placing the story of the woman in the middle of the other story allows time for the action to develop.

5.22–4   The *synagogue president* was the person responsible for arranging what went on in the synagogue, normally not a trained rabbi. Like the demoniac in the tombs (5.6), he *threw himself down at his feet*, but a different verb is used. The president abases himself before Jesus to plead for his daughter, but there is no sense of the worship that the demoniac offered. Even though he might have been expected to side with the scribes and Pharisees in their opposition to Jesus, he comes to the healer for help when his daughter is at the point of death, and pleads for him to lay his hands on her *so that her life may be saved* (literally 'that she may be saved and live'). There is no reason to suppose that the verbs carry Christian overtones; 'to be saved' means 'to be healed'.

5.25–34   As Jesus is going with the president of the synagogue, the woman with the haemorrhage comes and touches Jesus's cloak. REB softens the literal Greek both of 'she had suffered many things of many doctors' and 'and was not benefited but rather became worse', with its *in spite of long treatment by many doctors* and *she had become worse rather than better*, reflecting the different attitude towards the medical profession that we have. The implication of Mark's statement is that doctors were unable to bring healing and often fleeced their patients. Even before Mark wrote his book, such a view had been modified by Ben Sirach, who held physicians in high regard, declaring that their skill comes from God and urging the sick to call a doctor as well as praying and offering sacrifice (Sir. 38.1–15).

The woman's thought, *I shall be healed*, is literally 'I shall be saved', the same verb that the president of the synagogue used.

Twice the woman's illness is called an *affliction*. The

word is the same as that used in 3.10 (REB 'the sick'), and, as there, it need not imply that it had been sent by God as a punishment.

When Jesus looks round *to see who had done it* the verb is in the feminine in Greek. It is impossible to represent the nuance in English. To translate it as 'to see the woman who had done it' is too definite. Yet the feminine may indicate that Mark thought that Jesus possessed supernatural insight and knew who it was that had touched him as well as knowing that the touch had been deliberate and that healing power had passed from him to the woman.

Because she was ritually unclean, the woman should not have been out among the crowd and should not have touched Jesus, for contact made those whom she touched unclean. This may account for her fear, although Mark gives no hint that he was aware of the question of uncleanness. Rather she comes trembling *because she knew what had happened to her*. The verb *fell at his feet* is a compound form of the verb in the account of the synagogue president. She does not approach Jesus as more than a human healer. Only the supernatural evil spirits know who Jesus is.

In themselves the words that Jesus speaks to the woman (literally, 'Your faith has saved you, go into peace') again possess Christian overtones, but, while Mark's readers may have sensed this, it is not an integral feature of the narrative. It has sometimes been said that by confronting the woman in this way Jesus turned her superstition into faith, but this is to think in modern ways. Her faith was not Pauline faith in Christ for salvation, but confidence that Jesus possessed the power to heal her.

5.35–43   The account of Jairus's daughter can now continue. She was at the point of death when Jairus set out. While Jesus was delayed by the woman, she has died, and a message is sent from the president's house.

Mark again draws attention to the importance of faith. Jesus overhears the message and tells the president *Do not be afraid; simply have faith.* As with the woman, faith is contrasted with fear. In that story, however, the woman's fear was caused by the fact that she had obtained healing, though surreptitiously. Here the ruler could well have been afraid that once his daughter was dead Jesus could give no help. There have been other occasions of fear in Mark so far. The disciples were afraid in the storm (though

Jesus simply charges them with being cowards), but after Jesus had calmed the wind and sea they were overcome with a different kind of fear as they wondered who he might be (4.35–41). When the people from Decapolis find the demoniac in his right mind and are told about the fate of the pigs they are afraid (5.15), again because Jesus has shown himself to be such a powerful exorcist.

When Jesus arrives at the house he discovers that the customary wailing at a death has begun. He says, *The child is not dead; she is asleep.* Those at the president's house laugh at the suggestion. We might wonder if he was right, although it is also surprising that he can say this so confidently before he has entered the room where she is. If so, it could only be that he had supernatural knowledge. Does this mean, then, that this is not an account of bringing the girl back to life after all? It has been suggested that Mark and his Christian readers would have linked 'sleeping' with the Christian hope of a resurrection to life after death. Death is not the end, and so the girl is not irrevocably dead.

For the first time in the book, Jesus singles out *Peter and James and James's brother John* to go with him into the room where the girl is lying. Mark does not explain why these are privileged among the Twelve. In his narrative they are the first persons Jesus called to follow him, but on that occasion Andrew is included with the other three (1.16–20) and he is left out here. They are the first disciples named in the list of the Twelve in 3.16, where Andrew drops back to fourth place. By the time that Mark was writing, these three disciples must have become the most prominent and best known of the Twelve.

Mark gives the words that Jesus spoke to the girl in Aramaic *Talitha cum.* In miracle stories in the Hellenistic world words spoken in a foreign language were often thought to possess special power, and the Christian scholar Origen declared that they lose their power if translated. Whether this was Mark's view is uncertain, since he gives a Greek translation, not quite exact because the literal meaning is 'Lamb, get up', but accurate enough, since 'lamb' was apparently a term of endearment. The cure is immediate – the girl gets up and walks about. Some commentators find special significance in the fact that the verb *Get up* is 'arise', the verb used of the resurrection of Christ, but caution needs to be exercised, since it is the normal verb for getting up, and has already been used several times by Mark (e.g. 4.27). Although two of these occur in miracle stories (2.9, 11, 'stand up' and 3.3 'come and stand out here', literally 'rise into the midst'), there is no reason to suppose that Mark intended his readers to make a link with the resurrection.

Up to this point it has been only the demoniacs and the leper who have been ordered to say nothing about their healing, and in each case an explanation can be given. The evil spirits know who Jesus is, but either he does not want it to be generally known or he does not want the information to come from demons. The leper is to get official recognition that he no longer has leprosy and then to make the appropriate sacrifices rather than rush off telling everyone that he has been cured. Now the same command is given to the three disciples and the girl's parents. It seems an impossible instruction. How could bringing the girl back to life be concealed, especially as the mourners and a crowd were outside?

It may be that Mark added the command for a theological reason. The meaning of the miracles, and therefore the true knowledge of who Jesus is, can only be understood after the resurrection. Before Jesus is raised from the dead they would be regarded simply as the wonder-working of a divine magician. This may appear over-subtle. From the very opening sentence of his book Mark shows that his purpose is to present Jesus as the son of God. Even though the command is expressed in very strong terms (*he gave them strict instructions not to let anyone know about it*), it is possible that he meant no more than that they should not go rushing about telling everyone what had happened, and so draw even greater crowds.

Other ways of explaining the emphasis on keeping the exorcisms and healings a secret have been suggested. Mark (or the traditions that came down to him) inserted the commands for silence as a way of resolving the inconsistency between the fact that no one in Jesus's lifetime accepted him as the messiah and later Christians believed that he was. Jesus himself issued the commands because he realized that the true nature of his messiahship could only be revealed after he had been crucified and he was seen to be a suffering servant – to acknowledge that he was the messiah before this would have run the risk of triggering off a national uprising against the Romans. Neither is convincing, largely because the demands for secrecy are not all of the same kind, as we have seen. It will be better simply to read Mark's narrative in sequence and note exactly what is said on each occasion.

One further question remains. What is to be made of bringing the dead back to life? We may be tempted to suggest that at the time of Jesus's clinical death was difficult to determine and in fact the girl was in a deep coma from which Jesus roused her. If we find support for this hypothesis in the words of Jesus, declaring that she is not dead but asleep, we are faced with the problem that he has not yet seen the girl. If it is then claimed that he had supernatural knowledge, this goes beyond the strictly 'scientific' explanation that is being attempted. Alternatively, we may compare accounts of people whose heart and breathing stopped and who were resuscitated by doctors, though it needs to be noted that the 'death' in all these cases is only for a very short time, and that once the brain has been starved of oxygen death, or, at the least, damage to the brain is inevitable. As Mark tells the story, a considerable time elapsed between the girl having 'died' and Jesus reaching her. More importantly, as has been observed before, such rationalizing destroys the meaning Mark finds in the miracle. If the miracle has a natural explanation it can no longer arouse wonder and awe, or provide testimony to Jesus as the son of God. Mark's theology and Mark's narrative are of a piece and cannot be wrenched apart.

6.1–6   Jesus makes a return visit to his *home town* Nazareth (1.9) and teaches in the synagogue on the sabbath. Presumably he was invited to do so according to the common practice of asking visiting teachers to speak to the congregation. Synagogues were primarily places for teaching rather than worship in the Christian sense. Again Mark tells us nothing about what he said. His purpose is to record the rather cynical aphorism, almost a proverb, spoken by Jesus: *A prophet never lacks honour except in his home town, among his relations and his own family.* A secondary purpose is to record the further rejection of Jesus by his own people. The local scribes and Pharisees had opposed him and were now plotting with the men of Herod's party to bring about his death (2.6, 16, 18, 24; 3.2, 6). His friends and family supposed that he was out of his senses and tried to take charge of him (3.21, 31). The officials from Jerusalem accused him of being in league with Satan (3.22). Why the Jewish people rejected their messiah was a puzzle for the first Christians, as Paul shows in his attempts to find an explanation (cf. Rom. 9–11).

REB expresses the response of the congregation in vivid, idiomatic English that reflects the spirit of the questions they ask. Some manuscripts give the fourth question as: 'Is he not the son of the carpenter and Mary' rather than *Is he not the carpenter, the son of Mary*, and REB, which is rather sparing of footnotes, gives this as an alternative, showing that the arguments on either side are fairly evenly divided. Among the Jews, to designate someone by his mother, even if her husband had died, was something of an insult, carrying the suggestion that she was not married, but we cannot be sure that Mark was aware of this. By contrast, Origen in the second century found it impossible to believe that the son of God could ever have been a manual worker, and seems to have known the form of the text in the margin. Mark never mentions Joseph, and if we did not possess the later Gospels we should not know of his existence. Later Christian tradition took the brothers and sisters of Jesus to be his cousins, in an attempt to maintain the perpetual virginity of Mary.

In vv. 2 and 5 *miracles* are literally 'powers'. The words 'miracles' and 'powers' do not carry quite the same meaning. We recall that Jesus knew that 'power' had gone from him to heal the woman with the haemorrhage. The people in the synagogue accepted that Jesus gave wise teaching and possessed the power to heal people and cast out demons, and yet they *turned against him*. This is a little too positive. The word means 'stumbled' or 'took offence' (the same word that is found in 4.17, REB 'they quickly lose faith'). It was his lowly origins that prevented them from accepting that he was the messiah. As a result Jesus was *unable to do any miracle there*. Mark, unlike Matthew (Matt. 13.58) has no difficulty in presenting Jesus as being unable to perform any 'miracle' there because they were unreceptive, or in recording that *he was astonished at their want of faith*. Faith is important for Mark. Here, as earlier, it means accepting the authority of Jesus to teach and heal.

So Jesus left Nazareth and *went round the villages teaching*. Mark's narrative continues with 'and', and makes no greater break at this point than he does with the next sentence: 'And he called to him the Twelve'. The heading inserted by REB is misleading. Mark makes no sharp divisions in his narrative at all.

6.7–13   At last Jesus sends the Twelve out to do what he had appointed them for (3.14). The authority over unclean spirits that Jesus possessed is passed on to them, so that they *drove out many demons*. Exorcism is one of the main evidences for the authority of Jesus in Mark. They are to go in pairs, travelling light – *no bread, no pack* (more probably a beggar's collecting bag than a haversack), *no money in their belts* (literally 'copper', not even small coins, let alone silver denarii), with *sandals* but no *second coat*. They are to remain with their original host in a village, not seek better accommodation. If their message is not accepted they are to *shake the dust off* [their] *feet as* [they] *leave, as a solemn warning*. 'As a solemn warning' is literally, 'as a witness to them', and although it may be a warning to repent before it is too late, it seems more likely that Mark saw it as a witness that they have rejected God's coming reign.

They also *anointed many sick people with oil and cured them*. The mention of anointing comes as a surprise. Oil was commonly used to facilitate healing at the time, but this is ritual anointing, quite different from the action of the Good Samaritan, who bathed the Jewish victim's wounds with oil and wine (Luke 10.34). Jesus anoints no one, and the only other reference to anointing the sick in the whole New Testament is in James 5.14. We have suspected several times that Mark had Christians of his own time in mind as much as the historical life of Jesus himself, and this seems to confirm it. The instructions that Jesus gives the Twelve are effectively the practices of later Christian travelling preachers. According to Acts 8.14; 13.1–2; and 15.22, 39–40 the later apostles regularly travelled in twos. The *Didache* 11–12 also recognizes the existence of travelling Christian preachers, although by the writer's time some had clearly been sponging on their hosts and he warns against allowing them to remain more than two or three days without working to support themselves.

Curiously, according to Mark's account Jesus does not tell the Twelve what they are to say, and up to this point he has given them very little direct teaching. Mark says that *they proclaimed the need for repentance*. The word 'proclaimed' is that used for proclaiming the Christian gospel, but 'that they should repent' is no more than John the Baptist preached. What this proclamation actually was is therefore uncertain. Mark's reticence is similar to his failure to say what the authoritative teaching of Jesus actually was. The fact that they preached and had authority over the demons is more important to him than what they said. Possibly, however, he thought of the Twelve as preparing the way for the End and the establishing of the kingdom of God, as John the Baptist had prepared the way for the coming of the messiah.

6.14–29   To fill in the gap between the departure of the Twelve and their return Mark inserts an account of the death of John the Baptist. We possess a parallel, non-Christian account by Josephus who wrote in about AD 90. Josephus was a historian with access to official records. Mark draws on the stories that must have been whispered in the alleys and markets of many Palestinian towns.

This Herod (Herod Antipas) was a son of Herod the Great and ruled the tetrarchy of Galilee and Perea from 4 BC to AD 39. He was deposed and banished by the Romans when he made a request to be given the title 'king'. Apart from the bare fact that Herod had John executed, it is impossible to harmonize the two accounts by Mark and Josephus. They have two quite different backgrounds and were told for different purposes, and it is pointless to ask what actually happened or what Herod's motives were. Josephus is aware of the political situation and describes the execution of John as an attempt by Herod to get rid of a dangerous demagogue before he became a threat to his power. Mark tells his story from the perspective of the common people, who were interested in personalities, sexual scandal and the lurid detail of the presentation of John's head on a plate. Some of the details in Mark seem to be incorrect, and in several places the awkward and uncertain Greek (which is made even more difficult by occasional textual uncertainty) has been simplified by REB. Herod Antipas was properly Tetrarch, but he was doubtless commonly referred to as King. The relationships in Herod's family were complex. According to Josephus, Herodias was first married to another half-brother of Antipas, not to Philip, while Philip was married to Salome, not to her mother.

Now King Herod heard about Jesus, for his fame had spread. The story begins awkwardly. The Greek reads literally, 'And King Herod heard, for his name became known', without stating what Herod heard or mentioning Jesus. In the narrative sequence strict grammar makes it the activity of the Twelve that came to Herod's notice, but in the sentence itself it is more natural to follow REB. Some commentators suggest that this shows that Mark has incorporated into his narrative a story that already existed in the present form in the tradition that came down to him. Whether this is so is less important than trying to discover why Mark tells the story.

Mark introduces his account of the death of John the Baptist with some of the rumours about Jesus that were current: his power to work miracles showed that he was John, risen from the dead; he was Elijah; he was a prophet like the earlier prophets. Since Mark does not credit John with performing miracles, we might wonder why the miracles that Jesus performed should have suggested to anyone that he was John, but perhaps if John has risen from the dead that would be evidence of his power. Elijah did not die but was taken up into heaven (2 Kgs. 2.1–12), and Malachi 4.5 declared that he would return before 'the great and terrible day of the LORD comes'. REB has added 'of old' to indicate that *like one of the prophets* referred to the prophets in the Old Testament, with perhaps the further intention of showing that even the appearance of a prophet was something strikingly new – a long time had elapsed since the last prophet appeared and it seems to have been generally accepted that prophecy had come to an end. Mark tells us that Herod himself decided that Jesus was John, risen from the dead. We may wonder how Mark knew this, but it does not greatly matter. He knew about the rumours about Jesus that were current, but he has already shown his readers that none of the identifications was right. Jesus is still not recognized as the son of God.

Why did Mark include the account of John's execution at this point? We can only guess. It is hardly just to fill in the time between the sending out and the return of the Twelve, though it does that. If the main emphasis is placed on the introduction, the account of the way John was put to death provides the necessary background to the rumour that Jesus was John, raised from the dead, since the last we heard of John was that he had been arrested (1.14). There may be a further reason.

John the Baptist is important to Mark. He begins his book with John's appearance in the desert. He quotes passages of Scripture, which he claims were fulfilled in the coming of John, but gives no similar prophecies of Jesus. He uses the Christian word 'proclaims' of John's preaching. His description of John shows him to be a prophet like Elijah. He proclaimed the coming of the mighty one, who would baptize with holy spirit, and he baptized Jesus, though apparently without realizing that he was this mighty one. Jesus did not begin his preaching until John had been 'arrested' – and as we have seen, Mark implies that he was handed over by God to his enemies. It is rather curious that, although John proclaims the coming of the one who is mightier than he is, in Mark's account none of John's disciples transfer to Jesus. It may be that Jesus's first disciples had been baptized by John, but Mark gives no hint that this is so. Moreover, even after Jesus began his work of teaching, exorcism and healing, John's disciples remain separate, and are described as keeping a fast at the same time as the Pharisees do (1.18). Now *when John's disciples heard the news, they came and took his body away and laid it in a tomb*. The story of John in many ways runs parallel to the story of Jesus. Like Jesus he 'proclaims' repentance. Like Jesus he attracts great crowds and has disciples. Like Jesus he is 'arrested'. Like Jesus he is put to death by the secular rulers. Like Jesus his disciples take his body and lay it in a tomb.

Conflict and hostility appear in Mark's narrative as early as chapter 2, and John's arrest is full of foreboding. This account of Herod's action heightens the sense of menace.

6.30–4   Still continuing the narrative with a simple 'And', omitted by REB, which inserts another heading at this point, the disciples gather together and return to Jesus. Mark calls them *apostles* here, a name that later became almost a technical term for the Twelve, though Paul applies it to himself and others as well. Apart from 3.14, where 'whom he also called apostles' is almost certainly an addition to Mark's original book, the word occurs nowhere else in Mark's narrative. He probably slipped unconsciously into the term with which he was familiar, and there is no need to suppose that he intended to emphasize that the Twelve had been acting as 'apostles', messengers sent as the representatives of their master and with that authority.

They *reported to him all that they had done and taught*. The verbs reflect the description of their activities in vv. 12–13, but the verb here is 'taught' rather than 'proclaimed'. Mark hardly intended any difference between the two words. The authoritative teaching of Jesus was important to him, while both Jesus and the Twelve 'proclaimed' the gospel. There is no need to assume that Jesus was perturbed by the death of John the Baptist and needed time to think it through with his disciples. Mark implies that he realized that they were tired and needed to escape from the crowds. *'Come with me, by yourselves, to some remote place and rest a little'* ('with me' is not found in the Greek and 'some remote place' is 'a desert place').

Most scholars, intent on sifting out the traditions that Mark uses, suggest that vv. 30–3 were written by Mark to provide a setting for the next miracle that he is about to describe, but they form a natural sequence in Mark's narrative and we need not be diverted from the story as Mark tells it. Neither need we worry about how the crowd could get to the place across the lake faster on land than Jesus and the disciples did in the boat. Of greater concern is Mark's statement that when Jesus saw the large crowd on the shore *his heart went out to them, because they were like sheep without a shepherd; and he began to teach them many things*.

As often, Mark gives no account of what Jesus taught, but his description of Jesus's compassion for the crowd is somewhat inconsistent with Jesus's earlier statement that all his teaching to 'those outside' was in parables, so that they would not be able to understand. This does not trouble Mark who is rushing on to recount the miracle, which he tells with the same extensive detail that he gave to the miracles in chapter 5.

6.35–44   The question that comes immediately into the minds of modern congregations when they hear this story is 'what actually happened?' Some people accept it as Mark tells it. Jesus, because he was God, was able to turn five loaves and two fish into enough food to satisfy a large hungry crowd, and did just that. They imagine that it is a scientific problem and argue that God, as creator, is perfectly able to perform such a miracle. What they fail to come to terms with is the ethical problem that this raises. If God is able to multiply food so that a crowd in a lonely place can be fed, why does he do nothing for the millions of people who are starving in our present world? But then, how could he do so without ruining many farmers and causing economic chaos?

One common way of rationalizing the story is to suggest that Jesus persuaded those who had brought some food with them to share it with those who had not. It is often suggested that this in itself is miracle enough, given human selfishness, and carries a valuable spiritual message for the rich nations today. This is true, but that is not how Mark tells the story, and cannot be derived from his account. Those who had food with them would have had to have far more than they needed for everyone to have as much as they could eat and then for there to be 12 large baskets over.

Other, even less probable, suggestions are that the numbers in the crowd were exaggerated, or that, rather like modern eucharistic practice, only small fragments of bread and fish were given to each person. The exaggeration would have been extreme if the five small loaves are taken seriously, while the emphasis on the fact that the people ate their fill shows that a real meal was intended.

If literal fact and rationalizations are rejected, however, the story has to be taken as a legend without any historical foundation. Some are happy to accept this, and move directly to asking what Mark was trying to convey to his readers. Whether this is 'more rewarding', as one scholar suggests, may be doubted. Even if we find spiritual and ethical meaning in various kinds of fiction, it is surely different when the life of Jesus is concerned. Others will find such a dismissal of Mark's narrative intolerable, and will resign themselves to believing that there must have been some event that triggered off the legend, although it is impossible to discover what it was. They too should ask themselves how important historical fact is for the Christian faith. For the present we return to Mark's narrative.

From several features in it, such as the dialogue between

Jesus and the disciples, the fact that the grass was green rather than burnt up in the summer heat, and the exact number both of loaves and fish and the baskets of fragments collected up, some have claimed that the account must come from an eyewitness, perhaps Peter whom tradition linked with Mark as the source of his information about Jesus, and so support its being factual. The details may equally be part of an elaborated legend, much like the details in the account of the death of John the Baptist, added to emphasize the impressiveness of the miracle. And impressive it certainly is. The crowd *numbered five thousand men*. The amount of bread needed would have cost the equivalent of what it took a workman over six months to earn, a vast sum of money to fishermen. The food that Jesus multiplied to feed this large crowd consisted of only five small flat loaves and two fish. After they had all eaten their fill, 12 large baskets of scraps were collected up. Mark does not give a reason for doing this or consider how these baskets were obtained in the desert place. It is a prodigious wonder.

Even though Mark does not record the amazement of the crowd, as he does at the end of several other miracles, he clearly sees this as an expression of the power of Jesus, the son of God, and this must have been his main purpose in recounting the miracle.

Scholars have found varied symbolism in the story. Mark's Christian readers may have found echoes of their own Eucharists in the actions of Jesus, who *looked up to heaven, said the blessing* (literally 'blessed [the loaves and fish]' or 'gave thanks'), *broke the loaves, and gave them to the disciples to distribute*, but we cannot be certain that Mark intended the feeding of the crowd to prefigure the Eucharist, for offering thanks before eating was the normal practice, and Jesus would have had to break the loaves in order to give them to the disciples to distribute among the crowd.

Some scholars have pointed to the miracle performed by Elisha, when he fed 100 men with 20 barley loaves (2 Kgs. 4.42–4). Although there are some similarities, this was hardly the origin of Mark's miracle. Others point to the giving of manna in the wilderness (Exod. 16) and the fact that some rabbis taught that the messiah would again give his people manna. Mark shows no awareness of this.

Others note that one feature of the expected messianic age was a banquet, and suggest that Jesus acted like a host at such a banquet, but it would be odd if the Jesus who wished his identity to remain hidden should give a messianic banquet to outsiders. Other attempts to find symbolism are even more extreme – the five loaves symbolize the five books of the Law; the green grass shows that the wilderness has become fertile in the messianic age (cf. Isa. 35.1); the organization of the people in hundreds and fifties echoes the action of Moses in Exodus 18.21.

6.45–6   Why Jesus *made the disciples embark and cross to Bethsaida ahead of him* is not entirely clear. The verb translated 'made' is a strong one and normally means 'compelled', though it may have a weakened sense here. Mark adds *while he dismissed the crowd*, but gives no reason why he had to do this on his own. It has been suggested that it replaces the demand for secrecy, but if so Mark does not make it plain. Others invoke John's explanation that the crowd wanted to make Jesus king (John 6.15) and suggest that Jesus was afraid that the disciples would be caught up in the ferment. This must be rejected on the grounds that it moves too swiftly from Mark's narrative to the possible historical events in the life of Jesus. Mark must be interpreted without reference to the other Gospels, and there is no hint that the crowd wanted to make him king in his narrative. For the sake of the story that follows, Jesus had to be separated from his disciples.

After taking leave of them, he went up the hill to pray. Although the Greek word can mean hill, it is more usually translated 'mountain' elsewhere and may have special significance. It was on a mountain that Jesus chose the Twelve (3.13). Now, like Moses, Jesus goes up the mountain to meet God. In 1.35, rather similarly, Jesus left the crowds and went into the desert to pray.

6.47–52   This miracle is even more incredible than the feeding of the five thousand. Mark seems to go out of his way to exaggerate how uncanny it all was. The boat was *well out on the water* and it is *somewhere between three and six in the morning*, yet Jesus sees the disciples *labouring at the oars*. He comes *walking on the lake*, but then *he was going to pass by them* (the Greek is stronger: 'intended to pass by'), and only comes to them after they *cried out* because they *thought it was a ghost*. Mark emphasizes that *they all saw him*

– there is to be no doubt about it: he was walking on the water. As soon as Jesus *climbed into the boat the wind dropped* (the words are the same as in the story of stilling the storm). So it is not simply that Jesus walked on the water, but also, Mark implies, he calmed the wind, in order that they would no longer have to battle *against a head wind*.

Rationalizing seems impossible. The disciples, fishermen who knew the lake, could not have been mistaken and supposed that Jesus was walking on the water when in fact he was walking on the shore or paddling in shallow water, for Mark stresses that the boat was in the middle of the lake and Jesus comes up to them where they are. We have to accept that this incident simply could not have happened.

The ethical and theological problems are even greater. There was no reason for Jesus to walk on the lake. He was not even coming to help them, for he intended to go past them. That is a problem even for conservative scholars, who either deny that this was his actual intention or say that he was testing their faith. To argue that it reflects Exodus 33.17–34, where God reveals his glory to Moses by going past him, introduces a typology of which Mark says nothing explicit and is improbable in the face of his sparse Old Testament quotations. Moreover, to suppose that Jesus could walk on the lake is to deny that he was fully human. What we have here is little different from the wonder stories that are found in the apocryphal gospels, in which the boy Jesus makes clay birds fly and stretches a plank of wood that had been cut too short so that it becomes the required length.

Starting from the fact that Mark thought that it happened exactly as he describes, we have to ask how he interpreted it. It is usual to fasten on the reaction of the disciples. When they saw Jesus they *were terrified*. This, however, is not a sense of awe in the presence of the divine. It is abject fear. Jesus's words to the disciples, *'Take heart! It is I; do not be afraid'*, show this. It is a fear that has to be overcome. After he climbed into the boat and the wind dropped *they were utterly astounded*. Here is the wonder that is the reaction to other miracles.

Some suggest that Mark saw the walking on the water as a symbolic repetition of the crossing of the Sea in Exodus 14, but this is uncertain since he gives no hint that this is his meaning, and in any case in the Exodus the Israelites walked through the sea, not on it. If support is sought by linking the feeding of the crowd with the giving of manna, the connection can be no more than that both belong to the Exodus traditions, for the order is the reverse of that in Exodus. If Mark intended his readers to see Jesus as a greater Moses, he has concealed this very effectively. Others point out that the Old Testament often refers to Yahweh's victory over the waters, and in Job 9.8 he is described as treading on the depths of the sea (REB 'trod on the back of the sea monster'), but again there is little to suggest that Mark had this in mind. Even though he has earlier shown that Jesus is master of wind and sea (4.41), this hardly explains why he depicted Jesus as walking on the lake.

The only direct clue that Mark gives is totally baffling: *they had not understood the incident of the loaves; their minds were closed.* REB is unhelpful here and it is necessary to go back to the Greek. Literally this reads: 'for they did not understand about the loaves, but their heart was hardened'. It is not the 'incident' of the loaves, the entire miracle, but the loaves themselves. And their minds were not simply 'closed' in the way that we speak of someone who will not accept something which is obvious as having a 'closed mind' – their minds were supernaturally hardened. We may compare the hardness of the Pharisees' hearts in 3.5, and the lack of understanding of the crowd, which Mark held to be divinely intended (4.11–12). What the disciples should have understood about the loaves will be considered later (pp. 90–4).

6.53–6   Jesus and the disciples *completed the crossing and landed at Gennesaret.* Mark's geography is vague and there is no need to try to discover reasons for the destination being different from that in v. 45. He then provides a summary of Jesus's healing. *Scoured the whole countryside* represents 'they ran around that whole region', not perhaps looking for sick people to bring to Jesus, as REB implies, but with the idea that they rushed about saying that Jesus was there and bringing the sick people to him. Like the paralysed man, the sick are brought *on their beds* (the same word) and like the woman with the haemorrhage, they *begged him to let them simply touch the edge of his cloak,* and *all who touched him* (or more probably 'it', i.e. the edge of his cloak; the

Greek could mean either) *were healed* (literally, 'saved'). Whether the word translated 'edge' was the 'tassel' (REB mg.), which the Law decreed should be worn on the four corners of the outer cloak (Num. 15.38–9; Deut. 22.12), depends on how strictly Mark supposed Jesus observed the Law.

Jesus's clothes possess the power that he himself had, but this does not mean that they were regarded as an extension of his personality. In the same way that holiness or uncleanness could be transmitted to the objects that were touched, so Jesus's clothes were imbued with his power. It again reveals the distance that exists between our understanding of healing and that of Mark. New Testament healings are not suitable models for us. We saw earlier that Mark does not seem to have had a very high opinion of doctors (5.26). Moreover, a large part of Jesus's healings were exorcisms, the driving out of 'unclean spirits', demons who were themselves unclean and imparted ritual uncleanness to those who were possessed. We no longer believe that mental illness is caused by demons, we have rejected ideas of ritual uncleanness, and we do not accept that Jesus's clothes could have been filled with healing power – indeed, what 'healing power' can mean is extremely doubtful. We hold doctors in high esteem, and turn to medical science for healing. Even if we may have doubts about some claims by experts, we accept the scientific basis of medicine and the attempt to discover what causes disease, how it can be prevented, cured or held in remission, what drugs are effective and why those drugs work. We know diseases are caused by germs and viruses, and are aware of the effect that genes can have in some illnesses. Unless the resort to 'alternative medicine' is mere superstition, its effectiveness has to be proved by clinical trials as much as ordinary drugs. This raises important questions about healing services, which cannot be pursued here. All that can be said is that to assert that 'Healing was central to the ministry of Jesus', ought not to imply that the kinds of healings that Mark describes are possible in modern services of healing or that we should try to reproduce them.

7.1–8 After the series of miracle stories, Mark returns to conflicts with the Pharisees and scribes, again the official representatives from Jerusalem, as in 3.22. A few words and phrases in REB need to be clarified before the narrative is considered as a whole.

Defiled hands is literally 'common' hands, which Mark uses in the sense of ritually unclean.

REB mg. notes that 'some witnesses' (in fact many manuscripts) add *with the fist* after 'without washing their hands', while others add *frequently* or *thoroughly*. The latter appears to be an attempt to make sense of the strange expression. It seems probable that Mark wrote 'with the fist' and it has been suggested that this meant 'with a fistful of water', 'with one clenched fist in the other', or 'up to the wrist'. The Mishnah (m. Yad. 1.1) contains the statement that at least a quarter-*log* of water must be poured over the hands. A *log* was probably about a pint or half a litre, so that a quarter of a *log* was a very small amount, which shows that the intention is to remove ritual impurity rather than to clean the hands, and 'with the fist' might be an attempt to state this.

To translate 'the tradition of the elders' by *ancient tradition* is misleading, since the elders were the rabbis and the traditions were growing up within Judaism during the time of Jesus, elaborating on the Law in order to ensure that it was being fully kept.

As in the incident of plucking the ears of corn on the sabbath, the Pharisees and the scribes make their accusation against the disciples to Jesus. They are not keeping the Law strictly, as it had been interpreted by the rabbis. Mark adds an explanation: *(For Pharisees and Jews in general never eat without washing their hands, in obedience to ancient tradition)*. His intended readers are clearly Gentiles. Moreover, by saying 'Jews in general' (literally 'all the Jews') he shows that the division between his Christian readers and the Jews has already taken place. It may make us even more doubtful about the symbolism that many find in the last chapter. Would these Gentile Christians have known the Old Testament Scriptures sufficiently well to be able to pick up the obscure references that are never made explicit? Having mentioned ritual hand-washing, Mark adds that *on coming from the market-place they never eat without first washing* (ritual washings are meant), and that there are *many other points on which they maintain traditional rules* (literally 'which they have received to keep'), and gives as examples the ritual washing of various utensils, even though this is not relevant to the Pharisees' question. The rules, later much elaborated by the rabbis, go back to the Levitical laws concerning removing impurity from articles that have been contaminated with uncleanness. There is no evidence that any Jews, however scrupulous, washed after coming from the market-place, but it is possible that in predominantly Gentile towns some did so because of the fear that they might have incurred pollution. To avoid the problem, some commentators have suggested that it was food bought in the market that was washed (cf. GNB, 'nor do they eat anything that comes from the market unless they wash it first'), but it is difficult to derive this meaning from the Greek.

Jesus responds with a quotation from Isaiah and applies it to the Pharisees, whom he calls *hypocrites*. Almost all translators retain the transliterated word, which has firmly entered the English language, though CEV attempts a modern alternative with, 'You are nothing but show-offs' – and fails. This is the only time Mark uses the word, which in classical Greek meant 'actor', 'one who plays a part', and in the New Testament means 'dissembler', one who says one thing and does another. It does not fit the present situation, and probably comes from later Christian hostility towards the Jews. Jesus interprets the traditions of the elders as *the commandments of men* (we might wonder why REB did not go boldly for 'human commandments', and later 'human tradition'). *They teach as doctrines* is literally 'they teach teachings' – 'doctrines' is too theological. The whole quotation from Isaiah 29.13 is closer to the Septuagint than the Hebrew, but is not exact. The difficulty is rather greater than a matter of the original language. The quotation in the Hebrew form could not provide a reply to the Pharisees, for it does not draw a contrast between divine and human commandments. As Mark tells it, however, the story is logically consistent. Jesus is depicted as setting into sharp contrast the Law and the tradition of the elders, claiming that Isaiah spoke directly to this situation, and declaring that the Pharisees and scribes *neglect the commandment of God in order to maintain the tradition of men.* This is exactly the opposite of what the oral law was developed to achieve, and reflects the bitterness of the growing conflict between Christians and Jews.

7.9–13   To show that the Pharisees and scribes are neglecting the Law Mark adds an example of the way they are clever at *setting aside the commandment of God in order to maintain* [their] *tradition*. What precisely is condemned is uncertain. Corban is correctly translated by *set apart for God* (more literally, 'given'), but it is not clear what the son does. He may have vowed to give the money that would have supported his parents to the Temple, or in a moment of anger sworn a 'corban-oath' (apparently a common form of oath) that he would not support them and this was taken to be binding. An Aramaic inscription on an ossuary found near Jerusalem reads: 'Everything that a person will find to his profit in this ossuary is qorban to God from the one within', where the meaning can only be 'must be treated as if it were an offering to God', and this may well be what happened here. The son tells his parents that they must regard the money that would have supported them as if it had been dedicated to the Temple. Whichever it was, the point of the illustration is that the scribes are said to regard keeping the oath as more serious than caring for one's parents.

There are two problems with this. One is that the Mishnah records debates about precisely this question, and one line of tradition declared that honouring parents took precedence. It seems, therefore, that some, perhaps most, rabbis in the time of Jesus would have taught that God required that parents should be supported. The other problem is that keeping oaths is declared a sacred duty in the Law (Num. 30.2; Deut. 23.21–3), so that the problem is not a conflict between the Law and the tradition of the elders but between different commandments within the Law. The conclusion, *And you do many other things just like that*, is further anti-Jewish polemic.

It is doubtful Mark is offering teaching that has a direct bearing on the lives of his readers. Jews in his day would be unlikely to criticize Christians for failing to observe practices that only the most rigorous Jews observed, and while the question of vows was a live issue among Jews, it can hardly have troubled Gentile Christians. This stock anti-Pharisaic polemic reveals the hostility of later Christians to the Jews rather than teaching Christians how they should live. Jesus is depicted as utterly rejecting Judaism, and this is done by means of a caricature of Jewish ritual observance.

7.14–16   REB makes a sharper break than is found in Mark's narrative *On another occasion* springs from an attempt to produce a sequence that is historically credible, but Mark links this teaching closely with what precedes it. The Greek is literally, 'And calling the crowd again, he said to them, "Listen to me everyone and understand"'. This address to the crowd is slightly perplexing and some regard it as so inconsistent with Mark's view of parables in 4.11–12 that it calls that theory into question. But however straightforward Jesus's words, *'Nothing that goes into a person from outside can defile him; no, it is the things that come out of a person that defile him'* may seem to us, Mark regards them as a *parable* (7.17), which Jesus has to explain to the disciples. Moreover, 'Listen' was how Mark introduced the parable of the Sower (4.3), which also needed to be explained to the disciples. Even though Jesus says 'and understand', in Mark's view the crowd plainly did not, for even the 'insiders' failed to grasp the meaning.

7.17–23   *When he had left the people and gone indoors, his disciples questioned him about the parable.* The explanation is startling. *Do you not see that nothing that goes into a person from outside can defile him, because it does not go into the heart but into the stomach, and so goes out into the drain?* This immediately nullifies all the laws that distinguish between ritually clean and unclean food, and REB, correctly, takes *By saying this he declared all foods clean* as a comment by Mark, although the literal Greek is simply, 'cleansing all foods'. It has been suggested that in the original Aramaic the phrase meant, 'all the food being cast out and purged away'. If Mark rightly understood what Jesus said, it is difficult to understand why the question of whether the Old Testament food laws still applied was a matter of lively debate and disagreement among the first Christians, as Acts and Paul's letters clearly show. Possibly Mark added this comment because the saying had been interpreted differently by various groups of Christians. Some commentators claim that the words attributed to Jesus were invented by the early Church. Others suggest that Mark has turned some teaching that applied to a specific incident into a general rule, comparing his teaching on the sabbath in 2.23—3.6. There, it is claimed, Jesus dealt with the case in hand and did not abrogate keeping the sabbath. It was only later that Christians widened it in this

way after they had adopted Sunday as the main occasion
for worship. Yet others suggest that although the words
express a direct contrast, Jesus was really saying that the
food laws were less important than the moral ones.
Hebrew and Aramaic having no comparative forms of the
adjective, could only express direct contrasts.

Resisting the temptation to determine too hastily what
was historical, we continue to limit our attention to
Mark's narrative. Some difficulties remain. Jesus has just
condemned the scribes for neglecting the commandment
of God, yet here he apparently rejects some of those laws.
Moreover, here the issue concerns clean and unclean food,
whereas earlier the scribes had condemned the disciples
for eating food without previously washing their hands.
The link can be made only if it is assumed that the Jews
believed that the uncleanness passed to the food. This,
however, is a different matter from foods that were intrin-
sically unclean, such as pork, which is what Mark's comment refers to. (It is necessary to keep in mind that
washing the hands was not a matter of hygiene but of
ritual purity, so that to suggest that dirty hands contam-
inate food is to introduce modern scientific ideas into the
first-century narrative.)

Mark assumes that his readers do not observe the food
laws. If he himself was a Jew, the words also show that
some Jewish Christians had abandoned them as well. This
was a major departure from the Jewish way of life. Even
though there are very few references to the distinction
between clean and unclean animals in the Old Testament
apart from the lists in Leviticus 11 and Deuteronomy 14
(Gen. 7.2–3; Judg. 13.7; Hos. 9.3 are the main ones), it was
accepted that the whole Law was given by God. Why
some animals were 'clean' and could be eaten, and others
were 'unclean' has long been a puzzle. The *Letter of
Aristeas* (third to first century BC), Philo of Alexandria (an
older contemporary of Jesus) and the Christian *Epistle
of Barnabas* offer allegorical interpretations, seeing the
unclean animals as various vices, though Philo also suggested that the food laws were intended to restrain glut-
tony. Most Jews probably accepted that the laws were to
be obeyed simply because God had commanded them. By
keeping these laws the Jews showed the distinctiveness of
their religion and their separation from the Gentiles.

Jesus then defines the *evil things* that *come from within* and *defile a person*. All are moral wrongs. After *evil thoughts* comes a list of 12 vices. It is a straight list, but by inserting a semi-colon after 'malice', and linking 'acts of' with all six vices in the first set, REB attempts to show that the first six sins are in the plural, while the second six are in the singular. If the distinction is significant, it might imply that the first group are repeated actions while the second set are different vices, or possibly that two separate lists have been combined. Such lists are found elsewhere in the New Testament (cf. Rom. 1.29–31; Gal. 5.19–21; 1 Pet. 4.3), and were common in the Graeco-Roman world. Among Jewish writings may be noted the Hellenistic Wisdom of Solomon, where a list contains 'bloody murder, theft and fraud, corruption, treachery, riot, perjury, honest folk driven to distraction; ingratitude, depravity, sexual perversion, breakdown of marriage, adultery, debauchery' (Wisd. 14.25–6). Individually almost all the Greek terms in Mark's list are found in the Septuagint, but apart from short collections of commandments, as in the Decalogue, such lists are not found there.

Evil thoughts are not just ideas in the mind but evil designs that lead to evil actions. 'Machinations', which one scholar suggests, is perhaps too strong. 'Evil intentions' (NRSV, NJB) gives the sense.

Fornication is now archaic, though also retained by NRSV and NJB. CEV's 'vulgar deeds' is incorrect. NIV's 'sexual immorality' is better, though it begs the question as to what actions count as immoral. Although including adultery, the meaning is wider and covers all forms of unchastity, within and outside marriage.

Theft and *murder* have their normal meanings.

Adultery does not necessarily have precisely the same meaning as in modern usage. In the Old Testament 'adultery' was an offence against the husband, and a married man who had sexual relations with an unmarried woman had not committed adultery. Even if it is more likely that the term in this list had closely approached the current meaning today (a married man or woman having sexual intercourse with someone other than his or her spouse), the Old Testament meaning is a warning not to assume similar customs and understanding to our own.

Greed is better than the older 'coveting' (RSV). 'Avarice'

(NRSV, NJB) is inadequate. NEB had 'ruthless greed', but the revisers seem to have felt that this was too strong. It has been suggested that here it has sexual connotations, since it is associated with sexual sins elsewhere in the New Testament (e.g. Eph. 4.19 (REB paraphrases); 5.3; Col. 3.5; 2 Pet. 2.2–3), hence Moffatt's 'lusts', but this is doubtful as this meaning is not found in classical Greek though possibly it occurs in a papyrus.

Malice is rather too precise. The term refers to wickedness in general (as NRSV; cf. GNB 'do all sorts of evil things'). CEV's 'meanness' is wide of the mark.

Fraud in modern English is normally used of financial malpractice, and is too narrow as a translation of a word that means 'deceit', 'cunning' or 'treachery'.

Indecency probably gives the sense of the next word. In common parlance it carries the same kind of sexual connotations that the Greek does. 'Licentiousness' (NRSV) is archaic, and 'lewdness' (NIV) even more so. Moffatt has 'sensuality'. The word seems to refer to actions that are open and shameless, that shock public decency.

Envy is literally 'an evil eye'. It has been suggested that it referred to 'a malignant glance which casts a spell', and while it is true that this idea is found in many different cultures, in the Old Testament the word is used of envy and that is almost certainly the meaning here. GNB's 'jealousy' has a too narrowly sexual sense.

Slander is almost certainly the correct rendering in this list of wrong actions and refers to all abusive speech, although in the Septuagint it applies only to speaking evil against God

Arrogance occurs only here in the New Testament, although the adjective 'proud', 'arrogant' is found five times. 'Arrogance' is the meaning in classical Greek and probably is right, though 'pride' is preferred by most other translations.

Folly must be a moral defect in this list of vices, not just 'foolishness' (as RSV and CEV) or lack of intelligence, which means that the English translations do not immediately convey the right connotation. A possible alternative is 'foolhardiness', but this is still not quite right. It is difficult to find an English word that properly conveys the sense.

Rather than discussing whether the list is Jewish rather

than Pauline and wondering if it could come from Jesus himself, it is more profitable to take a hint from a scholar who cites a Buddhist list: 'destroying life, killing, cutting, binding, stealing, speaking lies, fraud and deceptions, worthless reading, intercourse with another's wife – this is defilement, but not the eating of flesh'. Morality is not the preserve of any one religion. Christians tend to select those Christian virtues that will be viewed favourably today and say less about attitudes that are unacceptable, such as the hostility towards 'the Jews' found in John's Gospel. But this should allow to every religion the same freedom to present their faith in the best light, and the high ethic that can be found within Islam, Buddhism and the Sikh religion should not be denied or despised. Neither should it be supposed that only an ethic sustained by religion is sound.

Mark, however, probably included this whole section for a different purpose. It is not that Jesus is debating, in rabbinic fashion, the relative importance of different parts of the Law, and setting moral commandments above ritual ones. Rather Jesus's teaching shows that he has authority over the Law, and since God gave that Law this is a very great authority indeed.

7.24–30   *He moved on from there into the territory of Tyre.* Mark makes a break at this point: 'And from there he stood up and departed to the region of Tyre'. Many manuscripts add 'and Sidon', but REB is probably correct in regarding this as a later addition either assimilating the account to that in Matthew or adapting it to 7.31. Why he went there is not made clear by Mark, who simply says that 'entering a house' he *would have liked to remain unrecognized* (stronger in the literal Greek: 'he wanted no one to know'). This suggests that he thought that Jesus's purpose was to obtain a period of seclusion from the crowds. He has depicted Jesus as trying to escape from the crowds on several occasions (1.35; 4.35; 6.30, 46). Certainly it was not a 'Gentile mission', for there is no account of Jesus giving any teaching to the local people. On the contrary, he is depicted as unwilling to heal a little Gentile girl. Although Mark is apparently writing for readers who are mainly Gentiles, he limits the mission of Jesus strictly to the Jews.

The woman who heard about Jesus and came to ask him to drive the demon from her daughter was a *Gentile* (the word is actually 'a Greek', but this is used in the New Testament for Gentile), *a Phoenician of Syria by nationality* (perhaps better, 'by birth'). She *fell at* [Jesus's] *feet*, as the unclean spirits and the woman with the haemorrhage had done (3.11; 5.33), not, however, as an act of worship or out of fear, but to support her request. She was confident that Jesus had the power to do what she asked, and thus possessed the 'faith' that Jesus required elsewhere. All this makes Jesus's refusal the more difficult to understand.

The narrative causes us considerable embarrassment, not just because of that refusal, but also because Jesus refers to the Gentiles as 'dogs', though within a figurative saying. Dogs were scavengers, not household pets and companions. To call someone a dog was highly offensive, and Jews frequently referred to Gentiles in this way.

Attempts have been made to soften Jesus's words by pointing out that he used a diminutive, but to call a Gentile a 'little dog' was hardly less derogatory. To suggest that he replied to the woman with a smile on his lips is an unwarranted supposition. To regard Jesus's reply as a test of the woman's faith does not excuse the use of such an offensive term. Even if Mark placed the emphasis on *Let the children be satisfied first* and implied that the Gentiles will be fed later, the reply is a rejection of the woman's request in deliberately insulting language. Jesus is acting as a normal Jew of his day. Some try to evade this by pointing out that the Old Testament prophets spoke primarily to their own nation, with few references to any missionary role, and that Jesus saw his task in the same way. Others suppose that Mark linked the miracles with the breaking in of God's kingdom to Israel; the woman did not recognize this and saw him simply as a miracle-worker.

The woman's reply is as clever as some of the replies that Jesus made to his opponents. *Sir, even the dogs under the table eat the children's scraps.* She accepts that she is a 'Gentile dog' and asks simply for the scraps that the 'children' (the Jews) drop. Although 'Sir' is the word for 'Lord', it was the normal term of respectful address, and does not indicate that she regarded him as any more than a travelling healer. Jesus accepts her response, but it is hardly possible to describe his words, which are literally, 'Go, the demon has gone out from your daughter', as exorcism at a distance. It is hardly an exorcism at all. The woman accepts his assurance, however, and returns home immediately, again revealing her faith, and Mark concludes the story with the woman finding her daughter cured.

That the woman succeeded in making Jesus change his mind is taken by some as an example of the way that a woman was able to teach Jesus something. Others feel that to change his mind is unworthy of the son of God. It is unlikely that Mark would have thought like a modern feminist, although this might be regarded as a valid insight for present-day readers, belonging as they do to a totally different culture. Those who are disturbed that Jesus should act as he did, should ask themselves if they are thinking of Jesus as a god walking about on earth rather than as fully human.

More serious is the question of whether Jesus's words and actions are out of character with what we know elsewhere. One response to this is to ask whether what is being compared is the character of Jesus drawn from the whole of Mark's Gospel, or it is an idealized Jesus.

7.31–7   Mark continues the narrative without a break: *On his journey back from Tyrian territory* (literally, 'And again he went out from the borders of Tyre') *he went by way of Sidon to the sea of Galilee, well within the territory of the Decapolis* – a curiously circuitous route to the eastern side of the lake. The people (and we discover that there is a crowd there) brought *a man who was deaf and had an impediment in his speech* to Jesus and *begged* [him] *to lay his hand on him.* Jesus is depicted as a typical healer of the time, putting his fingers in the man's ears and putting saliva on his tongue (the Greek is rather strange, but presumably if Jesus's fingers were in the man's ears he must have spat directly on his tongue). *Looking up to heaven, he sighed* (or 'groaned', perhaps expressing the difficulty of the healing or summoning up his healing powers) and then spoke the healing word in Aramaic, *Ephphatha*, which Mark translates into Greek, as he did in the raising of Jairus's daughter (5.41–2). Immediately the man's ears are opened and the 'fetter' on his tongue (the Greek is literally 'bond' or 'fetter', rather than REB's vaguer *the impediment*) loosed. Possibly Mark understood this as releasing the man from the bondage of demonic powers. Jesus then commands those who were present to tell no one. The narrative ends with the usual expression of astonishment, but this time two comments are added: *'All that he does, he does well'* and *'he even makes the deaf hear and the dumb speak'*.

Yet again the difference between the kind of healing that Jesus performed and modern medical practice is stark (see p. 74 and cf. pp. 16–17, 38–9 and 57), with the use of spittle and touch, and the uttering of what many readers in the Hellenistic world would regard as a magic spell. Accepting that Mark believed that everything happened exactly as he describes it, three features in this story need to be noted.

First, Mark is depicting Jesus as a typical wandering healer, using the same methods as other wonder workers, and possibly thinking of the miracle as an exorcism. The use of saliva in healing is recorded (though sceptically) by Tacitus, who says that a blind man threw himself at the feet of the Emperor Vespasian and asked him to 'anoint his cheeks and eyeballs with the water of his mouth' (*Hist.* 4.81).

Second, the words of the onlookers are so close to Isaiah 35.5–6 that many think it must have been intended as the fulfilment of prophecy. This reads: 'Then the eyes of the blind will be opened, and the ears of the deaf unstopped . . . and the dumb [will] shout aloud'. The Septuagint translation of the last phrase is 'and the tongue of the dumb will be distinct (or 'clear')', but remarkably the word it uses for 'dumb' is the same as that which REB translates as 'who had an impediment in his speech' in Mark. Some scholars suggest that 'He has done all things well' means, 'How exactly he fulfils the prophecies'. This is going too far. Mark does not mention the fulfilment of Scripture, and it is difficult to decide how he understood the incident. On the one hand Jesus's command to tell no one might mean that the miracle was regarded as evidence that he was the messiah, but on the other hand Mark treats the crowd as 'outsiders' to whom everything is taught in parables in order that they may not understand. This leads to the third feature.

Jesus's command to tell no one recalls the end of the story of Jairus's daughter (5.43), and the command to the man with leprosy to tell no one (1.43–4) as well as the way Jesus forbade the demons to declare who he was (1.34;

3.12; cf. 1.25). Here Mark adds, *the more he forbade them, the more they spread it abroad* (the Greek word is 'proclaimed', the verb used for Christian preaching).

It is time to tackle a question that was first raised by a German scholar, W. Wrede, at the beginning of the twentieth century, and which he called the messianic secret. Wrede argued that in the traditions that Mark used Jesus was presented as uttering these commands for secrecy as a means of explaining why he was not recognized as the messiah during his lifetime. Historically no one accepted him as the messiah, but because later Christians could not understand why they failed to do so, they invented the theory that Jesus intended the fact that he was the messiah to be a secret.

The theory troubled many other scholars, because it seemed to strike at the heart of the reliability of Mark as evidence for the life of Jesus.

Some argued it was a fact. Jesus tried to keep his messiahship secret because he knew that it would be interpreted in nationalistic ways and would lead to a rising against the Romans, and adopted instead the enigmatic title 'Son of Man'. Only after he had taught his disciples the true understanding of the kind of messiah that he was, and had been crucified and raised from the dead, would it be possible to speak of him as the messiah. There may well be some truth in this, but there are difficulties as well. Why did Jesus not give plain teaching to his disciples? Why did the statements of the unclean spirits make no impression on those who heard them? And how could the miracles be kept secret?

Others questioned whether Wrede was justified in lumping all the commands to silence together to fit his theory, claiming that different reasons could be found for them and that the secrecy was not universally imposed. Thus the leper is told to say nothing because he has to go straight away to the priests to have his healing confirmed and to make the required sacrifices. Jairus and his wife were merely told not to rush around spreading the news. The evil spirits were not to declare who he was because theirs would be tainted evidence. Because Jesus sometimes gave instructions for secrecy for good reasons, Mark may have generalized this and added the command for secrecy to some miracles where it was not appropriate.

Moreover, since Jesus was put to death on the charge that he claimed to be the messiah, there must have been some who thought of him in this way. These objections may also have some validity.

Probably too much has been made of the messianic secret in Markan studies, and it is time to move on. What remains important, however, is Wrede's recognition that Mark's account cannot be accepted as straightforward history just because it was the first Gospel to be written and has been linked with the reminiscences of Peter. The connection with Peter goes back to the church historian Eusebius, writing early in the fourth century. He quotes from Papias, Bishop of Hierapolis (*c.* AD 140): 'And the elder [generally supposed to be John, an older contemporary of Papias (not, of course, the Apostle John)] said this also: Mark, having become the interpreter of Peter, wrote down accurately all that he remembered of the things said and done by the Lord, but not, however, in order'. Papias goes on to say Mark did not himself hear Jesus or follow him, but was dependent on Peter. He claims that Mark 'made no mistake . . . for he made it his one care to omit nothing that he had heard and to make no false statement in it'. Many scholars, however, have questioned the reliability of this testimony.

As we have seen, Mark believed that Jesus was the son of God and told his story from that perspective. We know how impossible it is to write history exactly as it happened. However, why Mark wrote his book and what he intended by it, remain questions that it is impossible to answer on the evidence which we possess.

8.1–10   The next story is so similar to the account of the feeding of the five thousand (6.35–44) that almost all scholars treat it as a second version of that incident. The similarities include such details as the place being 'desert' (REB *this remote place*; the word is different from that in 6.32, 35, but related to it), a dialogue between Jesus and the disciples (though here Jesus takes the initiative, the disciples do not suggest that they would need to buy food, and the crowd has been with Jesus three days, not one), the actions of Jesus (but he does not look up to heaven and a different word is used for 'giving thanks', as REB indicates, adding 'to God', which is not in the Greek), the mention of fish as well as the bread (though here added rather as an afterthought and with the diminutive, with the same word for *blessed* as in 6.41), the fact that the crowd *ate and were satisfied*, the collecting up of the scraps left over, the dismissal of the crowd by Jesus, and the crossing of the lake (though this time Jesus is in the boat from the start, he does not walk on the water, and he and his disciples go to *the district of Dalmanutha* instead of Gennesaret). The numbers are different: seven loaves instead of five, a few small fish instead of two, seven baskets of scraps instead of twelve and different words for basket (in 6.43 the word is said by the Roman writer Juvenal to refer to a basket used especially by Jews; here the word is a general one for basket), and a crowd of 4,000 instead of 5,000, without defining them as 'men'. Mark certainly regarded it as a separate miracle, because he later draws comparisons between the two.

Since it is impossible to treat these miracles as historical, it does not matter whether Mark mistook two accounts of the same miracle as two separate feedings or not. Further discussion is left till later (pp. 90–4).

8.11–13   At this point Mark inserts another brief conflict with the Pharisees who *began to argue with him*. They came *to test him*, and *asked him for a sign from heaven*. Jesus *sighed deeply*, and replied, '*Why does this generation ask for a sign? Truly* ('Amen', as in 3.28) *I tell you: no sign shall be given to this generation*'. And Jesus then *left them, re-embarked, and made for the other shore*. This differs from the earlier stories in several respects, each of which is significant. The Pharisees come to 'test' Jesus – the verb is the same as when Satan 'tempted' Jesus (1.13). Previously they came with various accusations, claiming that Jesus or his disciples are not keeping the Law. Here they take the initiative by asking for a 'sign from heaven'. Apart from 13.4, 22, where signs are indications that the Temple is about to be destroyed and wonders performed by false messiahs, this is the only place in Mark's narrative where the word occurs. Jesus responds by sighing deeply, and then uttering a flat refusal, but not just to the Pharisees – he declares that no sign will be given to 'this generation'.

If we are to try to understand Mark's meaning it is necessary to push from our minds the changes that Matthew and Luke make to this very spare narrative. Mark does not present Jesus as calling the generation 'wicked' and 'godless' nor as addressing the crowd as 'a wicked generation', and he concludes the story with a blunt refusal by Jesus to give a sign, without any reference to the 'sign of Jonah' (Matt. 16.4; Luke 11.29–30).

While 'tempt' can be used in the sense of testing, and can have the good sense of giving someone the opportunity of showing their true colours, in Mark's account of the devil's 'tempting' Jesus it has overtones of enticing to do wrong. It is difficult to know how to take the verb here. REB offers a neutral sense – the Pharisees would be justified in challenging a teacher whose message differs from their own teaching by asking for his credentials. On the other hand, Mark is normally hostile to the Pharisees, so that he probably intends the testing to be a means of making Jesus do something that can form the basis of an accusation.

But what is the 'sign' they ask for? Even though Mark never uses the word of any of the miracles or exorcisms that Jesus performs, most commentators suppose that the Pharisees looked for a spectacular miracle. They then suggest that Mark's point is that they failed to accept the signs that were there before their very eyes, notably the feeding of the crowd that Mark has just recounted and to which he links this incident. But Mark does not say that the Pharisees were present at the feeding. The sign that the Pharisees request is described as 'from heaven', so that it would appear that they were looking for divine authentication of his authority.

The previous occasion when Jesus sighed was when he healed the man who was deaf and had an impediment in his speech (7.34, the verb is the simple form of that used here). The sense is different here, where it implies that Jesus was grieved (or perhaps angry) at the attitude of the Pharisees. His reply, however, is not addressed directly to them and they become the representatives of all those who reject him. In the Old Testament the term 'this generation' is often used in a derogatory sense, but there is no need to draw on this to explain Mark's account, for Jesus's words reflect the hostility between Christians and Jews in his own time.

Finally, Jesus's flat refusal to provide a sign fits in with Mark's portrait of the messiah whom no one recognizes because it is predetermined that they should not.

8.14–21   Mark's sequel must strike modern readers as contrived. Moreover, it is even more perplexing than the dialogue with the Pharisees, for the explanation of the feeding that Jesus gives is more cryptic than the fact of the miracles themselves, and seems to be totally unrelated to the saying about the leaven of the Pharisees.

REB's attempt to provide a translation in flowing English obscures some vital features, and it will be best to give an outline of the story, adding a few notes. The disciples *had forgotten to take bread with them, and had only one loaf in the boat.* Suddenly Jesus *began to warn them: 'Beware'*, he said, *'be on your guard against the leaven of the Pharisees and the leaven of Herod'*. (It is odd to find a reference to Herod. In 3.6 the Pharisees and the 'Herodians' (REB 'men of Herod's party') plot to bring about Jesus's death, and some manuscripts read 'Herodians' here. Although many scholars prefer to retain Herod as being more difficult to make sense of, and therefore unlikely to be a corruption of 'Herodians', it is certainly possible that Mark wrote 'Herodians'.)

The disciples' response to this warning is to *talk among themselves about having no bread* (the Greek might be translated 'because they had no bread', 'why they had no bread', or '[saying] "It is because we have no bread"'; moreover, some Greek manuscripts read, 'We have no bread'). Mark continues: *Knowing this, he said to them, 'Why are you talking about having no bread? Have you no inkling yet? Do you still not understand? Are your minds closed?* (literally, 'Do you have your heart hardened?', cf. 6.52 and the comment on p. 73). *You have eyes: can you not see? You have ears: can you not hear?'* (cf. the way Jesus addressed the crowd at the end of his parables in 4.9, 23). Instead of explaining the meaning of what he has just said, Jesus proceeds to talk about the two feedings. *'Have you forgotten?* (the Greek is 'and do you not remember?', not the verb 'to forget' as in v. 14). *When I broke the five loaves among the five thousand, how many basketfuls of pieces* ('baskets full of broken pieces' using the same word for 'baskets' as in 6.43) *did you pick up?' 'Twelve,' they said. 'And how many when I broke the seven loaves among four thousand?'* (the Greek repeats the question in a slightly different form: 'When the seven among the four thousand how many baskets full of broken pieces did you pick up', using the same word for 'baskets' as in

8.8). *'Seven,' they answered* (Greek, 'they said', as before). *He said to them, 'Do you still not understand?'*.

The logic of the dialogue seems to elude us completely, and commentators struggle to make sense of it, usually by arguing that Mark intends an almost Johannine symbolism. It may be best to list some of the difficulties.

After recording that the disciples had forgotten to take any bread with them, apart from one loaf, Mark says that Jesus gave his warning about 'the leaven of the Pharisees and the leaven of Herod'. The disciples, however, revert to the fact that they have no bread. Jesus's warning seems completely out of place, and it is difficult to find a logical connection.

Jesus's saying is figurative. In other words it is closer to the 'parables' that he addressed to the crowd than the plain explanations that he gave to the disciples, and yet he gives no explanation of the saying that the disciples have failed to understand.

Leaven is found elsewhere in the New Testament in a bad sense (e.g. 1 Cor. 5.6–8; Gal. 5.9), but Mark does not explain what the leaven represents. Matthew, who substitutes Sadducees for Herod, adds, 'Then they understood: they were to be on their guard, not against baker's leaven, but against the teaching of the Pharisees and Sadducees' (Matt. 16.12). Luke, who gives the saying a different setting, omits the reference to Herod, and makes Jesus say, 'I mean their hypocrisy' (Luke 12.1). Both obviously thought that further explanation was needed, but our intention is to try to interpret Mark, and he did not necessarily take it as either of the two later Gospel writers did.

Since they are all in a small boat it might seem hardly necessary for Mark to introduce Jesus's next words with 'knowing this', but perhaps it is to carry the narrative forward from the warning about leaven to a discussion about the two miracles. However, it adds to the sense of Jesus's supernatural powers (cf. 2.8).

Instead of explaining the meaning of his reference to the leaven, Jesus proceeds to draw attention to the precise numbers of people who had been fed, the number of loaves in each case, and, with greater emphasis, the numbers of baskets that had been filled with broken pieces, using the two different words for basket that occur in the two stories.

Jesus's final question, 'Do you still not understand?' leaves the whole episode in the air, without any explanation of why he has singled out the numbers of people, loaves and baskets, or how this relates to his warning about the leaven of the Pharisees and Herod.

Setting out some of the attempts of the commentators to make sense of all this will highlight the problem.

Some argue that Mark is responsible for inserting the saying about the leaven into the narrative, which gains in coherence without it. Omitting it, they then treat the remaining dialogue as concerned with the disciples' lack of faith – they have just seen two miracles of feeding and yet they are still anxious about not having any bread in the boat. This is inadequate, because Jesus talks about understanding, not faith. This might mean Mark placed the saying here, a trifle thoughtlessly, because he could think of nowhere else to put it. If this is so it might be further evidence that he included in his book all the material about the life and teaching of Jesus that he knew. On the other hand he may have seen some deeper connection between leaven and bread – but if this is so he has not disclosed what it was.

Some suggest that the complete passage should be interpreted in a way similar to that found frequently in John's Gospel: the disciples talk at cross purposes with Jesus and so fail to grasp the meaning of the two 'signs'. This, it is claimed, is brought out both by the misunderstanding of the saying about the leaven, which they mistakenly link with their having forgotten to bring any bread, and by their failure to recognize the true significance of the feeding miracles. They have seen two stupendous miracles with huge symbolic meaning and still do not grasp the symbolism or recognize who Jesus is and that he is always able to satisfy hunger (spiritual as well as physical).

Some look for meaning in the wider setting. This incident is preceded by the two feeding miracles, the account of the storm, on which Mark commented that 'for they did not understand about the loaves, but their heart was hardened', the healing of the deaf man who had an impediment in his speech, and the Pharisees' request for a sign, and is followed by the giving of sight to a blind man. This wider narrative is then interpreted as being concerned with being deaf and blind to Jesus as the 'son of God'. This is sometimes supported by reference to such Old Testament parallels as the giving of the manna, and by later Christian understanding of the feedings as a symbol of the Eucharist. There may be something in this, but it is selective, leaving most of chapter 7 out of account, and presupposes that Mark is intent on writing hidden symbolism. Some of the alleged symbolism, such as the link with the Eucharist, would have been meaningless to the disciples themselves, though Mark might not have realized this or it might have been unimportant to him if his purpose was theological rather than the recording of history.

Some, giving up on the leaven, fasten on the numbers and types of basket, arguing that to Mark the physical feeding of the crowds symbolized spiritual food given to Jews (twelve Jewish baskets of scraps) and Gentiles (seven ordinary baskets of scraps). Some go further and find the five books of the Law in the five loaves, and the seven 'deacons' who served the Hellenistic Christians in the seven loaves. This is most unlikely, since Mark would hardly describe Jesus as handing out the Law and the existence of the seven 'deacons' depends on Luke's account, which Mark may well not have known. An alternative reason for reminding the disciples of the numbers might be that they emphasize the magnitude of the two miracles, but this does not seem fully satisfactory, given the tremendous stress placed on the exact numbers. Was Mark really presenting an elaborate numerical cypher? It is impossible to say.

Any attempt to provide an explanation must produce one that fits into Mark's narrative as a whole. Several clues may help. Verse 18 is akin to 4.12, and taken with 6.52 appears to make the feeding of the crowds less miracles than 'parables' that need supernatural insight or special revelation. The reason for the disciples failing to understand is that their heart is 'hardened'. Yet the 'mystery of the kingdom' is given to them (4.12), and the elaborate questioning of 8.17–21 suggests that Jesus may have been trying to help the disciples to 'see'. If Mark believed that the two feedings were 'parables', he must have believed that there was a key which would reveal their meaning (cf. the parable of the sower, 4.3–9, 13–20). A strange feature of the dialogue is that the emphasis is placed upon the broken pieces left over rather than on the number of loaves and the crowds – what Jesus asks the disciples about is the number of baskets of broken pieces. One scholar suggests that the 'broken pieces' were not the scraps that the people dropped but the pieces that Jesus broke off and were not eaten, but Mark says the disciples 'picked up' the broken pieces. This, however, still does not explain the significance that Mark attached to the numbers twelve and seven, although some connection with Jews and Gentiles seems intended. And the 'one loaf' remains unaccounted for. It seems to have puzzled Matthew, who left it out (Matt. 16.5). Some point to Paul's reference to the 'one loaf' in 1 Corinthians 10.17, and suggest, rather improbably, that it provided a Eucharist for the disciples.

All this, however, fails to explain the 'leaven of the Pharisees' and 'leaven of Herod'. The combination of the Pharisees and the Herodians had a special importance for Mark. Here they may symbolize the hostility that led to the death of both John the Baptist and Jesus. This would fit in with 'to test him' (8.11), remembering that the verb is always found in hostile contexts in Mark and is linked with suffering. But to speak of 'leaven' remains odd.

Ultimately we have to concede that we have no idea what Mark's purpose might have been. The narrative as it now stands is incoherent, the symbolism, if such there be, is beyond finding out, and the whole episode stands upon two legendary accounts of impossible miracles.

8.22–6   The disciples had set out for Bethsaida (6.45), but had landed at Gennesaret, then gone to the territory of Tyre, before returning by way of Sidon to the territory of Decapolis and on to Dalmanutha. Now they reach Bethsaida at last. Mark's sense of geography is vague and he supposes that Bethsaida is a village rather than a town. Some see this as showing that his main concern is with the symbolism of Jesus's actions, but it may simply be that he did not know the area.

This miracle has several similarities with the healing of the deaf man in 7.32–7 (slight variations are noted in brackets): the people *brought* the man to Jesus and *begged* him to *touch him* ('lay his hand on him'); Jesus takes the man *out of the village* ('away from the crowd'); he *spat on his eyes* ('touched his tongue with spittle'); and *laid his hands upon him* ('put his fingers in the man's ears'). At the end of the first miracle Jesus 'forbade them to tell anyone', while after the second he *sent him home, saying, 'Do not even go into the village'* (the manuscripts differ to a considerable extent, many of them substituting or adding *Do not tell anyone in the village* (cf. REB mg.), which make the similarities even closer). But there are obvious differences: a blind man rather than a deaf one; the second healing is in two stages, and there is no mention of surprise by the onlookers or their proclaiming the miracle.

Those finding symbolism point out that the story of the deaf man follows Jesus's call to hear and understand his teaching (7.14, 18) and the account of the blind man follows the dialogue in the boat when the disciples fail to understand and see (8.17–18, 21). Thus the deaf man and the blind man stand for those to whom understanding is given, although this remains hidden from those who are still deaf and blind. It has even been suggested that the recovery of sight in two stages symbolizes the failure of the disciples to understand who Jesus is. On this interpretation the point at which they see clearly may be when Peter declares that Jesus is the messiah in the next chapter, or Mark may have regarded Peter's identification of Jesus as the first half of the cure, which is only complete after the resurrection when the disciples see clearly who Jesus is and understand the true nature of his messiahship. Alternatively, some scholars find the true parallel, not in the healing of the deaf man, but in the healing of blind Bartimaeus in 10.46–52, and argue that these two accounts of blind men recovering their sight mark off a central section of the book, in which the way of the cross, the meaning of discipleship, and true faith are presented.

The fact that resort to symbolism can lead to such a variety of interpretations should make us wary. The one thing that is clear about Mark is that he intends to present Jesus as the son of God who teaches with authority and has power to expel unclean spirits, heal diseases, and perform what we term 'nature miracles' (though he probably made no distinction between the three). How far he arranged the traditions that came to him in order to express an elaborate symbolism or found the main importance of the individual stories in their symbolic meaning is very questionable.

8.27–33   Most commentators make a strong break in Mark's

narrative at this point, often inserting a new heading and arguing that it is the beginning of a new section of his book, usually defined as 8.27—10.52. Thus one scholar heads it 'From Galilee to Jerusalem: The Character of Jesus' Messiahship Gradually Disclosed', and another 'The way of the Cross: teaching on discipleship'. REB, oddly, marks off 8.27—9.29, with the heading 'The cross foreshadowed'. Mark, however, continues his narrative in exactly the same way that he has done in the past: 'And Jesus and his disciples went into the villages of Caesarea Philippi', and we shall do well to follow him.

Mark has already recorded the various ideas about Jesus that were going around (6.14–16), and when Jesus asks the disciples about the rumours, they repeat them. *'Some say John the Baptist, others Elijah, others one of the prophets'* (it is not clear whether they mean that Jesus is one of the prophets come back to earth or, as earlier, 'a prophet like one of the prophets of old'). Jesus then asks them directly, *'And you, who do you say I am?'* and Peter replies, *'You are the Messiah'* (Mark uses the Greek word, 'the Christ' rather than a transliteration of the Hebrew or Aramaic). Jesus's response is the same as when he 'rebuked' the unclean spirit in the synagogue (1.25), when he 'insisted' that the unclean spirits should not make him known (3.12), and when he 'rebuked' the wind on the lake (4.39), though REB translates the verb in various ways. Here it has, *Then he gave them strict orders not to tell anyone about him.* While it would obviously be foolish to expect a Greek word always to be represented by a single English one, the different translations in REB obscure the fact that Mark depicts Jesus as reacting to the disciples in exactly the same way that he did to the demons. The unclean spirits, Mark has told us, 'knew who he was' (1.34), and although they call him 'the Holy One of God' and 'the son of God', Mark regards 'the Messiah' here as carrying the same meaning, or perhaps more precisely, Jesus as the messiah is the Holy One of God and the son of God, and he writes that Jesus insists that this should not be revealed to anyone outside the circle of 'the disciples' (presumably Mark means the Twelve, although he does not use the term, cf. 3.14, 16; 4.10; 6.7).

Jesus then proceeds to explain to the disciples what being the messiah means. First he substitutes the title *Son of Man*, which he has used twice before (2.10, 28). Then he declares that it is necessary for the Son of Man *to endure great suffering, and to be rejected by the elders, chief priests, and scribes; to be put to death, and to rise again three days afterwards*. Apart from Matthew 27.63, the phrase 'after three days' is unique to Mark, and, because it does not exactly fit the length of time between the crucifixion and the resurrection, some see this discrepancy as evidence that the prediction goes back to Jesus. Others think that it has the same meaning as 'on the third day' (the phrase used elsewhere in the New Testament), but the fact that Matthew and Luke alter it shows that they thought that it had a different meaning. Some trace the origins of the tradition to Hosea 6.2, but this is unlikely, for there the phrase is 'on the third day'. Mark makes no reference to Old Testament prophecy, in contrast to Paul (1 Cor. 15.4), and does not appear to have thought of the resurrection as a fulfilment of the Scriptures.

Mark then says that *He spoke about it plainly*. The Greek word refers to frank and open speaking, almost the equivalent of 'publicly'. REB makes Peter react violently, he *took hold of him*, but the verb means no more than 'took him aside', as all the main modern translations render it, and *began to rebuke him* (the same verb translated earlier as 'gave them strict orders'), whereupon Jesus *turning and looking at his disciples, rebuked Peter* (the same verb again). The 'rebuke' is surprisingly violent: *'Out of my sight'* (literally, 'Get behind me'), *Satan! You think as men think, not as God thinks'*. To ask why Jesus reacted so fiercely and to wonder whether it was because he himself was tempted to interpret messiahship in terms of power rather than suffering is to try too quickly to discover what actually happened, and probably to be influenced by the account of the temptations in Matthew and Luke. We must remain with Mark.

Mark took 'Son of Man' to be a title of Jesus, and he cannot have supposed that Jesus used an obscure term in order to conceal that he was the messiah. The previous history of the term and what the historical Jesus might have meant by it are of no importance to him. He depicts Jesus as accepting Peter's recognition that he is the Christ, but immediately substitutes the title Son of Man and speaks openly to the disciples about the way the Son of

Man must suffer, die and rise again. At the same time he insists that the disciples should tell no one.

Many scholars see this as the turning-point in Mark's narrative. Up to this point Mark records little of Jesus's teaching, and depicts him as the one who can perform great miracles, drive out demons and cure diseases. These display his authority as the son of God, but, apart from the demons, only those to whom 'the secret of the kingdom of God has been given' understand, and even their hearts are so 'hardened' that they fail to grasp his teaching or see the meaning of the miracles. Now at last Peter, possibly as the spokesman for the rest of the disciples, declares that Jesus is the messiah, but he has the wrong picture of the true character of the messiah and rejects Jesus's teaching. This explains Jesus's violent reaction. In the rest of his book Mark describes the way Jesus attempted to teach his disciples the true meaning of messiahship, but they still fail to understand, and arrive at the full Christian faith only after the resurrection. (It should be noted, however, that the disciples disappear from Mark's narrative after Jesus is arrested and never return, so that, on the basis of the book that we possess, they never understood!)

Some go even further and suggest that by placing almost all the miracles in the first half of his book and including most of Jesus's teaching in the second half, after Peter's declaration, Mark is deliberately opposing those who see Jesus as a 'divine man', a wonder-worker, instead of the suffering servant.

Neither of these interpretations fully corresponds with Mark's narrative. As we have seen, the 'secret' is not imposed on the traditions by Mark consistently, though it may have been part of some of the traditions he took up, and whether he held the idea at all remains doubtful. Instead, the important distinction is between the teaching given to the crowds and that given privately to the disciples. This is spelt out in 4.10–12. The parables spoken to the crowd conceal the secret of the kingdom of God, which is revealed only to the disciples. This is deliberate and reflects a sense of divine predestination. It is in the light of this belief that the present story is to be understood. Peter, like the demons, declares that Jesus is the messiah, but Jesus has to explain what being the messiah means. Peter still does not understand, however, and further teaching will be necessary. In much the same way, the miracles display Jesus's power and authority, but the disciples also fail to grasp their meaning, and the dialogue in the boat is part of his attempt to get them to see it.

8.34 The continuation of the story complicates matters somewhat. Jesus calls the crowd with his disciples and says: *'Anyone who wants to be a follower of mine must renounce self; he must take up his cross and follow me'*. This appears to be open teaching, when we expect it to be in parables that the crowd is destined not to understand. Christian readers of Mark's book would link it with the crucifixion of Jesus and the persecution that they themselves were suffering, even though his words were open to misunderstanding as being a call to join a revolt against Rome regardless of the consequences. This fits in with Mark's beliefs. He thinks of three cycles of suffering and death: that of John the Baptist, that of Jesus and that of his readers, and 'follow me' may mean to follow in Jesus's footsteps that led to the cross.

Possibly Mark then added a small collection of separate sayings because they were on a similar theme. The important thing, however, is to try to understand what he intended, and here the problems increase.

If all the sayings were addressed to the crowd as well as the disciples, and we accept the statement in 4.10–12, Mark held them to be 'parables'. However plain they may appear to us with centuries of Christian history behind us, it is worth testing out their meaning on this assumption.

8.35 *Whoever wants to save his life will lose it, but whoever loses his life for my sake and for the gospel's will save it.* The mention of 'the gospel' in this bald way is strange. Some of those eager to recover the words of Jesus treat it as an addition by Mark. Others think that 'for my sake' was also added by Mark or the earlier tradition, leaving the very general proverb, 'Whoever wants to save his life will lose it, but whoever loses his life will save it'. Attempting to get behind the words in our text is sheer guesswork, even though 'and the gospel's' is not found in the form of the saying in Matthew and Luke, and a few manuscripts omit 'for my sake'. Again the words would have a special resonance with Mark's persecuted readers, who might have understood them as a warning to those giving up the Christian faith out of fear, and providing reassurance to

99

the faithful that even if they are put to death their future life is secure. As part of Mark's narrative, however, the saying would be cryptic, since the crowd do not know that Jesus is the suffering messiah and would not know what losing one's life for the sake of Jesus could mean.

8.36–7   *What does anyone gain by winning the whole world at the cost of his life?* This is often regarded as a Jewish proverb, as is the following, *What can he give to buy his life back?* (more literally, 'For what shall a man give in exchange for his life?') Taken on their own they seem to mean that nothing is more valuable than life itself, and it is beyond price. Taken as 'parables', the hidden meaning would be similar to the previous saying: to abandon Christ is to lose one's life in the future kingdom of God, and against this loss no amount of worldly wealth is worth the price, and no ransom can be paid to escape the penalty of such apostasy.

8.38   *If anyone is ashamed of me and my words in this wicked and godless age* (literally 'this adulterous and sinful generation'), *the Son of Man will be ashamed of him, when he comes in the glory of his Father with the holy angels.* Although this seems closer to Jesus's words after Peter's 'confession', the saying is immensely difficult because Jesus appears to make a distinction between himself and the Son of Man. Again we must refuse to guess at what Jesus may have said. Mark held that Jesus was the Son of Man, so the saying must be interpreted on that basis, and we must push aside the question of what he meant by 'the Son of Man', whether a supernatural being other than himself or the elect community of Christians who will judge those who were ashamed of him. While it is somewhat odd that Mark represents Jesus as speaking of being ashamed of him and his words in the first half of the sentence and then declares that the Son of Man will be ashamed of them when he comes in the glory of his father, the distinction seems to be between the suffering and humility that Jesus now endures and his final glory when his power is fully revealed and exerted. Mark probably sees these words as addressed to those who have failed to recognize Jesus as the messiah. His readers, however, may well have applied them to those who fall away in a time of persecution – they will be excluded from the future glorious life with God and the angels.

9.1   The last four sayings are connected to the preceding
ones by the word 'For' (omitted by REB). Now Mark adds
another saying with his usual 'And' (also omitted by
REB). *He said to them, 'Truly I tell you: there are some of those
standing here who will not taste death before they have seen*
(more correctly, 'before they see') *the kingdom of God come
with power'.* This troubles many commentators since the
prediction was not fulfilled, and they attempt to evade the
obvious sense. Some of those who accept it as a genuine
word of Jesus suggest that the kingdom came in the trans-
figuration, or the coming of the Holy Spirit, or at some
other point during the lifetime of at least some of the disciples. Others lay the emphasis on 'with power', and contrast the way the kingdom came with Jesus but was not
perceived, and the time in the future, perhaps after the
resurrection, when the disciples will realize that it has
come (cf. NRSV 'until they see that the kingdom of God
has come with power'; REB changed the NEB's 'before
they have seen the kingdom of God already come in
power', which expressed this view, although by keeping
the perfect tense of 'they have seen' the revisers leave the
possibility open and probably still imply it). Given the
horrendous history of the world, it can hardly be maintained that God's rule has been established at any time
up to the present, so that we have to accept that Jesus
expected the kingdom to come in the near future and was
mistaken. Some try to soften this by emphasizing that the
doctrine of the incarnation carries with it human limitations, including limited knowledge, or by urging that the
saying should be understood as asserting that God's purpose will ultimately be achieved. One commentator says
that the vindication which Jesus expected took place in the
resurrection, although the final coming of the kingdom
remains still in the future, so that he was wrong in one
sense but right in another. This is inadequate, since there
is a vast difference between the expectation of the first
Christians who looked for the coming of the Son of Man in
the near future, and any expectation of his coming that
Christians might hold today after 2,000 years of history. In
spite of the reiteration of 'Christ will come again' in many
liturgies, few Christians today really expect an earthly
return of Jesus or even the establishment of God's rule on
earth. Mark, however, depicts Jesus as making this pre-

diction, and at the time that he was writing it seems that this belief was still alive. The frame of reference in 1 and 2 Thessalonians and 1 Corinthians is similar to that of Mark. It appears that a detailed expectation about what was going to happen at the end of the world grew up, although the delay in the coming of Christ in glory soon became a problem, as 2 Peter 3 shows.

In this discussion I have mostly retained the word 'kingdom', since any alternative appeared awkward. This is largely a matter of English idiom, but the word has a wider connotation than any single English one. In 6.23 Herod promised Herodias's daughter any request 'up to half my kingdom', where 'kingdom' must mean his possessions and the territories over which he ruled rather than his authority. In 3.24 Satan's 'kingdom' is his power, but includes the demons subservient to him. In 1.15 the future kingship that God will assert seems appropriate, but the precise meaning is somewhat uncertain in the two parables in chapter 4. The emphasis is on the 'mystery' in 4.11, but 'kingdom' carries overtones of its future arrival. Here what 'some of those standing here' will see is the full assertion of God's royal power at the end of the world, when the Son of Man comes in glory.

9.2–8   *Six days later Jesus took Peter, James, and John with him and led them up a high mountain by themselves.* Although Mark attaches this with his usual 'And', the precise 'after six days' is almost as unique as the story he now tells. It may well be that Mark sees the transformation of Jesus and the voice from heaven as confirmation of Peter's identification of Jesus as the messiah. There are several similarities to Exodus 24.16 where the cloud covered Mount Sinai for six days, and on the seventh Yahweh called to Moses out of the cloud, although Mark does not state the connection. Whether six days had become the traditional length of time required for self-purification before approaching God is also uncertain.

REB tells the story with its usual vigour and only two words and phrases need to be mentioned before we turn to the meaning of the episode.

Rather unfortunately it retains the traditional *was transfigured*, which goes back to Tyndale and is also used by NRSV and NJB, although the verb is translated 'transformed' in the other two places in the New Testament where it occurs (Rom. 12.2 and 2 Cor. 3.18). The Greek word is the one from which we get 'metamorphosis', and should have been translated 'transformed' or 'was completely changed' (CEV).

They saw Elijah appear and Moses with him represents the Greek 'And Elijah with Moses appeared to them'. The verb means 'to see', but in the passive (as here) it means 'to become visible, to appear'. It is used of visionary experiences, as when a vision appears to Paul (Acts 16.9), and often there is something supernatural about the appearance. Luke and Paul use it of the risen Christ (Luke 24.34; Acts 9.17; 1 Cor. 15.5–8).

Peter, James and John accompanied Jesus into the bedroom of Jairus's daughter (5.37), and they are again singled out. The Greek emphasizes that they were completely alone with Jesus on the high mountain. Mark attempts to describe how utterly *dazzling* Jesus's clothes became – *with a whiteness no bleacher on earth could equal.* What he is depicting is the glory that belongs to Jesus as the son of God. It is a secret no longer. His true nature is revealed, if only to the three disciples.

Mark does not explain why 'Elijah with Moses' then appear. Note that they are named in that order and not in historical sequence; Matthew and Luke reverse the order (Matt. 17.3; Luke 9.30); to Mark Elijah is more important than Moses, cf. vv. 9–13. They talk with Jesus, but what they said is not recorded and they play no part in the rest of the story. Contrast Luke, who supplies a conversation that fits in with the rest of his Gospel with its emphasis on Jerusalem (Luke 9.31). Do they represent the Law and the prophets? Hardly, when all the emphasis is on Elijah, who is put first, and there is no firm contemporary evidence that he could stand for the prophets. Both experienced theophanies (Exod. 19.16–25, 34.5–8; 1 Kgs. 19.9–18), but this seems an inadequate reason. The suggestion has been made that they foreshadow the resurrection since in Jewish tradition both were taken up into heaven. But the death of Moses is described in Deuteronomy (Deut. 34.5–6, though cf. Josephus *Antiquities* 4.8.48 [323–6]; Philo knows the same tradition), and if this were intended Enoch would have been a better companion for Elijah (cf. Gen. 5.24). Since Mark does not tell us what he made of their appearance, we are left in ignorance.

Many commentators find it strange that Peter addresses Jesus as *Rabbi* after he had declared that he was the messiah. However, it does not necessarily mean that he was treating him as a Jewish rabbi. The meaning of the word developed from the literal 'my great one', and could be used as a respectful term of address to any one of higher rank than the speaker. From the first Christian century it was normally ordained teachers of the Law who were addressed in this way, but the term could still be used more widely. Even as late as the third century AD a rabbi who had been the leader of a band of robbers before he became a teacher of the Law said: 'There [among the robbers] they called me rabbi, and here [in the rabbinic school] they call me rabbi'. This may explain the curious fact that Jesus is not actually giving teaching on any of the four occasions when he is called rabbi, and it may also mean that when Jesus was addressed as 'teacher' it carried the same overtones of respect.

Peter's response, *'It is good that we are here'*, probably means that it is fortunate that they are there so that they can build booths for Jesus and the two visitors. Whether the Greek can mean that it is good for the disciples to be there to see Jesus in his glory and to see Elijah and Moses is doubtful. *'Shall we make three shelters?'* is not a question but proposes a definite action: 'Let us make three shelters'. In the secular world the word was used of a soldier's tent. In the Septuagint it is the word for a nomad's lodging (Gen. 12.8), the shelters of branches in which the Israelites lived during the Feast of Booths (Lev. 23.42), and the Tent of Testimony (Exod. 27.21). Some think that Mark had the last of these in mind, but by his comment, *For he did not know what to say*, he implies that Peter's proposal was rather stupid, or at the least inappropriate. He does not explain what Peter might have meant or what was wrong with his proposal, and we are little better placed to do so. Did Peter want to retain the experience for longer? Was it an attempt to entertain the visitors? Was his mistake that, by proposing to honour Jesus, Elijah and Moses in the same way, he was ranking Jesus on a level with the other two, and so still failed to recognize Jesus's unique status as the son of God? It is impossible to know.

Mark's explanation of Peter's words is that the three disciples *were so terrified*. This is not a religious sense of awe nor the wonder that follows several of Jesus's miracles, for which Mark uses different words (1.27; 2.12; 5.42; 6.51), but utter terror, similar to that which the disciples felt after Jesus rebuked and silenced the storm (4.41) and when they saw Jesus walking on the water (6.50). Mark uses the word 'terrified' only here, though it is a compound of the simple verb 'to be afraid'.

The *cloud* is a stock symbol for God's presence, so that the voice coming out of the cloud is God's, as when Yahweh spoke to Moses on Sinai (Exod. 24.16). REB's *casting its shadow over them*, gives the impression that the cloud was in the sky and 'they' (probably just Jesus, Elijah and Moses, rather than all six of them) were standing in its shadow, but the meaning is more probably that the three men were enveloped by the cloud.

The voice echoes the words spoken to Jesus at his baptism: *'This is my beloved Son'*. As the voice at the baptism declared to Jesus that he was God's son, so here the voice declares this to the three disciples. Peter had said that Jesus was the messiah. Now he and the other two disciples are told that Jesus is the son of God. Does Mark see this as reinforcing what Jesus had said to the disciples earlier, that he was the Son of Man (and so the son of God) rather than the (Jewish) messiah? The message continued: *'listen to him'*. Some commentators point out similarities with Moses's promise that Yahweh will raise up a prophet like himself and the command, in almost identical words, 'it is to him you must listen' (Deut. 18.15). Jesus, however, has greater authority than any prophet. Given the importance that Mark attaches both to the identity of Jesus as the son of God and to his teaching, there is no need to look beyond the present narrative.

Although Mark does not state that the cloud then lifted, revealing only Jesus on his own, this is the implication of the narrative. The transformation of Jesus and the appearance of Elijah and Moses are now over, and the disciples are alone with Jesus. This is the end of the incident. It is most unlikely that Mark intended to teach that the disciples should no longer heed Elijah and Moses, Jewish prophecy and Jewish Law, and look to Jesus alone.

The question that comes to our minds is what actually happened? The most obvious rationalization is to treat the experience as a hallucination or a mystical vision. The mystics often speak of shining light, and some of them claim to have seen religious figures from the past and to have conversed with them. Some scholars draw on accounts of men whose facial appearance was changed during periods of intense prayer, although this does not explain the shining clothes and the two other figures. It hardly looks like a misplaced resurrection story, as other scholars propose. Others again give a purely symbolic interpretation, suggesting that the story had no historical basis but drew on the account of Moses on Sinai. The three disciples represent the Christian community and Jesus is revealed in the glory of his (second) coming. To Mark there would have been no problems at all. It happened exactly as he describes it. Jesus was transformed. His clothes became dazzling white. Elijah and Moses were actually there. God spoke from the cloud in words that could be heard and in the disciples' own language. There is no way to get behind this, and we have to accept it as part of Mark's portrait of Jesus as the son of God.

9.9–13   *On their way down the mountain, he instructed them not to tell anyone what they had seen until the Son of Man had risen from the dead.* Although this is similar to the demands for secrecy that have been seen earlier in Mark's narrative, it is distinctive in two ways. The secret is to be withheld from the other disciples, and Peter, James and John can (or even must) reveal it after Jesus, the Son of Man, has risen from the dead. The first feature is part of the general question of why these three disciples were singled out. The second accords with the theory that the 'messianic secret' was invented in order to explain why Jesus was accepted as the messiah only after the resurrection, but it can be understood in a different way. If the suffering that John the Baptist, Jesus, and the Christians of his own time endured is central to Mark's understanding, to declare the glory of Christ without his suffering would run counter to the way he interpreted Jesus's life. Jesus is the messiah of glory, but he is equally the crucified messiah and it is essential that both are accepted.

The disciples *seized upon those words, and discussed among themselves what this 'rising from the dead' could mean.* REB seems to take this as meaning that their discussion about the Son of Man rising from the dead arose directly from this statement by Jesus. Most English translations agree with REB in taking the next words of the disciples as a question *'Why do the scribes say that Elijah must come first?'* although it is possible that it is a statement: '[But] the scribes say that Elijah must come first' (in Greek, questions are indicated only by the punctuation, not by word order, as is usual in English). Either way, their response does not seem to follow naturally from their discussion about rising from the dead, and several attempts have been made to trace a logical sequence of ideas. The most drastic is to argue that Mark has combined two different sources, and that the disciples' question originally followed Jesus's prophecy in 9.1. The meaning would then be that the disciples wondered how the kingdom of God could come before Elijah had appeared. But Mark must have thought that his narrative made sense.

It has been suggested the disciples' question is related to the command to tell no one until after the Son of Man has risen from the dead. Since Elijah will appear publicly before the coming of the messiah and they have seen Elijah, they wonder why they must keep silent. Will not all the people see him soon? This, however, fails to connect the question with their perplexity about rising from the dead.

Perhaps Mark meant that the disciples obeyed his command to say nothing until after the resurrection, but were puzzled at the three things that Jesus had said about the Son of Man – he would suffer and be put to death, he would rise again, and he would come in the glory of his Father (8.31, 38). The two sayings, therefore, set out succinctly the whole of Mark's view of Jesus, the Son of Man. He would be persecuted and put to death. He would rise from the dead. He would reappear in glory. The disciples failed to grasp this and, as with the parable of the sower, Jesus has to explain it to them.

He points out first that the teaching of the scribes is correct. *'Elijah does come first to set everything right.'* The scribes based this on Malachi 4.5: 'Look, I shall send you the prophet Elijah before the great and terrible day of Yahweh comes'. The prophet was speaking of the day of judgement, but as we have seen, Mark, and probably many Jews in the time of Jesus, understood it as meaning that Elijah would prepare for the coming of the messiah. Jesus added a further statement about the Son of Man, but in the form of a question: *'How is it, then, that the scriptures say* (Greek, 'it is written', correctly explained by REB) *of the Son of Man that he is to endure great suffering and be treated with contempt?'* But nowhere in the Old Testament, or even in any other Jewish writings from the time of Jesus that have survived, is there a prophecy of the suffering of the Son of Man. Some trace the reference to the suffering of the faithful Jews in Dan. 7, but this assumes that Jesus interpreted the Son of Man as the community. Mark certainly did not. Jesus, in his view, is the Son of Man, so that for him this cannot have been the scripture to which Jesus referred.

This question about the Son of Man is closely related to the next sentence: *'However, I tell you, Elijah has already come and they have done to him what they wanted, as the scriptures say of him'*. Again there is no biblical prophecy of the suffering and death of Elijah. It is true that Jezebel set herself against Elijah and sought his death (1 Kgs. 19.2), and perhaps the idea is that Herodias managed to achieve what Jezebel failed to do. This, however, is not strictly prophecy. As with the Son of Man, it appears that Mark believed that everything in the life of John the Baptist and Jesus was foretold in Scripture, even though he could not quote any specific text.

Although Mark does not provide a key here, his readers will recall that he began his book by quoting a prophecy that declared that John the Baptist was the herald, preparing the way for the messiah (1.2–3), and describes in considerable detail the events leading up to his death (6.17–29). Jesus began his work only after John was 'delivered up', with its overtones of divine purpose (1.14). Moreover, he reports the way it was rumoured that Jesus was Elijah, and rejects the identification (6.15; 8.28). It is John the Baptist who is Elijah. He is the forerunner of the messiah, but suffers in the same way that the messiah will suffer. When we recall the stern warnings of Jesus against wanting to save one's life and being ashamed of him and his words (8.35, 38) the triple cycle of suffering is complete.

9.14–29   The healing of the boy *possessed by a spirit that makes him dumb* (the Greek has 'a dumb spirit') is described in even greater detail than the accounts of Jairus's daughter and the woman with the haemorrhage. The disciples, the crowd and the scribes are all involved. There are other oddities. The disciples (and here it seems certain that Mark meant the other nine members of the Twelve) had been given the authority to drive out demons (3.15), yet they were unable to do so. The crowd was *overcome with awe* (in the New Testament the word is found only in Mark (also 14.33; 16.5) and means 'to be amazed, alarmed, or distressed') when they see Jesus, although he has said and done nothing yet. Mark does not say what the scribes were arguing about. When Jesus asks 'them' *'What is this argument about?'* (literally, 'What are you discussing with them?'), it is the father who replies by saying that he had brought his son *for you to cure* (the Greek is simply 'to you'). The scribes play no further part in the story. Jesus's reaction to the father's account of the demon's actions is to complain about the *unbelieving generation* (earlier he had described 'this generation' as 'adulterous and sinful' rather than 'unbelieving', 8.38). The spirit is *dumb* and so does not announce who Jesus is or enter into conversation with him, but shows its power by throwing the boy into *convulsions* (a strong word, found rarely and meaning 'to tear (to pieces)', 'to pull about'). Instead of immediately driving the demon out, Jesus enters into a further conversation with the father, who for a second time describes what the demon has done to his son. This leads to a discussion about faith – to the father's *'If it is at all possible for you, take pity on us and help us'*, Jesus replies, *'Everything is possible to one who believes'*, at which the father cries out, *'I believe; help my unbelief.'* Jesus makes no further response to the father, but when he *saw that the crowd was closing in on them* ('running together', a word found only here in the New Testament), he commands the *deaf and dumb spirit* to come out and never return. The reaction of the spirit is dramatic – it *shrieked aloud and threw the boy into repeated convulsions* before coming out, *leaving* [the boy] *looking like a corpse* (the Greek is simply 'and he became as if dead'). Finally Jesus *took hold of his hand and raised him to his feet, and he stood up* (we are reminded of the way he took the hand of Peter's mother-in-law (1.31) and of Jairus's daughter (5.41)).

A tentative explanation can be given to some of these features.

The repetitions and awkward sequence of events may show that Mark combined two separate accounts of the incident, but again our present concern is with the narrative as Mark sets it out and we assume that it made sense to him.

The hostility of scribes is a continuous feature of Mark's book (2.6, 16; 3.22; 7.1, 5; 8.31), alongside that of the Pharisees (2.16, 24; 3.6; 7.1, 5; 8.11), and Mark appears to picture them as contesting the ability of the disciples to cast out demons in much the same way as they accused Jesus of driving them out by the power of Beelzebul. Perhaps they are an example of the 'unbelieving generation', who fail to accept that Jesus is the son of God.

If Mark linked the experience on the mountain with Moses on Sinai, the alarmed amazement of the crowd may reflect the way the people were afraid to approach Moses when his face shone as he came down from the mountain (Exod. 34.29–30), but as has been seen earlier, there is absolutely no evidence that he regarded Moses as a type symbolizing Jesus, and he makes no explicit reference to the Old Testament. That he thought that the appearance of Jesus still held something of the glory that the three disciples had seen is possible, though uncertain.

The emphasis on faith is remarkable. Mark has mentioned faith several times earlier in his narrative (2.5; 4.40; 5.34; and the verb in 5.36), each time in relation to a miracle, but never in quite this concentrated way. The 'unbelieving generation' seems to include everyone, including the disciples, and some think that by adding *'How long shall I be with you? How long must I endure you?'* Mark was indicating that the lack of faith was a failure to realize that the miracles are part of the breaking in of the kingdom of God and of the work of Jesus as the son of God. Yet when Jesus picks up the father's 'If it is possible' and asserts that 'everything is possible to one who believes', faith seems to be confidence in the exorcist's power to drive out the demon from the boy, as it usually is in Mark's narrative.

In the end, however, the difficulty in driving out the demon appears to be not the father's lack of faith but the power of the demon. Mark stresses the way it tears the boy apart, even at the very moment of leaving him, and the father vividly describes all the things that it has done to him, trying to destroy him (Mark's readers might recall that Legion destroyed the herd of pigs in 5.13). Even after it had been driven out it left the boy as if dead, as though it had achieved its purpose, and Jesus has to act in the same way that he did with Jairus's daughter.

The sequel is as unique as the account of the exorcism. In exactly the same way that Jesus answers the disciples' questions in private and explains the meaning of the parables to them, so when Jesus *went indoors* (literally, 'into a house'; cf. 7.17 and 4.10), he replies to their question *'Why could we not drive it out'* with *'This kind cannot be driven out except by prayer'* (many manuscripts add 'and fasting', but this is almost certainly a later addition, reflecting the practice of the early Church). The statement comes rather strangely after the account of the exorcism, since the narrative contains no reference to Jesus's praying before expelling the demon. Moreover, in the story it is faith not prayer that is singled out. To argue that it is a separate strand of tradition that Mark, a little illogically, has placed here fails to explain what meaning it had for Mark. Perhaps he had in mind the practice of his own church, and thought that this was a good place to put this saying. On the other hand he may not have thought of prayer as a means of achieving the healing, but have seen it as utter trust in God, who alone can drive out demons.

Exorcism appears to have been very important for Mark. He recounts a large number of exorcisms and says that the disciples were given authority to cast out demons (3.15: 6.7). Yet curiously he includes only two pieces of teaching about exorcism. In 3.23–9 the teaching is said to be 'in parables' and no private explanation is added. Clearly he sees Jesus as the strong man who is invincible in his encounters with the demons and can pass this authority to his disciples. The exorcisms are of cosmic significance in the battle against Satan and appear to be an essential feature of the period between the coming of John and the coming of Jesus at the end of the world. Here, then, Mark may be saying that during this time Christians are to maintain the struggle with evil through continuing to cast out demons, and the words are an encouragement to his readers to do this.

One commentator gives the story the heading 'The Epileptic Lad'. The symptoms are certainly those that modern medicine would diagnose as epilepsy, but Mark's account only makes sense if we lay aside such attempts to interpret it from a modern perspective and accept that, at the time, everyone would have accepted that a demon had entered the boy and caused the actions that his father describes. They would also have believed that Jesus drove the demon out exactly as Mark tells his story. The 'cure' is a straight exorcism by the son of God, who can exert his authority over the most powerful spirits ('this kind'). To recognize the completely different attitude to illness is extremely important for Christians today. It is impossible to combine modern medical practice, which controls epilepsy with drugs, and first-century beliefs in possession by demons, and to move directly from this story to claim that the Church today has a similar healing mission is false and dangerous.

Many today evade the problem of demon possession, and direct their attention to the father's faltering faith. He wants to believe for the sake of his son, but cannot escape his doubts and cries in deep anguish, 'Help my unbelief'. At a time when many members of the churches feel very insecure in their faith, this may serve as an encouragement, but for Mark the faith is either faith that Jesus can drive out the demon, or the acceptance that the son of God is bringing in God's rule. Some commentators suggest that he saw the story as teaching members of his own church who had attempted exorcisms and failed, that this was due to lack of faith and a failure to pray sufficiently intensely. It again needs to be made clear that when we pray for those who are ill, we are not praying as those first Christians did, that the demons that bring about disease will be conquered, but are holding the sick up to God and asking that he will be with them in their illness.

9.30–32   From this point the amount of teaching that Jesus gives to the disciples (Mark seems to mean the Twelve) greatly increases (see comment on 8.27–33). We must be careful to keep closely to Mark's narrative and not impose upon it ideas about the life of the historical Jesus. Mark simply emphasizes that Jesus *did not want anyone to know* where he was because *he was teaching his disciples*.

Immediately after Peter's 'confession' Jesus had told the disciples that 'the Son of Man had to endure great suffering, and to be rejected by the elders, chief priests, and scribes; to be put to death, and to rise again three days afterwards' (8.31). The present prediction is slightly different: *'The Son of Man is now to be handed over into the power of men, and they will kill him; and three days after being killed he will rise again'*. There is no reference to the 'elders, chief priests, and scribes', and the verb is 'is handed over' (the present tense refers to the near future) into the 'hands of human beings'. The verb is the same as that which describes the 'handing over' of John the Baptist in 1.14, and the action of Judas Iscariot in 3.19, and has the same theological overtones. Although the stress on divine necessity in the earlier prediction is absent, the meaning is probably that God will hand the Son of Man into human hands. It is probably wrong, therefore, to translate the verb 'is going to be betrayed' (NIV, cf. NRSV), for there is no direct reference to the betrayal by Judas. Neither is there any reference to the suffering of the Son of Man; just the statement that human beings will kill him. This places a certain emphasis on the rising again 'after three days', as in 8.31.

In 8.32 Mark said that Jesus spoke about it 'plainly' or 'openly', and Peter clearly knew what it meant because he reacted by rebuking Jesus. Here Mark says that the disciples *did not understand what he meant* (perhaps 'said' would be better – the Greek is 'the word' or 'the saying' – but the sense is much the same), *and were afraid to ask*. Mark is often accused of deliberately stressing the failures of the disciples, who seem little different from the crowd, and this is sometimes seen as part of the 'messianic secret'. In the narratives, however, Peter has already declared that Jesus is the messiah, and the lack of understanding must apply either to the reference to the Son of Man or to the idea of the resurrection, probably the latter (cf. 9.10). Their fear is not awe in the presence of the messiah, although it may indicate the distance that Mark sees between the teacher and his disciples. It may be just that they were afraid of looking stupid.

9.33–41   This is one of the most tangled passages in the book. It seems to bear some relation to later incidents and teaching (cf. 10.42–44), and commentators are too ready to import ideas from the other Gospels to explain it. Taken on its own there is no indication that Jesus was concerned with the humility of the child, far less with its innocence. The point of the story as Mark tells it lies in the attitude of others towards the child, not that the child is an example to follow. But the narrative is by no means straightforward.

113

9.33–5   Jesus is still in Galilee and now enters Capernaum, and *when he had gone indoors* (literally, 'when he was in the house') *he asked them, 'What were you arguing about on the way?'* They are silent because they were discussing who was the greatest. Jesus then sits down and *called the Twelve.* Apart from the account of the appointment of the Twelve Mark uses the term rarely, and calling them 'the Twelve' comes oddly here, when Jesus has been alone with his 'disciples' (presumably the Twelve) from v. 30. Some think that Mark has combined different traditions. The meaning of the first saying is a little uncertain. Although all modern translations and almost all commentators agree with REB in taking a future tense 'he shall be' as a form of imperative, 'he must', introducing the idea of service, the Greek may be an announcement of judgement – those who seek pre-eminence will be made last of all and servant of all in the kingdom of God. Earthly positions will be reversed.

9.36–7   To this Mark attaches a second saying, set into the account of Jesus's taking a child, setting him in front of the disciples, and putting his arm round him. The words, however, do not seem to relate closely to what has gone before, *'Whoever receives a child like this in my name receives me; and whoever receives me, receives not me but the One who sent me'.* What does 'receiving a child in my name' mean? Why the sudden introduction of the strange idea of 'receiving' God, which many modern translations try to make easier by saying 'welcomes' ('receive' often means 'receive as a guest', cf. 6.11)? And what is the connection with the previous saying? It is extremely forced to suggest that true greatness lies in performing services to people such as this child. The emphasis is placed on 'in my name' rather than the insignificance of children, such actions being accepted as being done to Jesus and ultimately to God. Some think that 'in my name' means 'when my name is confessed' and indicate an allusion to baptism ('because my name has been invoked over him or her'). On the other hand it may mean 'for my sake' in the sense 'because this is the action I desire', or even 'because this child in his human need is my representative'. Some despair of finding a logical sequence of ideas and treat the two sayings as entirely separate, each with its own introduction. On this view vv. 33–5 teach the reversal of earthly position in the future kingdom, while vv. 36–7 make the quite different point that Jesus stands as the representative of God and the 'little child' (either a believer or a person in need) stands as a representative of Jesus.

9.38–40   Exorcism was practised by Jews and pagans as well as by Jesus and the disciples, so that there would be nothing strange in finding someone driving out demons. What may appear surprising is that the exorcist uses the name of Jesus, but we know from Greek papyri that it was not unusual for pagan exorcists to invoke powerful names, so perhaps these Jewish exorcists invoked the name of Jesus because he had become famous as being especially successful in driving out demons. Perhaps Mark sees the story as offering guidance to people in his own church, who wonder how they should behave towards those who work miracles using the name of Jesus as a powerful spell without being members of the church. Jesus teaches that no one who uses his name in exorcisms is likely to revile or insult him, even if they are not active disciples. The story is rather loosely attached to the previous one. Jesus and his disciples are pictured as still in the house and continuing to discuss matters of concern. That it is John who asks the question is unusual. Some think the name was already embedded in the tradition that Mark took up. He then adds a proverbial saying, *He who is not against us is on our side* to express the underlying theme.

9.41   At this point, or perhaps even earlier, Mark's narrative seems to disintegrate. Suddenly he introduces a completely separate idea. *Truly I tell you: whoever gives you a cup of water to drink because you are followers of the Messiah will certainly not go unrewarded.* The Greek is awkward and there are differences among the manuscripts. Literally the words translated 'because you are followers of the Messiah' read: 'in name (some manuscripts have, 'in my name') that (or 'because') you are Christ's' (perhaps taken as a proper name, as in 1.1, rather than 'the messiah's'). Commentators are fascinated by these variants, emphasize the differences between the sayings, and seek to discover what the original words might have been on the lips of Jesus. Here we stay with Mark's intention. The reward comes not for simple humanitarian action but for help given because those receiving it are Christians. This is not moral teaching, but belongs to a world in which Christians are sharply separated from pagans.

115

If Mark saw a connection between the different parts of this section, those giving the cup of water will be non-Christians. Perhaps the background is deep hostility and persecution, so that a minor act of kindness is sufficient to merit reward in the future kingdom. However it is interpreted, Mark seems to have believed that the final battle between the messiah and the demonic powers was now taking place.

Jesus's reaction to John's question is both attractive and disturbing to us today. Attractive, because it appears to support the prevailing ethic of toleration, and disturbing because it presupposes a war between good and evil spiritual powers.

9.42–50 The stuttering of the narrative continues. A completely new idea, causing *the downfall of one of these little ones who believe*, appears in v. 42, attached with Mark's usual 'and'. Jesus declares that it would be better to be drowned than to commit this wrong. Three separate sayings, again added with 'and', speak of *hand*, *foot* and *eye* as the agents of an individual's downfall, now described as going to *hell, to the unquenchable fire*, with the further description in v. 48: *where the devouring worm never dies and the fire is never quenched*. Again there are differences between the manuscripts. As REB footnotes show, some texts add the extra clause found in v. 48 to the two previous references to hell in vv. 43 and 45, but it is generally agreed that this is not original. There are other smaller variations, and after 'who believe' many manuscripts add 'in me', although it seems likely that this has come into the text of Mark from Matthew's account (Matt. 18.6) at some time.

Almost all the commentators hold that vv. 42–50 were put together on a catchword principle. The link word in v. 42 is uncertain. A child was mentioned in vv. 36–7, so that it may have seemed appropriate to add a saying about *little ones*, taken to mean 'children'. On the other hand, the 'little ones who believe' may be disciples, when the connection would be with v. 41 ('because you are Christ's'). *Downfall* (literally 'cause to stumble', the same verb as in 4.17, REB 'they quickly lose faith', and 6.3, REB 'they turned against him') attracted the next three sayings, though their theme is not the same. Then the mention of the *unquenchable fire* in these sayings led to the addition of a completely different saying about being *salted with fire*,

and the reference to salt attracted two further sayings in
v. 50. Although this does not seem unreasonable, it has
probably been accepted too lightly. To us the idea of catchwords appears to be a purely mechanical method of collecting independent and unrelated sayings. The ancients
may not have separated language and logic in this way.
The section, therefore, raises three questions that need to
be addressed. What does each of the sayings mean individually? How did Mark understand the passage that he
has constructed? And if Mark, rather than his tradition,
collected the sayings in this way, what does it suggest
about his knowledge of the traditions?

9.42   The sayings about 'stumbling' are all addressed to the
disciples. Most commentators think that this verse refers
to the shaking of a believer's faith in Jesus. This, however,
does not explain why 'little ones' is used. We might wish
that Jesus was condemning those who abuse children, or
destroy their innocence, but this is hardly the meaning the
words had for Mark. If he had persecution in mind, he
may have taken it as a strong word against the persecutors
of Christians in his own day.

9.43–8   The next three sayings have been interpreted as implying moral demands (the verb 'to cause to stumble' meaning 'to lead into sin'). One suggestion is that by Mark's
time Christians were applying the verb as a technical term
to those who found something in Christ that stopped
them from going on to full discipleship. Another scholar
has argued that in the time of Jesus amputation of foot or
hand was imposed as a punishment, so that the contrast
is between loss of hand or foot and execution. The true
contrast, however, is between *life* and *hell*. The Greek
word is 'Gehenna', originally the valley outside Jerusalem
where sacrifices were offered to Molech (2 Kgs. 23.10), and
later used as the city rubbish heap. It was then taken
metaphorically as the place of punishment of the wicked.
The punishment was probably thought of as destruction
rather than torment, and this provides a better contrast to
'life'. It is the fire that is *never quenched*, not those who are
thrown into the fire. While this is not the traditional
Christian idea of everlasting torture, the most severe punishment in the future is threatened for those who sin, so
that anything is better than that. Yet 'causing to stumble'
is vague and colourless. It has to be given a content by

Mark's readers before the words can have any real meaning. This can hardly be described as moral teaching. Rather it fits the pattern of the sharp division between good and evil, between Christ and the demonic powers, that has been noticed several times already in this section of the book.

9.49   The meaning of *Everyone will be salted with fire* is uncertain. That some of Mark's early readers could make little of it is suggested by the fact that some manuscripts add: 'and every sacrifice is salted with salt' (cf. Lev. 2.13, but despite the emphasis on salt, the symbolism is not clear, although some scholars link it with maintaining the covenant), and some have only this addition on its own (and there are other minor variations). Perhaps the meaning is that everyone (presumably every disciple) will be tested in the fire of persecution. It may refer to the final judgement. But none of this fully explains the reference to salt in relation to fire. Mark gives no hint that he has any Old Testament allusion in mind, and may not have had any clear idea about the meaning of this obscure sentence.

9.50a   Many think that the next saying bears no relation to what has gone before beyond the word 'salt', and refer to Matt. 5.13 and Luke 14.34–5 for its meaning. It is always dangerous to turn to the later Gospels to explain Mark. Perhaps it is attached less artificially than many suppose. There is a violent change of metaphor, it is true, but in the context of testing and judgement Mark may well have seen it as a warning to maintain the Christian character and allegiance during the period before the end of the world and the coming of the Son of Man, rather than a statement about the quality possessed by the disciples, 'seasoning' the daily life around them. (It is perhaps unnecessary to point out that in Mark's day the salt derived from the sea contained many impurities, and so could lose its taste when the sodium chloride was washed out.)

9.50b   On this interpretation the next saying may continue the same theme: 'Instead of allowing yourselves to become salt that has lost its saltiness, take care to maintain among yourselves that which is the saltiness of the salt', that is the full Christian allegiance to Jesus, or maybe the rigorist Christian ethic. In a setting of persecution it would mean that Christians should be willing to suffer and resist the pagan way of life. On the other hand, many commentators place the emphasis on *be at peace with one another*, wrench the saying out of its context, and point out that 'sharing salt' symbolized eating together, the ultimate sign of unity and fellowship.

It is certainly possible to find connections between these sayings apart from the catchwords. If Mark has in mind the threat of persecution, they all fit into place.

The difficulty in finding a coherent argument running through this collection of teaching may provide an answer to the third question: how many of the traditions that contained teaching by Jesus did Mark know? It is vital to avoid approaching Mark by way of the other Gospels, and assume that all the teaching that is found there was available to Mark and he made a selection from it. Many scholars make this assumption and give various reasons for his actions. He wished to supplement the traditions in his church, traditions that consisted entirely, or chiefly, of Jesus's teaching. His intention was to present Jesus as the son of God, the Son of Man, rather than to collect his teaching. He deliberately selected those pieces of teaching that seemed to him either most important or most in keeping with his main theme. But why should we assume that Mark knew any more of the sayings of Jesus than he has included in his book? If he put in all that he knew, it would explain why there is relatively so little (though there is more than most people imagine). It would also explain why he has placed some of the sayings where they are – he had to place them somewhere, and since they had no context in the traditions that he knew, he placed them where he thought they fitted best. It would explain why he said that Jesus always taught the crowd in parables and explained their meaning to his disciples, yet includes very few parables and fails to give an explanation to two of those in chapter 4. And it would explain why the most common form of address to Jesus is 'Teacher' and Mark stresses the authority of his teaching, yet has less of the actual teaching than Matthew and Luke – he included every fragment of teaching that he possessed, but it was relatively little. Some argue from 4.2, 33–4 (and even less plausibly, 12.38) that Mark intended to give only a selection from a larger collection of traditions, but all that these verses show is that Mark believed Jesus gave more teaching than he records. It does not follow that he possessed that teaching. It may seem a little odd that he did not know the Lord's Prayer, but then, did Paul?

10.1   Continuing with 'And' in his usual way, Mark describes the arrival of Jesus in Judaea. The sentence is extremely awkward and difficult to fit into the geography of Palestine, and REB has smoothed it out. Differences between the manuscripts show that early copyists were aware of the problems. It does not matter beyond showing again Mark's uncertainty about the geography of Palestine. *Once again crowds gathered round him, and he taught them as was his practice.* So there are crowds in Judaea as well as in Galilee.

10.2–9   The debate about divorce presents enormous problems of interpretation. It is not clear why Mark put it here rather than with the other stories of conflicts with the authorities in chapters 11 and 12. Some have found a 'catechism of discipleship' in the whole section 10.1–31, but this fails to explain the presence of the crowd and the different types of material that have been collected together. Mark does not make it clear who the questioners are. REB takes the verb as impersonal and translates it *He was asked*, but this involves omitting 'and Pharisees (or the Pharisees) came and asked him', which the vast majority of manuscripts read, though with some variations. The question is put to Jesus *to test him*, and this places it alongside the account of the request for a sign (8.11–12). The questioners are clearly hostile, and given Mark's overall pattern throughout the book, it seems as good as certain that Mark wrote that the question was asked by the Pharisees. Mark would hardly have described anonymous questioners as 'testing' Jesus. REB again uses the neutral verb 'test', but as in that earlier questioning of Jesus, it has overtones of trying to trip Jesus up. The question, *Is it lawful for a man to divorce his wife?* as in the debates about keeping the sabbath in 2.23–8; 3.1–6, is to discover whether Jesus's teaching is contrary to the Law. Jesus replies with another question, to which the Pharisees respond by referring to Deuteronomy 24.1–4.

The law about divorce is explicit, even though the main point in Deuteronomy concerns remarriage with one's divorced wife after she had subsequently married another man who had also divorced her or died. It is taken for granted that a man can divorce his wife, giving her a certificate of divorce. What is forbidden is remarriage with her first husband, and this is on the grounds of purity not ethics.

Jesus replies, '*It was because of your stubbornness that he made this rule for you*'. REB translates 'hardness of heart' by 'stubbornness', which hardly seems to give the right sense here, but is clearly an attempt to avoid the false overtones of a literal translation. The meaning is not that men are 'hard hearted' in the sense of showing no compassion, but that they are disobedient. Those English translations that try to avoid 'hardness of heart' struggle: 'because you are so hard to teach' (GNB), 'because you are so heartless' (CEV), 'on account of your perversity' (Goodspeed). Jesus then quotes Genesis 1.27 and 2.24, almost exactly as the Septuagint. REB's *and is united to his wife* possibly carries the wrong overtones. The Greek means 'adheres closely to', 'is devoted to'. Jesus says that *what God has joined together, man must not separate*. The verb originally meant yoking two animals together, but it was widely used of marriage. Indeed a pagan writer used the same verb when he said of two lovers: 'who can separate those whom a god has joined?' Jesus goes behind the Law to God's purpose in creation, and it would be relatively straightforward were it not for the addition in the next three verses.

10.10–12   Mark appears to treat Jesus's reply to the Pharisees as a divine revelation that was hidden from everyone except the disciples, to whom God chose to make it plain (cf. 7.18–23). Perhaps he regarded the final aphorism as a 'parable' that needed to be explained.

The private teaching given to the disciples is startling. In direct contrast with the law in Deuteronomy, Jesus forbids remarriage after divorce. Strictly this would permit separation so long as neither party remarried, and this is how Paul understood the ruling (1 Cor. 7.10–11), but it is not certain that Mark took the words in this sense. Moreover, the way he presents the saying envisages a pagan society in which a wife could divorce her husband, a practice that was contrary to normal Jewish custom. It also involves taking adultery in the sense we give to the term today (contrast the Old Testament, cf. p. 80).

Apparently this rigorist teaching did not survive very long. Matthew, who is legislating for a Jewish-Christian church, makes important changes, turning the words of Jesus into a legal pronouncement, omitting the right of a woman to divorce her husband, and permitting the man to divorce his wife for 'unchastity' (Matt. 19.3–9).

Many scholars emphasize how radical and humane Jesus's teaching was, putting women on an equality with men, refusing easy divorce to husbands, and going behind the legalism of the Law to return to God's purpose for men and women. Before we rush too quickly to this conclusion, we should look more closely at Mark's narrative. In the same way that he interpreted the teaching that nothing going into a person from outside can defile them as declaring all food to be ritually clean as a general principle (7.14–23), so here he takes Jesus's reference to Genesis as forbidding divorce (and incidentally also declaring that adultery is sinful). But he is not concerned with proclaiming an ideal or perfectionist ethic. Nor is he setting out the will of God in an absolute form that can be completely fulfilled only in the new world of God's kingdom (cf. 12.25). This is a rigorist ethic that can be demanded because the time before the end of the world is short. It is true that this is not mentioned here, but the teaching has to be interpreted in the light of Mark's total perspective. There is the same urgency here as in cutting off hand or foot or gouging out the eye if these cause 'stumbling'. Matthew found it to be unworkable once the end of the world was delayed and the Church continued as a permanent society.

10.13–16 GNB and CEV give this incident the title 'Jesus Blesses Little Children', but it is doubtful whether Mark understood it in this way, despite the conclusion, [Jesus] *put his arms round them, laid his hands on them, and blessed them*. It has often been suggested that Jesus's words, *'Truly I tell you: whoever does not accept* (Greek, 'receive') *the kingdom of God like a child will never enter it'*, was an isolated saying on the grounds that it expresses a different idea from the command to allow the children to come *for the kingdom of God belongs to such as these*, and that the narrative is complete without it, but they are both part of the story as Mark tells it. Why the kingdom of God belongs to children has been much debated and a variety of reasons suggested – they are unselfconscious and receptive, they are little and helpless, they are unsophisticated, it is God's inscrutable will that those who have not reached the age of the Law (12 years old) should inherit the kingdom, and that it is the younger generation who will be the generation of the last times and will live to see the coming of the kingdom. It has been argued that the Greek should be translated, 'whoever does not receive the kingdom of God as one receives a little child', but besides being a doubtful way to take the Greek, this is alien to the culture of the times. Links have sometimes been made with infant baptism, though this was hardly in Mark's mind. It seems most probable, in view of Mark's teaching elsewhere about the reversal of positions in the kingdom, that he took the meaning to be that, since children as insignificant members of society will occupy important positions when the kingdom arrives, so those who wish to enjoy the privileges of the kingdom must accept humble status.

This is far from the way the story is interpreted in churches today, where it is seen as calling us to take special care of children and make sure that they are welcomed into our services. We may again remind ourselves that texts have an 'afterlife' and the meanings that we attach to them are not necessarily 'wrong' because they differ from those that they had for the original writer, but we should not suppose that these reinterpretations have any special authority just because they are derived from stories that are found in the Bible rather than in secular literature.

The meaning of 'the kingdom of God' in these two statements still needs to be considered. 'God's kingship' fits 'receiving the kingdom' (i.e. submitting oneself to God's authority), but not 'entering the kingdom', and it is impossible for 'God's kingship' to belong to children. In these two sayings the kingdom must be the society over which God reigns, so that the promise is that children will enjoy the riches of the new world that God will bring in when he asserts his power at the end of the world.

10.17–22 The story of the rich man raises many problems. REB tells the story in modern terms but gives the essential meaning, apart from two phrases. To *win eternal life* introduces ideas more suited to a national lottery. The Greek is 'inherit', which, from the original meaning of entering into an inheritance, developed the general sense of 'to obtain' and then more specifically participating in the messianic salvation. *His heart warmed to him* is simply 'loved him'. It is difficult to understand why REB flinched from the obvious translation, though CEV apparently felt some qualms as well, with its feeble 'liked him'. Perhaps they felt it unseemly for one man to 'love' another, or thought that 'love' carried false overtones.

Before discussing the story as a whole, one other phrase needs to be considered.

In the list *Do not defraud* takes the place of the commandment 'do not covet', and the commandment to honour father and mother is placed last instead of first. The order of the other commandments varies in the manuscripts, and some substitute 'do not commit fornication' for 'do not kill'. Several good manuscripts omit 'do not defraud', as do Matthew and Luke, but it is inconceivable that a later scribe would have added it. No satisfactory explanation has been given for these changes.

The emphasis in the stories such as this one lies in the final aphorism by Jesus, but this story differs from the others in several ways.

Jesus rejects being addressed as 'good'. This so offended Matthew that he makes nonsense of the story by altering Jesus's words to, 'Why do you ask me about the good?' (Matt. 19.17). Although Mark believes that Jesus is the son of God he retains the tradition that came down to him.

Jesus quotes the ethical section of the Ten Commandments with approval as permanently valid. Some say that he singled out those commands that concern personal relationships, but this does not seem to be the emphasis.

The final saying is not an aphorism but an exhortation to the questioner. We are then told the reaction of the man to Jesus's words, and Mark has added an 'explanation', given to the disciples.

Much of the discussion about this story centres on Jesus's demand to *sell everything you have, and give to the poor*. Because it is manifestly impracticable for all Christians to do this, attempts began to be made very early in the history of the Church to evade the straightforward meaning, either by limiting the demand to the rich man and his special situation and denying that it is an example for all would-be disciples, or making a distinction between Christians who seek perfection and give up all their possessions and the rest who must continue to maintain an earthly existence. This second interpretation seems to have been current as early as the time of Matthew, who introduces Jesus's words with, 'If you wish to be perfect' (Matt. 19.21). This fails to take account of Mark's view of history. He does not contemplate a continuing life of the Church reaching out into the distant future, but expects the end of the world to come soon. Hence what is important is to have *treasure in heaven*, and everything must be sacrificed to obtain this.

10.23–31   The explanation is introduced by an aphorism: *'How hard it will be for the wealthy to enter the kingdom of God!'* The idea of the future kingdom of God and of rewards for being disciples are marked features of this section of Mark's narrative. When the rich man asked what he had to do to gain 'eternal life', Jesus replied by promising 'treasure in heaven' if he sold all his goods and followed him. Now he speaks three times of the difficulty of entering the kingdom of God, to which the disciples respond, *'Then who can be saved?'* After Peter has, a trifle indignantly, pointed out that the disciples have left everything to follow him, Jesus promises rich rewards 'in this age', and 'in the age to come eternal life'.

The actual words of the narrative in vv. 23–31 are easy enough to understand; its meaning is more difficult to follow. Three small points may be disposed of first.

'Children' (a different word from that in v. 15) was often used by teachers of their students. In modern language it has patronizing or sentimental overtones that are alien to Jesus's use of the term. Curiously only CEV appears to be sensitive to this, and solves the problem by omitting any term of address.

A few good manuscripts omit *for those who trust in riches* (cf. mg.), probably rightly. The words sound like an early attempt to soften the rigour of Jesus's words.

The striking exaggeration of the comparison with a camel passing through the eye of a needle is not to be weakened by suggesting that the word 'camel' was really 'cable', or that there might have been a door in the walls of Jerusalem through which a camel could squeeze, though with considerable difficulty.

The astonishment of the disciples is natural. In Judaism riches were taken to be a mark of God's favour and a reward for obedience to his commands, even though in the Old Testament (and indeed elsewhere in the ancient Middle East) the pious often called themselves poor when they prayed to God. Moreover, it was the rich who had the leisure to keep the Law in all its refinements, whereas the poor, struggling to make a living, often broke some of the commandments and could not always keep themselves clean from ritual impurity. Jesus, therefore, is reversing the common view of riches.

His teaching, however, goes far beyond saying that those who put their confidence in riches will be unable to enter the kingdom of God. He almost goes so far as to say that it is impossible for a rich man, and draws back only with the further assertion, *'For men it is impossible, but not for God; everything is possible for God'*.

The 'kingdom of God' is equated with 'eternal life', and Jesus speaks of entering the kingdom of God three times (cf. v. 15). Clearly the phrase cannot mean God's kingship or his authority, and is most naturally taken to be the future society that God is going to bring in at the end of the world.

10.28   The break introduced at this point in REB is unfortunate, and even if the paragraphing was intended to make the passage easier to read, it obscures the fact that Mark has written a continuous narrative. Peter's response is slightly less vigorous in the Greek, but it is still dramatic: 'Look, we have left everything and followed you' (GNB). This evokes the promise of a recompense *'in this age a hundred times as much'* and *'in the age to come eternal life'*. An early critic of Christianity mocked the suggestion that Christians would have a hundred mothers, but we should not be deflected from the central issue because of Jesus's characteristic exaggeration. The problem lies in the promise of rewards and the conception of the two ages. We take the second difficulty first.

Mark is writing when it is still possible to look for the (second) coming of Christ in the very near future. He works with the picture of two ages, the present age, which will continue until God brings in the age to come, when Jesus will return and God's rule will be finally established. It is difficult to express this in modern language because it is totally alien to our own way of thinking. To understand Mark we have to push aside all our knowledge of the vast extent and great age of the universe, the idea of evolution, and the belief that life on earth will continue unchanged until it is ended by some natural catastrophe or through human action such as nuclear war or pollution that has got out of control.

This means that Mark did not regard Jesus's teaching as given to a Church that was to have a continuing existence in the world. The End will come soon, and this is a rigorist ethic for the period before Christ returns. What is of supreme importance is to have 'treasure in heaven', to 'enter the kingdom of God', to 'inherit eternal life' – the phrases all mean the same thing: enjoyment of the age to come. Riches tie the rich man to the present age. This is what is wrong with them, not that the rich show no concern for the poor, or that there should be equality for all. Probably Mark thinks of the reward for those who have given up all as becoming a member of the Christian community that forms their new family, persecuted though that family is. *And persecutions besides* is not an ironical addition, but a description of the experience of that Christian community. This, however, will last only until the End. Christian fellowship, even though this involves persecution, is an adequate reward for leaving everything and following Jesus because it is only for the period before the End and that period will be brief. The full reward, however, is eternal life in the age to come. Only on such a belief in the imminent coming of the kingdom of God at the end of the present age is such a rigorist ethic feasible. The concluding verse reiterates the reversal of fortunes in the future age, which was seen earlier (9.35).

Recognizing how Mark understood this teaching solves the problem that it is an impractical dream, but it still leaves the question of the promise of rewards. Many judge that offering material rewards for moral actions demeans the morality and makes the motive unethical. Yet the promise of reward is firmly embedded in Mark's narrative and there is no reason to suppose that it was not equally a part of the traditions that came down to him. Peter asked what they would get out of it, and Jesus promises a rich reward. This is the blunt fact and it cannot be evaded by claiming that the rewards are spiritual, or by emphasizing the persecutions. Perhaps it is an inescapable consequence of believing in the present evil age and the imminence of the age to come.

10.32–4   REB correctly shows that Mark begins a new section here. *They were on the road going up to Jerusalem, and Jesus was leading the way*. The account is a little awkward and it is not entirely clear what is being described. 'Leading the way' is actually 'going ahead of them', and in the context 'them' ought to refer to the disciples (i.e. the Twelve). The account continues, *the disciples were filled with awe*, but the verb is the same as in 1.27 and 10.24, and the phrase should be 'and they were amazed', still without naming the disciples. Mark continues, *while* ('and') *those who followed behind were afraid*. These appear to be the crowd, because *once again* [Jesus] *took the Twelve aside*, to give them private teaching. Probably the picture is of Jesus striding towards Jerusalem, with the Twelve and a crowd of other people following him, when he took the Twelve aside *and began to tell them what was to happen to him*.

The prophecy is more precise than the two earlier predictions (8.31; 9.31). Although Jesus speaks of the Son of Man, Mark, as usual, understood it to be a prophecy about Jesus himself. The significant words have already been discussed, and it is necessary only to point out that the predictions *'they will condemn him to death and hand him over to the Gentiles. He will be mocked and spat upon, and flogged and killed'* agree more exactly with what took place. Commentators debate whether this is an invented prophecy or not, but if we remain with Mark's narrative the question is not important. Mark is emphasizing the inevitability of the crucifixion within God's purpose, and the repetition of the prophecy stresses this and forms part of his threefold pattern of suffering by John the Baptist, Jesus, and later Christians.

10.35–45   With the request of James and John, Mark returns to the theme of the kingdom. The section appears to contain four separate themes, the prophecy about the cup and baptism (vv. 38–9), the statement that God alone has decreed who shall have the chief places in the future kingdom (v. 40), teaching about the importance of service in the Christian community (vv. 42–4), and a theological explanation of the death of Jesus (v. 45). It is not part of our purpose to discuss if the passage has been compiled from different traditions. We stick with what Mark has written and attempt to understand it as a connected narrative.

10.35–40   REB's *'do us a favour'* is almost comic, as if they were going to ask him to lend them 50 shekels (curiously NJB and CEV offer the same translation). If the literal 'we want you to do for us whatever we ask of you' (NRSV, NIV) is regarded as stilted, we may follow GNB: 'Teacher, there is something we want you to do for us'. The request is to be granted positions of honour and power in the future kingdom where they expect Jesus to be king. To this Jesus gives two answers, '*Can you drink the cup that I drink, or be baptized with the baptism that I am baptized with?*' and '*to sit on my right or on my left is not for me to grant; that honour is for those to whom it has already been assigned*'. Both are highly significant.

Given the importance that the (second) coming of Jesus had for Mark, the climax of the first part of this narrative is the second statement, the meaning of which is exactly caught in REB's paraphrase. The future kingdom is a replica of earthly kingdoms, and God has already decided who will sit on Jesus's right and left. Jesus accepts that he will be the king in the future kingdom, but his relation to God is not clearly defined. It has been suggested that the disciples expected Jesus to inaugurate a temporary earthly paradise when he reached Jerusalem and took his words in this sense, but the reference to 'in your glory', together with their amazement and fear as they followed him towards the city, makes it much more likely that Mark had the kingdom at the end of the present age in mind.

The first reply to the disciples, however, is just as important to Mark. Those who are to receive honour in the future kingdom must suffer exactly the same fate that awaits Jesus. To us 'cup' and 'baptism' immediately suggest the Eucharist and the sacrament of baptism, and no doubt they carried these overtones for Mark. Yet this is not the immediate sense of the question. In the Old Testament the cup is a symbol both of joy (Ps. 23.5; 116.13) and of punishment and suffering (e.g. Ps. 75.8; Isa. 51.17, 22; Jer. 25.15–17; Ezek. 23.31–4). Here it symbolizes persecution and probably martyrdom. As the Son of Man will drink the cup of suffering so his followers must drink that cup – and Mark's fellow Christians were probably already doing so. In popular Greek thought the verb 'to plunge', 'to immerse' (here translated in its usual Christian sense, 'be baptized') was used metaphorically for being overwhelmed by various kinds of misery and calamities, and here it also seems to refer to martyrdom. Even if Mark could hardly have avoided thinking of the Eucharist and baptism, this does not mean that he regarded the suffering as redemptive. Rather it is part of the general theme of recapitulation. Jesus as Son of Man will suffer, be killed and return as glorious Lord. In the same way the disciples will suffer in the persecutions that will reach their climax in the period preceding the End, and will then share the splendour of the kingdom.

10.41–4   Not unnaturally the remaining ten disciples *were indignant* at the presumption of James and John, and Jesus reiterates his teaching about the reversal of values that he gave when the disciples were arguing about which of them was the greatest (9.33–7). Earthly positions will be reversed in the kingdom of God and those who seek pre-eminence will be made last of all and servants of all. He makes a contrast with earthly political states: *'You know that among the Gentiles the recognized rulers lord it over their subjects, and the great make their authority felt'*, but it is not clear in what situation the contrasting humble service is to be given. It has been suggested that there was a crisis in Mark's church where indignation, anger and mistrust had flared up and the leaders attempted to secure positions of power and prestige. Mark meets this situation by setting out the way of discipleship in suffering and service. This is very doubtful. If Mark wished to respond to such a situation there were other ways of acting than by inserting a paragraph in a book that was mainly concerned with collecting traditions about Jesus and presenting them in a continuous narrative. Moreover such an interpretation seriously undervalues the importance that the End and the (second) coming of Jesus had in Mark's thought. In any case the validity of attempts to discover details about the community to which Mark belonged by analysing the way he presents the ministry of Jesus is highly questionable.

10.45   The final saying, *'For the Son of Man did not come to be served but to serve, and to give his life as a ransom for many'* stands apart from the rest of this episode. It goes beyond the idea of the Son of Man as a servant and declares that he gives his life as a 'ransom'. There has been an enormous discussion about it. Most of that debate has centred on whether Jesus actually said it – naturally, perhaps, for if we could be sure that it is authentic it would shed important light on how Jesus understood his death – but it has proved impossible to reach any agreement.

The noun 'ransom' occurs only here and in the same saying in Matthew 20.28 (Luke has no parallel to the present episode, but in response to a dispute among the disciples at the Last Supper as to which was the greatest, Jesus says, 'I am among you like a servant' (Luke 22.27, literally 'as one who serves'), without any reference to a ransom). The verb 'to ransom' ('redeem') is found only in Luke 24.21 ('we hoped that he was the one who was going to redeem Israel'); Titus 2.14 ('Jesus Christ, who gave himself for us that he might redeem us from all iniquity') and 1 Peter 1.18 ('knowing that you were redeemed from your vain manner of life handed down from your ancestors, not by corruptible things, silver and gold, but by precious blood as of an unblemished and spotless lamb, even Christ's'), and a related noun in 1 Timothy 2.6 ('who gave himself as a ransom for all'), each of which REB paraphrases so that the presence of the word is concealed. Another related noun with a similar meaning occurs rather more widely, mainly in Paul's letters and in Hebrews (e.g. Rom. 3.24; Heb. 9.15).

In secular language the word 'ransom' was mainly used for the release of slaves. In the Septuagint the noun and the verb are used of the payment of money to free a slave (Lev. 25.47–55) and as a substitute for the sacrifice of the firstborn (Exod. 13.13–16). Josephus uses it of the bar of gold that the high priest promised to give to the Roman general Crassus 'as a ransom' for everything else in the Temple, and also says that Herod was prepared to pay 300 talents as a 'ransom' for his brother to ransom him from the enemy (*Antiquities*. XIV.7.1 [107]; XIV 14.1 [371]).

It is often claimed that Jesus was influenced by the suffering servant in Isaiah 53, but it has been decisively shown that the links with that chapter are tenuous. 'Ransom' has no links with 'a sacrifice for sin' (Isa. 53.10). The Greek word for 'to serve' here is never used in the Septuagint, and the Septuagint translated the Hebrew word for 'servant' or 'slave' by two different Greek words, neither of which is applied to Jesus in the Gospels. I would add that, as we have seen, Mark alludes to the Old Testament so rarely that it is not to be expected that he had Isaiah 53 in mind.

It is usual to say that 'many' has the sense of 'all', on the basis of the way it was used in Hebrew and Aramaic.

Evidence is drawn from the Qumran writings, where the community is often referred to as 'the many'. Since the group regarded themselves as the true Israel, it is argued that 'the many' were the people of God, and that this is the meaning of the word here. Yet at Qumran one of the punishments for breaking the community rules was exclusion from 'the many', particularly exclusion from the common meals. So the idea of exclusion cannot be so easily disposed of. We have seen that Mark believed that the parables were told deliberately to exclude outsiders, and that the disciples were singled out to receive private teaching. He makes a strong division between the close followers of Jesus and those who fail to understand his teaching and do not join the company of his disciples. Past battles over predestination may have influenced the interpretation of many scholars, and these must not be allowed to blind us as we examine the saying. Neither must our own emphasis on toleration and inclusion distort our vision.

The ransom is 'for' many. The preposition has several different meanings. Those holding a substitutionary theory of the atonement take it to mean 'instead of'. Others point out that it can mean 'for the sake of' or 'on behalf of', implying that Jesus's 'giving' of his life in some way benefited 'many'. Combining this with the claim that the contrast is between the one man Jesus and 'many' in the sense of all, several commentators interpret the saying as meaning that God uses Jesus's sufferings to bring salvation to us all.

Our present purpose is to try to discover what Mark meant. This is made more difficult because the saying is so isolated in the book. There is no other allusion to Jesus's death as a ransom, and much of the narrative expresses ideas that would appear to deny any need for such redemption. Jesus declares that the sins of the paralysed man are forgiven, without even requiring penitence, apparently on the grounds of the faith of his four friends rather than that of the man himself. He offers healing freely, even to those who are ritually unclean and who have broken the requirements of the Law by coming among the crowd and touching him. His defeat of the demons implies a battle against their power rather than the need to suffer and die in order to secure release. On three occasions Jesus predicted his death, but in none of these predictions did he say anything about its purpose. The words that Mark records appear to regard the execution of Jesus as the same as the execution of John the Baptist, the one decisive difference being that he will rise again after he has been killed. Finally, the saying stands in a very loose relation to the debate that it concludes.

One proposal for finding a coherent sequence of thought fastens on the contrast between being served and serving. It was expected that the Son of Man would be a ruler, as in Daniel 7, taking 'the son of man' as an individual. This is now reversed: the Son of Man is a servant. From this it is alleged to be a small step to the idea that the Son of Man gives his life on behalf of others. A comparison is sometimes made with the description of the Jewish martyrs in 4 Maccabees (probably written between 63 BC and AD 70), where it is said that 'they became, as it were, a ransom for the sin of our nation', and 'through the blood of these righteous ones and through the propitiation of their death, the divine providence rescued Israel' (4 Macc. 17.21–2; cf. 6.28–9, where Eleazar prays when tortured and on the point of death, 'Be merciful to your people and let our punishment be a satisfaction on their behalf. Make my blood their purification and take my life as a ransom for theirs'). Although the word translated 'ransom' is different from that in Mark and means 'giving up one's life for another' or 'in return for sparing the life of another', it shows that such ideas were current among Jewish thinkers. Some find the concept in the Community Rule at Qumran, but the Hebrew word is 'to make atonement', which is translated by several different words in the Septuagint.

It certainly looks as if this is additional evidence for thinking that Mark included all the teaching of Jesus that he knew, and placed the sayings where he thought was most appropriate. After all, he had to find somewhere to put them.

This raises the question of how we are to understand Mark's account today. The difficulty is rather different from that which the miracles pose. It is not that a scientific knowledge of the world has created problems, but that traditional Christian dogma is too easily attached to the saying. Although no doctrine of the atonement has ever been officially adopted by the Church, and many different theories have been proposed, Christian theology has asserted that Jesus made an atonement for human sin and so brought salvation to the human race. All the theories explaining the atonement wish to find support in the New Testament, and there is a strong tendency to interpret the present saying in ways that fit the reader's beliefs. Texts continue to live into the present, and on the way readers give them different meanings, or at the least, changing emphases. There is nothing wrong with this, so long as it is not supposed that the way the text is now read was the way the first readers read it or that the meaning now given to it was the meaning that Mark intended. This text expresses in admirably succinct form the combination of service and sacrifice that most Christians find in the life and death of Jesus. Perhaps we should leave it at that.

10.46–52 Suddenly Mark describes another miracle, which is marked by considerable detail including the name of the blind man who is healed, and the exact place where it took place. *They came to Jericho; and as he was leaving the town, with his disciples and a large crowd, Bartimaeus (that is, son of Timaeus), a blind beggar, was seated at the roadside.* The interpretation of the name is not in Mark's usual style, to which REB has assimilated it. The Greek reads 'the son of Timaeus Bartimaeus'. Perhaps this is a pointer to the fact that Mark quoted the story in exactly the form in which he received it from tradition. Other features in the story add their own hints that this was so. This is the only place in Mark where Jesus is called 'the Nazarene' (REB 'of Nazareth') by the narrator. Earlier it was the man possessed by the unclean spirit who addressed Jesus in this way (1.24), and later it will be used by other actors in the drama. Bartimaeus is the only person in Mark's book who addresses Jesus as 'Son of David'. Moreover, this is the only place where *Rabbi* occurs in the alternative form 'Rabbouni' (REB gives this form of the word in John 20.16, but not here). At the end the miracle lacks the usual account of the wonder of the onlookers and Jesus's command to silence. Instead Mark simply says that Bartimaeus *followed him on the road*, implying that he became a disciple.

The miracle is often contrasted with the healing of the blind man at Bethsaida (8.22–6). There Jesus spat on the man's eyes, and the cure took place in two stages. Only after Jesus laid his hands on the man's eyes for a second time did he see everything clearly. Moreover, on that occasion Jesus sent him home and told him not even to go into the village. Here the healing is instantaneous and is achieved by Jesus's words, and when he could see again, Bartimaeus followed him.

Some have seen great significance in Mark's placing of these two miracles. They are said to mark off the section of the book in which Jesus teaches the disciples about his future suffering, death and resurrection and the meaning of discipleship. It has also been suggested that the first healing carries symbolic meaning: either it points to Peter's 'confession' as the full recovery of 'sight' by the disciples, or it teaches that even after that recognition of Jesus as the messiah the disciples still saw only with clouded vision.

The messiah was expected to be a descendant of David, and 'son of David' had already become a title for the messiah. In the Psalms of Solomon, which probably come from the first century BC, the psalmist prays: 'See, Lord, and raise up for them their king, the son of David, to rule over your servant Israel in a time known to you, O God' (Ps. Sol. 17.21). The blind man's address to Jesus is a recognition that he is the messiah, and this may be the 'faith' that Jesus says has healed him, rather than just the confidence that Jesus, as a powerful wandering healer, could give him back his sight. Some commentators have suggested that it is this confession of Jesus as the messiah that makes him a disciple who now 'followed' Jesus. Whether more than this was in Mark's mind is difficult to determine. Some argue that the story of Bartimaeus shows that those who have faith know the truth about Jesus, in contrast to the disciples, who still fail to understand. They place some emphasis on Jesus's statement that the man's faith has 'saved' him, but REB is right in translating the word as *healed* (cf. 5.23, 28, 34; 6.56); the word does not have overtones of spiritual 'salvation' here. Some make the further claim that the account of the miracle introduces the final section of the book, in which Jesus boldly claims to be the messiah and his true identity is revealed.

It is difficult to believe that Mark had such complex ideas in mind. A much simpler reason for the placing of the present healing here is that the tradition contained a reference to Jericho. Since Jesus in Mark's narrative travelled to Judaea only once this was the only possible place where he could put it. It just would not fit anywhere else.

11.1–10   To those who have been following Mark's narrative the next incident must appear most surprising. Up to this point Jesus attempted to conceal who he was, and when Peter declared that the disciples believe that he was the messiah he immediately taught them that the Son of Man would endure great suffering and be put to death, rising again after three days. Now suddenly he deliberately enters Jerusalem as a king. The change of policy is as sudden as it is dramatic.

It looks as if Jesus had made the arrangement to borrow the colt, giving as a kind of password, *'The Master needs it'*. The alternative, that it reveals his supernatural knowledge, is less probable. *Master* is the word elsewhere translated 'Lord' (1.3; 2.28; 5.19). It is unusual to find it here, since Mark's normal term for Jesus is 'teacher'. If it refers to Jesus, it would mean that at this point he referred to himself as 'Lord'. This appears to be the meaning adopted by REB, with its capital letter. Some suggest that the colt's master was meant, the reply being intended to reassure casual bystanders. Although this is possible, it hardly fits the mood of the story as a whole. Some suggest that Jesus commandeered the ass, in this way exerting his authority. This may be going too far. How the words are interpreted affects the rest of the reply, *'and will send it back here without delay'*. If 'the master' is Jesus, it would be part of the password and the meaning would be that Jesus would return it as soon as he had completed what he borrowed it for. If 'the master' referred to the colt's owner, it means that the person who objects to the disciples' action in taking the colt will then permit the disciples to bring the colt to Jesus.

The strewing of garments and leafy branches on the road may have been the normal practice when a king arrived (cf. 2 Kgs. 9.13). The cry of the crowds, *'Hosanna! Blessed is he who comes in the name of the Lord!'* follows the Septuagint of Psalm 118.25–6, except that 'O Lord, cause us to prosper, we pray' is omitted and 'Hosanna' is transliterated (the Septuagint translates the word – correctly – as 'O Lord, save, we pray'). In the psalm, the one who comes is a pilgrim coming up to Jerusalem for one of the festivals, probably Booths (Tabernacles). The next two sentences, *'Blessed is the kingdom of our father David which is coming! Hosanna in the heavens!'* (literally, 'highest heights') have no Old Testament parallel. The entire cry puzzled Matthew and Luke, who both made extensive changes. Mark's version is highly nationalistic. It looks for the restoration of the Davidic kingdom, the time when Israel had its greatest empire. It has been claimed that by the time of Jesus 'Hosanna' had become an exclamation of praise. Mark appears to have interpreted it as a triumphal cry, welcoming the messiah (the one who comes), as most congregations do today, rather than its original meaning of 'Save!'

And Jesus engineered all this! Did he really at last present himself in the capital city, the city of David, as the messiah? Much is often made of the fact that he rode on a donkey rather than a war-horse, but a donkey was as much a royal mount as a horse. There seems little doubt that Mark saw Jesus as claiming to be the messiah, deliberately riding into Jerusalem rather than walking as the other pilgrims did, and as he had done in all his travels up to this moment. If due weight is to be placed on the three predictions of his suffering and death, the only conclusion that can be drawn is that he threw down a challenge to the authorities, making it certain that they would take him to be the leader of an insurrection against Rome. The messiah had to die. By his actions he ensured that his prophecy would be fulfilled.

11.11 The final days of Jesus's life are precisely dated by Mark. On this first day (our Sunday) Jesus *entered Jerusalem, went into the temple*, and did nothing more; he just *looked round at everything*, before going out to Bethany, presumably having sent the colt back to its owner.

11.12–14 *On the following day* (Monday) occurs what to us is the strangest of all Jesus's actions. Jesus felt hungry, noticed a fig tree in the distance, went to it, and found nothing on it *for it was not the season for figs*. Yet he proceeded to curse the tree: *'May no one ever again eat fruit from you!'*. Commentators try to wriggle out of the straightforward narrative by suggesting that it is a legend that grew out of the presence of a withered fig tree near Bethany, or that it was an acted parable that carried the meaning that Jerusalem or the Temple would be destroyed, or that some such parable as that found in Luke 13.6–9 has become a story about Jesus. It is commonly claimed that, whatever its origin, it had symbolic meaning for Mark. The fig tree represents Israel. It had produced no fruit when the messiah looked for figs. Therefore, it is under divine judgement and will be destroyed. Support is found in Old Testament passages such as Hosea 9.10, 16–17; Micah 7.1; and Jeremiah 8.13. It is sometimes suggested, further, that in the messianic age the fig tree will again bear fruit, for in other texts the fig tree is a sign of prosperity (Mic. 4.4; Hag. 2.19; Zech. 3.10). In addition, the fact that the cursing of the tree and its withering are separated by Jesus's actions in the Temple is said to be Mark's way of drawing attention to the parallels. The unreasonableness of Jesus's expectation when it was not the season for figs is explained away by suggesting that the original story was set in the autumn Festival of Booths and the statement was added when it was transferred to the spring Passover, or that Jesus was looking for the buds that would produce figs later in the year, or that Mark's comment is a hint to the reader to treat the story symbolically not literally.

None of these attempted explanations is satisfactory. Where Mark finds fulfilment of Old Testament prophecy he provides quotations. Here he gives no hint that he had any Old Testament texts in mind. The statement that it was not the season for figs is an integral part of the story as he tells it and should not be brushed aside. Mark may well have believed that the fig tree should have provided figs out of season for the Son of Man when he wanted them. He certainly regarded Jesus's words as a curse and the events as actually happening as he describes them. His reason for placing one story within another is normally to allow time for the first story to proceed (cf. 5.21–43; 6.6b–31), and this is the reason here, not elaborate symbolism. Finally, the lesson that Jesus draws from the incident and explains to the disciples is the power of prayer, not God's judgement on Jerusalem (11.20–4).

Most commentators have been led into making these improbable explanations through an attempt to vindicate the historical actions of Jesus. But Mark's narrative hangs together perfectly. Admittedly his moral and religious sensitivity is very different from our own, but his book must be interpreted on his terms, not ours.

11.15–19   It is natural for us to picture the Temple as a church, but in fact the roofed building was only a small part of the whole complex, most of which was in the open air. There were areas where women and non-Jews could go, and it was in this part of the Temple that animals for sacrifice were sold ('those who bought' were the pilgrims), and where the money-changers exchanged Greek or Roman coins for the Jewish money in which the Temple tax had to be paid. According to the Mishnah the tables were set up both in the provinces and in the Temple in the days before the Passover (m. Shek. 1.3). It seems that the inhabitants of Jerusalem carried goods through the Temple courtyards as a short cut, a practice later Jewish tradition forbade (m. Ber. 9.5: '[A man] may not enter into the Temple Mount with his staff or his sandal or his wallet, . . . nor may he make of it a short by-path; still less may he spit there').

Jesus then explained his actions. *'Does not scripture say, "My house shall be called a house of prayer for all nations"? But you have made it a robbers' cave.'* The first quotation is from Isaiah 56.7, and follows the wording of the Septuagint, which here exactly translates the Hebrew. In the second sentence only 'robbers' cave' is derived from Jeremiah 7.11, again in the same words as the Septuagint. The full sentence in Jeremiah reads: 'Do you regard this [Septuagint 'my'] house which bears my name as a bandits' cave?' (REB). Jeremiah condemns the moral wrongdoing of the Israelites in terms that are akin to the Ten Commandments and declares that far from protecting them, the Temple has been defiled by their actions. It is curious that Jesus criticizes those who were facilitating the offering of sacrifice, and commentators frequently try to find some moral wrongdoing by asserting that the dealers were making huge profits out of the pilgrims who had to get their money changed and buy animals that had been certified as fit for sacrifice. Jesus, however, does not mention this. His complaint appears to be that by setting up the tables in the only part of the Temple open to non-Jews they are preventing them from worshipping God.

The chief priests and scribes now *looked for a way to bring about his death* (literally, 'how they might destroy him', the same word as in 3.6), but *the whole crowd was spellbound by his teaching* (a curious word for REB to use; it is the same word that Mark uses in 1.22 and 6.2, where the people are 'amazed' at Jesus's teaching, and in 7.37, where the people's 'astonishment knew no bounds' at the healing of the deaf man). Mark continues his careful dating of the events: *when evening came they went out of the city.*

11.20–4   *Early* on the Tuesday morning *they saw that the fig tree had withered.* The sequence of thought may be this. Peter's *'Rabbi, look, the fig tree which you cursed has withered'* shows that Mark regarded Jesus's words as a curse that would have a physical effect on the tree. Despite the almost unanimous opinion that the saying about removing mountains is figurative (like the saying about the camel and the eye of a needle), it may be that Mark believed that in the period of the end-time in which he and his readers were living such miracles would take place. This is followed by an unequivocal statement that those who believe that their requests will be granted will have *'whatever you ask for in prayer'.* To Mark, Jesus's cursing of the fig tree is an example of that absolute faith in God which makes it possible for Christians to perform any miracle. The large number of miracles in Acts, including what is a virtual curse directed at Elymas (Acts 13.6–12), show that the ethos of the early Church was very different from our own.

11.25   To this Mark has added further teaching about prayer that is more akin to the type of teaching recorded by Matthew and Luke than the rigorist ethic and teaching about the end of the world found elsewhere in his book. Verse 26 (see mg.) is omitted by several good manuscripts, and was almost certainly added by a later copyist from Matthew 6.15. It may be that v. 25 was also added to Mark's original narrative, but more probably it is further evidence that Mark was intent on including every scrap of teaching that he knew and placed isolated fragments where he thought it most suitable. It is the only passage in the entire book where forgiveness is made dependent on moral action and where the teaching is more suitable for the ongoing life of the Church than in the period between the coming of John the Baptist and the End, and is in strong contrast to 2.1–12; 3.28–9; and 4.12.

11.27–33   This is the first of another set of stories, where Mark's interest lies in the conflict with the authorities and the aphorisms that Jesus utters (cf. 2.1—3.6). It is closely linked to Jesus's actions in the Temple on the previous day (the suggestion that it concerned his authority to teach when he was not a licensed rabbi may be dismissed). Not unnaturally, the Jewish leaders question Jesus's authority for interrupting the offering of sacrifices as he had done by overturning the tables of those changing the money for paying the Temple tax and the seats of those selling the pigeons. Presumably their question was intended to commit him to some assertion of his authority that would make him liable to a religious or political charge. His response by asking about John's authority is essentially a clever evasion, although it reveals yet again Mark's interest in John the Baptist and the important part he plays in his narrative. Some think that Jesus's question implies that John's authority came from God as does his own. Others find in it a hint that he is the messiah, since John was the forerunner who announced his coming.

12.1–9   The sequence of stories of conflicts with various questioners is broken by this parable. It fits the general setting, however, in that *they* (the chief priests, scribes and elders) *saw that the parable was aimed at them*. But does this mean that, contrary to what Mark said in 4.10–12, the parables were readily understood by their original hearers? Probably not. Mark speaks of the parable being 'aimed at them', not 'that he was referring to them' (as Matt 21.45). Rather than meaning that the opponents identified themselves with the tenants, Mark may well have intended that they realized that in some way the parable was a threat directed at them, but they did not understand what it meant.

How, then, did Mark interpret the parable? Once again it is vital to avoid allowing our interpretation to be contaminated by Matthew and Luke. It is equally important not to rush hastily into questions of whether it goes back to Jesus himself. The concept of Israel as a vineyard is found in Isaiah 5.1–7, and putting a *wall* round it, *hewed out a winepress*, and *built a watch-tower* are all very close to the Septuagint. The sequel, however, is completely different. In Isaiah the 'choice red vines' yield 'wild grapes' and because of this God's judgement falls on the vineyard, which is destroyed. Isaiah explains that the vineyard is Israel. In Mark attention is directed at the tenants. After they had beaten and killed a succession of servants who were sent to collect the owner's share of the harvest, he

141

sent *his beloved son* (probably this implies his only son), but the servants *killed him, and flung his body out of the vineyard.* Jesus then declares that the owner *will come and put the tenants to death and give the vineyard to others.*

Since Mark regarded parables as allegories, his interpretation must have been similar to that which modern congregations give it. The owner is God, the tenants are the Jewish leaders, the servants are the prophets, and the son is Jesus, the 'son of God'. Whom the 'others' represent is not clear. Some think they are the Gentiles, who by Mark's time were probably a majority in the Church, but since the tenants are the Jewish leaders, these other tenants must be leaders of some sort – the Roman authorities perhaps, or the leaders of the Christian Church. The emphasis, however, does not lie here, but is placed on the judgement of the present tenants. In a different form it is another prediction of the crucifixion, but there is no reference to the resurrection. In one sense the teaching is Christological, since the 'beloved son' is set apart from the servants, but the main emphasis appears to be placed on the judgement of the Jewish leaders.

12.10–11   To this Mark has attached a quotation from Psalm 118.22–3, exactly following the Septuagint translation. Whatever the words meant to the psalmist (in the psalm they come in a loose collection of various types of material), Mark would have applied them to his own day. Accepting his allegorical interpretation of parables, Jesus is the stone, rejected by the Jewish leaders but now made the *main corner-stone.* This reversal is God's doing. This is not necessarily a reference to the resurrection. What it certainly foretells is the eventual triumph of Jesus.

12.12   The dispute with the 'chief priests, scribes, and elders' is rounded off by Mark's assertion that they *wanted to arrest him* (the word was used earlier when Herod 'seized' John the Baptist (7.17), but it is doubtful that it provides another example of the parallels between Jesus and John, since it is a very common word, used in a variety of ways). Again Mark points out that they were *afraid of the people* ('crowd', cf. 11.32), and *went away* (REB's *left him alone* gives a slightly wrong slant; the Greek is 'and leaving him they went away').

12.13–17   Mark now attaches accounts of a succession of Jewish groups and individuals who come and question Jesus, not all with the evil intent of the Pharisees and men of Herod's party (cf. 3.6 for their earlier plotting together), who *were sent to trap him with a question* (the Greek has 'and they sent', which REB takes as impersonal, but in the narrative it is implied that the Jewish leaders sent them).

The question was designed to force Jesus into proving that he was a rebel against Rome by rejecting payment of the poll tax, or, if he accepted that such payment should be made, to destroy his influence with the crowd. The questioners' flattery reveals their *duplicity* ('hypocrisy' in the Greek), and Jesus recognizes that they are *trying to catch* [him] *out* (literally 'tempt' or 'test' me, as in 1.13; 8.11; 10.2). The poll tax (this is the meaning of the word translated more generally as *taxes*) was paid in Roman coinage, and Jesus asks to see one of these coins. The most common kind of denarius, a small silver coin, carried the emperor's head surrounded with a laurel wreath on one side and the head of his mother on the other. The inscription was abbreviated, as on English coins, and read: 'Tiberias Caesar, Son of the Divine Augustus, Venerable Supreme High Priest'. How offensive this was to pious Jews is obvious.

Commentators offer a range of interpretations of the words: Jesus showed that his questioners themselves accepted Roman government and were using Roman money and revealed their duplicity; Jesus held the quietist view that so long as the Roman state did not interfere in the religious life of individuals it was morally indifferent and taxes should be paid; Jesus accepted that the state came within the divine order and to obey it was not inconsistent with loyalty to God; in the light of his expectation of an imminent end of the world when the political power of Rome would be destroyed, Jesus held the state to be relatively insignificant compared to the kingdom of God; or Jesus swept away the whole principle of ready-made formulae that could be applied to every situation, the essential fact being that everything belongs to God.

It may be that the story was retained in the tradition because the relation of Christians to the state and paying the poll tax were of great importance to the early Christians when their loyalty to Rome was being questioned, but that does not seem to be Mark's purpose in including it here. The story is set in a series of conflicts with opponents, the overall theme of which is the failure of each successive group to trap Jesus and weaken his standing with the people. Ultimately the stories reaffirm his authority as the messiah. At the end the Pharisees and Herodians are *completely taken aback*, or perhaps, 'felt grudging admiration'. This concluding comment appears to indicate that Mark regarded the aphorism, *'Pay Caesar what belongs to Caesar, and God what belongs to God'* primarily as the means by which Jesus evaded the trap, and did not regard the incident as presenting positive teaching similar to that in Romans 13.1–7.

12.18–27   Mark explains that the next group of questioners, Sadducees, did not believe in the resurrection. They present him with what was probably a stock example to show how foolish such a belief was. The law, the essential provisions of which are set out fully but not quoted exactly after either the Hebrew or the Greek, is found in Deuteronomy 25.5–10, and comes from the time when the Israelites did not believe in life after death. A man's future existence continued in his descendants (the masculine is deliberate – it was a male-dominated society). Even in the time of the Deuteronomist, however, this particular regulation appears to have been dying out, since it is limited to cases where the brothers were still living together in the family home and it is accepted that a sanction must be applied against a brother who was unwilling to perform his duty. It was hardly a live commandment in the time of Jesus.

12.24–5   Jesus's reply is in two forms. First, he declares that there will be no marriage in the resurrection life, but those who rise will be *like angels in heaven*. Many who have enjoyed happy married lives will feel that this is rather bleak comfort, and it may be some consolation to realize that Mark's intention is not to provide teaching about the nature of life after death. Commentators who take it to be positive teaching try to escape from the idea that Jesus believed that life in heaven would be a pale, unemotional existence by suggesting that he is rejecting narrow conceptions of marriage and wished to remove its limitations by looking to a wider and deeper set of relationships. This is to impose modern ideas upon a first-century story.

12.26–7   Second, he quotes from Exodus 3.6. The argument is that God would not have described himself as the God of dead people. This is not the meaning of the Hebrew original, where God's words are simply to identify who he is, but Mark takes it as a decisive refutation of the denial of any resurrection by the Sadducees. The emphasis is not, as is sometimes supposed, on 'I am', for the verb is absent from Mark's text, which also omits 'the God of your father' (the Hebrew is in the common form of a noun clause that has no verb, while the Septuagint begins the sentence with 'I am the God of your father').

The debate has parallels in rabbinic literature and contains both a 'proof' of life after death and a description of the kind of life that those who are raised will enjoy. In this it seems to be closer to the kind of positive teaching that is common in Matthew.

Few commentators go beyond considering the question of the original form of the story and the authenticity of the sayings, the beliefs of the Sadducees, and the meaning and cogency of the arguments. It has been suggested that Jesus's spiritual view of the resurrection, freed from the crudely materialistic features that are found in many Jewish writings of the time, would have been attractive to Mark's Gentile readers. But again we need to ask if Mark intended to present positive teaching. The incident is set within the series of conflict stories, and it is clear that his main aim was to show the failure of members of all the sects of Judaism to trap Jesus. The key to the narrative is to be found in the two final Greek words, translated by REB as *You are very far from the truth* (literally, 'you err greatly', i.e. 'you are quite wrong'). This is not the admonition of a teacher but the triumphant climax of a battle in which Jesus utters his aphorisms with authority.

12.28–34   Mark introduces the next, and final, debate with the comment that *one of the scribes observed how well Jesus answered*. The Greek is literally, 'he had answered them well', and by omitting 'them' REB loses the point that the scribe recognized that Jesus had routed his Sadducee rivals.

The question concerning *the first of all the commandments* has been generally regarded as at the heart of the ethical and religious teaching of Jesus. Matthew and Luke differ from Mark and agree between themselves in some details, while each gives a different stress to the teaching, Matthew expressing anti-Jewish polemic by speaking of the Pharisees coming together and one of them trying to catch him out ('test' him), and Luke being concerned with moral exhortation and adding the parable of the Good Samaritan (Matt. 22.34–40; Luke 10.25–37). All this provides commentators with much to debate. We stick to our purpose of trying to understand Mark.

Jesus's answer combines the *Shema'* (Deut. 6.4–5) and Leviticus 19.18b. Unlike the other Gospels, Mark quotes the whole of the *Shema'*, to some extent combining the form in the Hebrew and the Septuagint. At the end of the story he gives the scribe's reply and Jesus's commendation. Both Jesus and the scribe, therefore, affirm that there is only one God, but the scribe, after restating Jesus's reply in different words, adds that keeping these two commandments *means far more than any whole-offerings and sacrifices*. Jesus recognizes that the scribe has replied *thoughtfully* and says that he is *not far from the kingdom of God*. Then follows a very important statement: *After that nobody dared put any more questions to him* (the Greek is especially emphatic). The questioning is at an end. The victory is complete. The son of God who teaches with authority is triumphant.

The conclusion has an air of finality and marks the end of this group of conflict stories. Yet this final story differs from the others. The scribe is not hostile to Jesus. He responds positively to Jesus's reply and Jesus appreciates his thoughtful response. Yet Mark's purpose in the whole section from 11.27 to 12.34 is to present Jesus as being challenged by all the Jewish parties that he has mentioned in his book and decisively routing each of them. The teaching is almost incidental. The picture he wishes to present is that of Jesus the victorious messiah. This final story, however, does not quite fit his purpose. Perhaps this is another little pointer suggesting that Mark included all the teaching that he knew. He put this story here because it seemed a suitable place.

To us, of course, the teaching is not incidental. We seize on every word that the historical Jesus may have spoken and attempt to apply it to the moral problems of our own day. Even so, we would do well to hesitate and reflect before we grasp these two commandments too eagerly. In a politicized and secular society we tend to fasten on the second commandment, even if we do not omit the first altogether. Moreover, the teaching is so generalized that almost any ethic can be derived from it, and it is easy to use it to support a morality that springs from our own culture.

Before leaving this story we need to notice Jesus's striking words: 'You are not far from the kingdom of God'. Again it is hardly possible to substitute 'the kingship of God' or 'God's authoritative rule'. The kingdom is a place to which individuals can be near. If this is a figurative expression, the meaning will be that the scribe has grasped the nature of God's character, though possibly with the overtones that he has not submitted himself fully to his authority.

12.35–7a   Despite so firmly marking the end of this collection of stories Mark continues his narrative with 'and', adding that Jesus was still teaching in the Temple. Having vanquished all the Jewish parties, he now goes on the offensive. *'How can the scribes maintain that the Messiah is a son of David?'* is a rather astonishing denial of what had become a general title for the messiah and has strong support in the Old Testament (cf. Isa. 9.6–7; 11.1–5; Jer 23.3–4; 33.14–17) as well as in later writings (cf. Pss. Sol. 17.21–43). After the manner of rabbinic debate, Jesus quotes Psalm 110.1. The psalm was attributed to David and was apparently held to be messianic prophecy (*when inspired by the Holy Spirit*), even though there is little evidence that the rabbis interpreted it as such at the time. Jesus fastens on the fact that David addresses the messiah as 'my Lord'. Many Old Testament scholars describe the psalm as a 'royal psalm' addressed to the Israelite king, and few would accept Davidic authorship. This need not worry any except those who cannot allow any error in the Bible, for Mark (and Jesus) was a man of his time and has to be understood within the society and culture in which he lived.

Commentators are anxious to discuss whether Jesus could have thought like this and spoken these words, and many hold that the sayings came from the Christian community and belong to later theological debates about Jesus. It seems likely that Mark understood Jesus to be asserting that the messiah was greater than David. It is strange to find rabbinic-type argument, but this could well be part of the tradition that Mark took up, especially if he included all the traditions he knew and kept closely to their wording. To him Jesus is primarily the Son of Man

147

and son of God rather than a Jewish messiah, and this story would provide confirmation. It is part of the open revelation of the 'secret' that began with the entry into Jerusalem and continued with Jesus's actions and words in the Temple.

Some scholars find in the stories of Jesus's actions in the Temple a veiled reference to Malachi 3.1, 'Suddenly the Lord whom you seek will come to his temple', but apart from the word 'Lord', Mark gives no hint that this is in his mind. Again we need to be careful about assuming later Christian interpretations and finding biblical references where Mark does not make them explicit.

But do Jesus's words mean that he rejected the Davidic descent of the messiah, and by implication also denied that he was a descendant of David? Again because they turn too rapidly to the genealogies in Matthew 1.2–17 and Luke 3.23–38, and to such passages as Romans 1.3; 15.12, many commentators believe that this is impossible. But Mark has the title 'son of David' only in 10.47–8, where Bartimaeus addresses him in this way, and even though Mark does not depict Jesus as rejecting the title in that story, this is no evidence that he himself accepted it. We need to remember that he never mentions Joseph and says nothing about Jesus's life before he was baptized by John. He mentions Jesus's family only once, and then speaks only of his mother and his brothers and sisters (3.31). There is no evidence, therefore, that he accepted that Jesus was descended from David. It shows yet again how important it is to read Mark on its own. According to Mark, Jesus's descent was unknown. Moreover, because he believed that Jesus was the son of God, the title 'son of David' was both too lowly and carried false nationalist overtones.

12.37b–40   Mark's narrative flows on and REB's paragraphing and punctuation are questionable. Probably no break should be made here. The crowd listen eagerly to the teaching about the son of David and Jesus continues to teach them. The meaning is slightly ambiguous. REB may be right to begin a new sentence at *Those who eat up the property of widows*. This makes it refer to a separate group from the scribes. Perhaps those condemned were trustees appointed to look after the property of widows, who took exorbitant fees. On the other hand, it may still be part of the warning about the scribes and suggest that their apparent piety enabled them to prey on the widows' religious devotion. In this case [They] *will receive a sentence all the more severe* is a separate statement.

The warning about the scribes is much shorter than in Matthew and Luke, and some think that Mark's introduction, *As he taught them* (literally 'in his teaching'), shows that he selected it from a larger body of teaching known to him. This puts too much weight on the phrase, which simply links it to the previous story. It seems much more likely that this attack on the scribes was among the traditions that Mark knew and he placed it here because it continued the series of conflicts, even though it comes rather oddly after Jesus's commendation of a scribe who was 'not far from the kingdom of God'. The oddity is increased by its being addressed to the crowd even though it is plain teaching, not a parable, and this may confirm that Mark had to find a place for an independent story among his traditions.

Those who find a reference to the Lord's appearance in the Temple in Malachi 3.1, note that a little later in that chapter the prophet declares judgement on those who 'wrong the widow'. But this is only one crime among others that the prophet condemns. Judgment, he declares, will also fall on 'sorcerers, adulterers, and perjurers, . . . those who cheat the hired labourer of his wages, and . . . who thrust the alien aside'. Moreover, as we saw earlier, Mark gives no overt indication that he had Malachi 3 in mind. Possibly a later copyist made the link, for a small number of manuscripts have 'and orphans' after 'widows' as in Malachi, although the common connection of widows and orphans may be the reason for the addition.

12.41–4   The next story is attached with the statement, *As he was sitting opposite the temple treasury* (probably one of the chests shaped like trumpets that stood round the court of women), and may equally have been a separate piece of tradition that came down to Mark. The account is usually regarded as positive teaching, showing that Jesus sided with the poor. By placing it as the conclusion of a series of conflict stories, Mark may have treated the aphorism of Jesus as a condemnation of the rich, for he regarded riches as one of the major hindrances to the complete dedication to Jesus that was necessary for entering the kingdom of

God. The *tiny coins* were the smallest in circulation in Palestine, and together the two coins amounted to less than a fiftieth of what a labourer might expect to earn in a day. We may note that the widow is said to have *given all that she had to live on*, a reckless disregard of the self that belongs to the rigorist ethic seen earlier in the sayings about denying oneself (10.17–25; cf. 8.34–7). She could have given only one coin, and retained one to buy food for herself. She threw in both.

13.1–2   Mark's narrative flows on. *As he was leaving the temple, one of his disciples exclaimed, 'Look, Teacher, what huge stones! What fine buildings!'* This was Herod the Great's temple, magnificent in its splendour, and erected at his own expense. It was begun in 20 BC, and Josephus, who gives a detailed account, says that the inner sanctuary was completed in 18 months, and the whole building was finished in 8 years (*Antiquities* XV.11.1–6 [380–425]; a slightly different description is given in *War* V.5.1–6 [184–227]). Josephus says some of the stones were 25 cubits in length, 8 in height and 12 in width (about $38\,\text{ft} \times 12\,\text{ft} \times 18\,\text{ft}$ or $11.7\,\text{m} \times 3.7\,\text{m} \times 5.5\,\text{m}$) – 'huge stones' indeed. Jesus's response is a firm prediction of the temple's destruction: *'Not one stone will be left upon another'*.

13.3–37   This leads into the longest continuous body of teaching in the whole book. Its importance for understanding Mark cannot be overestimated. There is a discouragingly large mass of literature on this chapter, but many of the studies are concerned with the problem of authenticity and an analysis of sources rather than with Mark's own understanding of what he has recorded. Whether Mark constructed the discourse from a Jewish-Christian apocalypse or from independent sayings, he has carried out his work in a far more thoroughgoing way than anywhere else in the book. Jesus speaks without any interruption for 33 verses. There are no references to a fresh start or even the insertion of such phrases as 'and he said to them' (contrast 2.27; 4.2, 21, 24; 6.10; 7.9; 8.21; 9.1). The audience remains the same for a longer time (contrast the changes in 4.10; 7.14, 17; 8.34; 10.23, 41). Despite alleged inconsistencies, a series of phrases marking the time shows that Mark intended to describe a sequence of events – *the end is still to come* (v. 7, Greek, 'but not yet [is] the end'), *These are the first birth-pangs of the new age* (v. 8), *Before the end* (Greek,

'First') *the gospel must be proclaimed to all nations* (v. 10), *then those who are in Judaea must take to the hills* (v. 14), *If anyone says to you then* (v. 21, Greek prefaces 'And then'), *after that distress* (v. 24), *Then* (Greek 'And then') *they will see the Son of Man coming in the clouds* (v. 26), *and* (Greek 'and then') *he will send out the angels* (v. 27). The unity of the chapter is further emphasized by connecting links – *these things* (vv. 4, 8, 29, 30), the repetition of *Be on your guard* (vv. 5, 9, 23, 33; the Greek word is 'look', as in the warnings in 8.15 and 12.38, and provides an important link with the disciples' exclamation in v. 1).

It has sometimes been argued that the large number of warnings reveals a stress on exhortation that is unique in Jewish apocalypses, but this should not lead to the conclusion that Mark was not concerned about prophesying the events at the end of the world. *Keep watch* (v. 33) and *Keep awake* (better, 'be watchful', 'be on the alert', vv. 35, 37) might perhaps be said to have an ethical sense, though the exact meaning of the last is uncertain, but the other imperatives draw attention to the events that are to come and to possible misunderstandings of those events. Thus 'Be on your guard' in vv. 5 and 23 warns against the false teachers (hence the call not to believe them in v. 21), and this is reinforced by the statement, *I have forewarned you of it all* (v. 23). The reason why the disciples should not be afraid of the coming wars (v. 7) is that the wars are part of God's predestined plan. *Such things are bound to happen* is not an assessment of what is probable but an assertion of divine necessity, and within that plan these events precede the End, which is *still to come*. Five exhortations in vv. 14–18 call for flight to the mountains and urge prayer that the worst sufferings of winter may be avoided, while the curious *let the reader understand* (v. 14) is most satisfactorily explained as an aside by Mark, akin to that in 7.19, calling attention to the hidden meaning of the *abomination of desolation*. In vv. 28–9 the imperatives draw attention to the enigmatic meaning of the fig tree as pointing to the way in which the signs will indicate the imminent approach of the End or the coming of the Son of Man. The imperatives in vv. 9 and 11 urge endurance under persecution. The whole setting has a strongly predestinarian cast, seen in the straight description in future tenses and the fact that the disciples will be passive mouthpieces of the Holy Spirit. Whatever pastoral concern is to be found in the chapter, the basis for the warnings is the certainty that a course of history has been predetermined and only awaits its unfolding, and the imperatives tie the discourse into a unity.

Mark has linked the destruction of the Temple with the events of the End. The double mention of 'these things' (v. 4, obscured in REB because it translates the first 'these things' as 'this') emphasizes that that destruction is part of those events. The prediction then takes its determined course.

13.3–6   The teaching is given to the inner circle of Peter, James and John, but this time Andrew joins them. Jesus begins with a warning against those who will come in his name and lead many astray (vv. 5–6). Mark envisages the coming of these false teachers or false messiahs either as the first stage of the final events or, more probably, a danger throughout the period (there is no time sequence in v. 6, and false Christs and false prophets are mentioned in v. 22).

13.7–8   The disciples asked when these things would happen, and this is picked up five times (vv. 7, 11, 14, 28, 29), a further indication that Mark regarded the whole prediction as a unity. The prophecy of the future begins at v. 7, with the prediction of *wars and rumours of wars*. Despite the statement that these wars are not the End, they are described as *the first birth-pangs of the new age* (v. 8, literally 'these things [are] a beginning of birth-pangs'). The 'not yet' cannot, therefore, mean that the end events have been postponed, even though the wars take place. Those end events are now set in motion and move remorselessly to the End itself.

This is reinforced by Mark's 'it is necessary' (v. 7; REB's *such things are bound to happen* misses the stress on divine predestination). 'It is necessary' was applied to the suffering and death of Jesus in 8.31 (REB 'had to') and the coming of Elijah (9.11, REB 'must'), and appears once more in this sense in this chapter (v. 10, REB 'must'). It has been argued that Mark portrays Jesus as the one who accurately predicted what his readers know has already happened: finding the colt (11.2–6), Jesus's passion and resurrection (8.31; 9.9, 12, 31; 10.32–4), and later in the narrative will predict the man carrying the water-jar (14.13–15), Judas's betrayal (14.17–21), and Peter's denial (14.30). Some of the predictions in chapter 13 have already taken place, so that Mark's readers may be confident about the coming of the Son of Man. Several of these are wrongly identified as predictions (11.2–6; 14.13–15), and Mark's emphasis is not on Jesus as 'predictor' but on the certainty of the divine purpose and plan. The point is not postponement but a recognition of the sequence of events that must take place before the Son of Man finally comes.

13.9–13   A change of theme is often found at v. 9, and commentators show a greater readiness to accept vv. 9–12 as going back to Jesus. If, however, our understanding of the chapter is not to be distorted by hasty questions of authenticity or by a reading of Mark in the light of Matthew and Luke, we must accept the sequence of thought. This section follows naturally and easily on the earlier prophecies. Having foretold war, earthquake and famine, Mark proceeds to describe sufferings more directly affecting the Christians – persecution and family divisions. Verse 10, however, stands out so strikingly from the surrounding sentences that almost all commentators treat it as inserted by Mark. This may be right (though we should not be too quick to deny that it may have been part of the tradition that came to him), but that does not excuse us from attempting to make sense of the narrative that he has produced. The saying should certainly not be seen as teaching a delay in the coming of the Son of Man, an interval that has been described as 'the time of God's patience', and so allows us to retain a belief in the 'Second Coming' even after two thousand years of history. Mark may have meant it as an interpretation of v. 9, perhaps teaching that to witness before a pagan tribunal will be to preach the gospel and in this way help to hasten the coming of the Son of Man and the kingdom of God by fulfilling the preconditions of their appearing. Alternatively the thought may be that the persecutions arise as a consequence of the Gentile mission. *Before the End* (REB has correctly interpreted Mark's 'first') this mission will take place according to God's predetermined plan and will result in the persecution and divisions within families that form part of the sorrows that inaugurate the new age. It is just possible that this is a further pointer to the accuracy of Jesus's predictions. By the time that Mark is writing his narrative the gospel has been widely proclaimed across the Roman world.

As we have seen, Mark has mentioned 'the holy spirit' only three times before this (1.8 (without the article); 3.29; 12.36), with 'the spirit' a further twice (1.10, 12), yet three of these have overtones of the end-time (1.8, 10; 3.29). Whether he linked the outpouring of the spirit with the messianic kingdom (cf. Isa. 11.1–2; 61.1; Joel 2.28–9) must remain doubtful, since he quotes none of these passages. Here the spirit comes in the midst of the persecutions rather than bringing the joys of the new age. Again it needs to be emphasized that Mark could not possibly have held the later trinitarian doctrine, and his under-standing of the spirit is akin to Old Testament beliefs (see on 1.8).

Despite these persecutions and other horrors *whoever endures to the end will be saved.* 'The end' (which does not have the article in the Greek) might mean 'right through' or 'finally' (i.e. up to martyrdom), and need not refer to the end of the world, though this is the most natural interpre-tation. To Mark these persecutions are a further stage of the birth-pangs that had begun with the wars, earth-quakes and famines in vv. 7–8, and the passage has a firm place within the chapter, whatever sense it may have had within the earlier tradition.

13.14–20   So much has been written about *'the abomination of deso-lation'* that anything said in a short commentary is bound to sound dogmatic, but this cannot be avoided. A new stage is introduced with *But when you see,* yet in view of the shortening of the days of distress in v. 20 and the final act of the drama in vv. 24–7 it seems that the appearance of the abomination is still part of the birth-pangs, though some think it points to the events immediately preceding the End. Almost certainly the term is derived from Daniel 12.11, and the masculine Greek verb 'standing [where he ought not]' (REB *usurping a place which is not his*) shows that some form of anti-Christ is intended. Again most interpretations are distorted by theories about the origin of the chapter and how much of it goes back to Jesus him-self. So long as we restrict our aim to recovering what Mark teaches, all is relatively clear.

Mark's aside to the reader shows that he regarded the reference to the abomination as a cryptic saying, almost a cypher, but he does not decode it. The geography is Palestinian (*those who are in Judaea must take to the hills*), and the distress would suit the Jewish War. It is impossible to know whether Mark is referring to the desecration of the Temple (Caligula ordered that his statue should be erected there in AD 40, but died before it was carried out) or its destruction (it was burned after the capture of Jerusalem by Titus in AD 70), or, indeed, if he knew of either event. The basic problem is that the kind of prediction that is found in this chapter carries its own logic, but that logic is very different from the logic of normal thought. Inevitably metaphors and pictures derived from experiences of warfare are used to describe what is believed to be the final conflict between the forces of good and evil, but this does not necessarily mean that a historical battle is excluded. The 'War Rule' from Qumran (probably written at about the turn of the eras) illustrates the difficulty very well. The weapons and tactics correspond to the art of war practised by the Romans, but the war is between light and darkness, even if it contains ideas of a holy war against the Gentiles. One scholar has argued that the phases of the battle described in the scroll are fixed in advance and its duration predetermined. As in Mark 13, no clear distinction is made between historical events and those belonging to the end-time. Terrestrial and transcendent features are intermingled. War in Palestine could well be regarded as part of events leading to the destruction of the present world order, especially as the Temple had great significance for Mark (cf. 11.11, 15–18 – and later, 15.38). As in the 'War Rule', all is predetermined and God by his divine fiat shortens the time of distress for the sake of the elect (*his own, whom he has chosen*, 13.20). The harshness of the suffering is emphasized, and if such phrases as *and will never be again* (v. 19) are more than exaggeration, they may indicate that Mark supposes that such dire suffering will not recur before the End comes. In any case Mark's idea of 'history' and the passing of time are very different from ours.

13.21–3   Although many commentators take the reference to false messiahs and false prophets as evidence that this passage comes from a different source from vv. 5–6, it is perfectly possible to trace Mark's thought through what is now a consistent whole. False leaders and prophets appear throughout the period before the End and Mark reiterates the warning against them. To meet their false teaching and the wonders they are able to perform, he declares the accuracy of Jesus's prediction: *'I have forewarned you of it all'*.

13.24–7   Then comes the final scene. With a solemn *in those days, after that distress* (introduced with a strong *But*), Mark introduces the portents in the heavens, the cosmic events that are frequently mentioned in the Old Testament and later Jewish literature of this type. REB prints vv. 24–5 as poetry. Even if there are some poetic rhythms, this should not lead us to suppose that it is a quotation or a separate piece of tradition. Commentators are divided as to whether Mark understood the language about the sun, moon and stars as figurative or literal. The present inter-pretation assumes that Mark takes everything as literal, his description indicating the break-up of the cosmos. It is perhaps unnecessary to add that this does not mean that Christians in the twenty-first century have to hold the same belief.

The sequence of events flows on remorselessly, until, finally (REB has *Then*; the Greek is 'And then'), the Son of Man comes. Scholars have debated whether the Son of Man goes up (as the Son of Man in Dan. 7.13 went up to the Ancient of Days) or comes down (from heaven). In Mark's picture it can only be that Jesus as the Son of Man descends from heaven to gather the elect and take them up to heaven. The angels are agents of the messiah and the gathering of the elect has parallels in Jewish writings. Commentators express surprise that other features from these writings, such as judgement and punishment of evil, and descriptions of the bliss of the elect are missing, and nothing further is said about the fate of the abomination of desolation, but Mark was not reproducing Jewish writ-ings. Most of this chapter seems to have come from Christian tradition, as similarities with Paul's description in 1 and 2 Thessalonians suggest. His account reaches a satisfactory conclusion with the glory of the Son of Man and the gathering of the elect.

Whether Mark constructed this discourse from isolated sayings or longer sources, or even took over a relatively complete apocalypse, the result is quite different from any other of Jesus's teaching elsewhere in his narrative. It has a unity and development lacking elsewhere. We are presented with a sequence of events in a tight framework of temporal adverbs and conjunctions, linked together with backward and forward references. This does not mean that it is alien to the rest of the book. Rather, it suggests that the events of the End were important to Mark. It probably provides the key to his thought. This is very difficult for readers today, but before we discuss this the rest of the passage must be examined.

13.28–31   The conclusion of the discourse (vv. 28–37) is more akin to some of the other collections of teaching in Mark. The structure is looser and there appears to be less concern with consistency. Yet the themes are the same. Scholars who regard the main purpose of the chapter as exhortation appeal largely to these verses. There is a repeated stress on watching. And while the suddenness of the End and ignorance about the exact time when it will come receive a certain emphasis (vv. 32, 33, 35, 36), there is no suggestion that the End lies in an indefinite, long distant future.

Assuming that Mark did not intend to set out a different view of the future from that in the main part of the discourse, it is necessary to find some overall pattern of thought. Jesus begins by telling the disciples to *'learn a lesson from the fig tree'*. 'Lesson' is 'parable' and this is the last time Mark uses the word. It has an unusual sense here, as the REB translation shows. This is perhaps why it can occur here in teaching addressed to the disciples, not the crowd. Jesus draws a parallel between the budding of the tree, pointing to the approach of summer, and the appearance of 'these things'. In a way the 'parable' is really the interpretation. REB offers a paraphrase, *'In the same way, when you see all this happening, you may know that the end is near, at the very door'*. This blurs several important features. 'All this happening' obscures the fact that the literal 'these things' points back to the same word in vv. 4 and 8. The Greek then reads, 'know that it (or he) is near, at [the] doors'. What is near is not stated. 'It' may be the final act of the drama, the coming of the Son of Man, the events in vv. 26–7, or even the whole sequence of events, everything from v. 5 to v. 27, while 'these things' (the sign that the disciples sought) may refer either to the cosmic events of vv. 24–5, or to the whole sequence of events beginning with the wars in v. 7. Alternatively 'he' may be the Son of Man, but this seems less likely. Although 'near' in relation to 'doors' is spatial, the meaning is temporal, as in our colloquial phrase. The 'sign' is the initial stage of the End, and the events foretold will occur in a relatively short space of time, for once they have begun 'it is near, at the doors'.

All attempts to avoid the obvious sense of Jesus's assertion, *the present generation will live to see it all* – the whole drama will take place within the lifetime of those present during the earthly ministry of Jesus – can only be described as evasion. This sentence, however, is making a different point from the previous one. There the close connection between the anticipatory birth-pangs and the final consummation is stressed, but no mention is made of the date when the whole sequence will begin. Here this is expressly stated, rather more emphatically than in REB: 'Amen I say to you that this generation will certainly not pass away until all these things happen'. Indeed, the prediction is reinforced by the declaration, *Heaven and earth will pass away, but my words will never pass away.*

13.32   The statement that no one knows about *that day or hour* is often thought to contradict the imminent expectation of v. 30, and therefore to be an addition to explain the delay of the End. Yet again, commentators worry over whether it goes back to Jesus or not. We retain our purpose of trying to make sense of Mark. It is true that the delay in the coming of Christ caused problems in the early Church, as can be seen from the assertion in 2 Peter 3.8–10 that the 'day of the Lord' will assuredly come, even though (or because, as an explanation of the delay) one day with God is as a thousand years. Nevertheless, it seems inconceivable that Mark should say in one breath that the Son of Man would come during the lifetime of the contemporaries of Jesus and in the next that it might be delayed almost indefinitely, or that, having laid such emphasis on the exact prediction of what was to happen and having stressed the certainty of Jesus's predictions, he should reject all attempts to discover and interpret the signs of its coming. One suggestion is that he meant something like this. The events of the end-time are predetermined by God and will occur in the way that has been described. By discerning the early stages of the sequence it will be possible for those who have been granted divine insight to recognize that the Son of Man will come very soon. This total event will happen during this generation, but the precise moment of its occurrence is known only to God. It is this combination of an imminent hope with uncertainty about the precise time that gives force to the urgent call to watch in vv. 33–7.

13.33–7   The admonitions to be watchful are as loosely assembled as the sayings at the end of several of the other collections of teaching. Commentators suggest they were added on the catchword principle and observe that there is a certain tension between the implication of a long absence of the *man away from home* and the work allotted to each servant in v. 34, on the one hand, and, on the other hand, the emphasis on the master's coming *suddenly*, and finding you *sleeping*, with the detailed four periods of the night in vv. 35–6. The contrast need not be as great as is often supposed, and is largely due to allowing our interpretation to be contaminated by the parable of the talents in Matthew 25. Treated on its own the emphasis is placed on the *door-keeper*, who is ordered to *stay awake*. To infer from the absence of the householder 'away on a journey' that Mark envisaged a long period in which Jesus would be absent from his church is to misunderstand his intention, for the sense of urgency is acute throughout the whole passage. Such a sense of urgency is hardly compatible with the idea that Jesus might come at any time in an indefinite future that stretches out for thousands of years, which Mark would not have envisaged.

No specific content is given to the command to watch (as REB mg. points out, many manuscripts add 'and pray', but even if original it hardly adds much to the very general command). Two different verbs are used, translated as *keep watch* and *keep awake* by REB. They are fairly common in the New Testament and mean little more than remaining awake and being prepared for whatever may occur and thus being ready to take any necessary action. To try to discover what Mark had in mind we have to go beyond the words themselves to his total view of the End and his ethical thinking.

In this discourse Mark has linked the prophecy of the destruction of the Temple with the prediction of an ordered and predetermined sequence of events, some historical, some transcendent, but not sharply differentiated from each other. Together they constitute the final epoch and lead to the End, the coming of Jesus, the Son of Man, and the gathering of the elect. The period of the first and last of these events is short and the time of their coming is imminent, although not precisely defined, since God alone knows when the End will be and has 'cut short' the period of distress (13.20). Christians must prepare themselves for the coming of the Son of Man: they must watch and not sleep.

Such is the drama as Jesus teaches it to the four disciples. It is now necessary to relate it to the rest of Mark's narrative.

Many scholars have insisted on maintaining a rigid separation between the Son of Man sayings that refer to the suffering and death of Jesus and those that refer to his (second) coming. However, the two themes are linked in 8.27—9.1, where Jesus is identified as the Son of Man, his sufferings, crucifixion and resurrection are foretold, Peter is rebuked, there is a call to strenuous discipleship, and a threat or promise is made that this action will be recognized when the Son of Man comes in the glory of his Father, and the tightly packed section is rounded off with the statement that some of those standing there will still be alive when the kingdom comes in power. The coming of the Son of Man must refer to his coming in the clouds with great power and glory (13.26). Further, since the coming of the kingdom of God in power follows immediately on this prophecy it must have a closely similar meaning. The Son of Man comes in the glory of his Father and this manifests to humanity the kingdom of the Father in its full power. The closeness of the link is confirmed by the statements 'there are some of those standing here who will not taste death' and 'the present generation will live to see it all' (9.1; 13.30).

Because Mark is writing between the resurrection and the future coming of the Son of Man, he cannot have regarded the two events as identical – a period, shorter or longer according to whatever date is given to the writing of the book, must have intervened. It is in this period that the disciple 'takes up his cross' and 'loses his life' for the sake of the gospel, for no disciples were caught up in the crucifixion of Jesus. The time for strenuous discipleship, therefore, is the interval between the resurrection and the (second) coming.

14.1–2   Mark makes a major break at this point. Once he has started, however, he continues with his usual linking of each paragraph by 'and'. Some commentators point to the fairly tight sequence of events and suppose that the account of the last days of Jesus's life had already taken the shape of a connected narrative before Mark wrote it down, but there is little reason to think this. In any case, this is what Mark wrote and we must presume that it represented his own understanding.

There are more differences between the Greek manuscripts in these final three chapters of Mark than in the earlier part of the book, and it is clear that in a number of places copyists have introduced phrases and sentences from the other Gospels. Some of these additions are recorded in the REB mg.

The date is precise: *It was two days before the festival of Passover and Unleavened Bread*, yet exactly what Mark means is uncertain. Originally they were separate festivals, but because the Passover was eaten on 15 Nisan and Unleavened Bread was celebrated from 15 to 21 Nisan they effectively became one. The crucifixion took place on the day before the sabbath (i.e. Friday (15.42)) and the Passover was eaten on what to us would be Thursday evening (14.12). If Mark used Roman reckoning the plotting was on Tuesday. If he was counting inclusively, and this is more likely (cf. 8.31, where Jesus declares that the Son of Man will rise 'after three days') it was on Wednesday.

The chief priests and scribes wish to avoid a riot and decide not to arrest Jesus during the festival, yet this is precisely what they subsequently do. Mark does not explain why they changed their minds, but since he makes a great deal of Judas's treachery, it may be that he thought that this provided them with an opportunity to seize him away from the crowds.

14.3–9   Mark moves back to Bethany. Jesus is now having a meal in the house of *Simon the leper*. Questions immediately arise in our minds. If Simon was still suffering from the skin disease, why was he hosting a meal? Jesus may have shown his willingness to associate with outcasts by being there, but since he was a healer, why did he not cure the man as he had cured the leper earlier in Mark's narrative? Perhaps Simon had recovered from the disease but the name stuck. Or possibly he fell victim to leprosy later. We shall never know.

The woman broke convention by coming into a meal attended only by men, and while it was usual to anoint honoured guests, her action reveals exaggerated extravagance. The perfume, which cost almost the equivalent of the wages a labourer earned in a year, was entirely used up and the flask that contained it broken. Commentators compare the widow's gift to the Temple treasury. *Some of those present*, presumably not close disciples of Jesus, are indignant. Their complaint that the money raised by the sale of the perfume might have been *given to the poor* need not be regarded as hypocritical. Jesus responds by defending the woman's action: '*It is a fine thing she has done for me. You have the poor among you always, and you can help them whenever you like; but you will not always have me*'. This does not reveal a lack of concern for the poor. Still less does it teach that no social system can be devised that will eliminate poverty. Rather the stress once again is on the shortness of the time – not before the End, but before Jesus is taken away. This is the urgency that justifies the woman's flamboyant action. If the incident is used as a defence of costly church ornaments or as a repudiation of socialist policies, it must be recognized that this was not how Mark intended it.

Jesus's defence of the woman continues: '*She has done what lay in her power* (the Greek is terse: 'What she had she did'); *she has anointed my body in anticipation of my burial*' (or, with a slightly different emphasis, 'she has anointed my body beforehand for burial'). Some have suggested that this interpretation arose out of the inability of the women to anoint the body of Jesus in the tomb after the crucifixion, but that was due to his resurrection and would hardly be the likely cause. The threat of the crucifixion casts a heavy shadow over the whole of this final section of Mark's narrative, but it had been there almost from the first.

Feminists have cavilled at the way Jesus then declares that '*what* [the woman] *has done will be told as her memorial*' but fails to give her a name, so that in effect she is denied a memorial. Mark's emphasis is upon her action, both as giving an enormously costly gift to Jesus and as anointing his body for burial. Since flasks that contained the perfume were often broken and placed beside bodies in tombs, her action may emphasize that symbolism.

'Wherever the gospel is proclaimed throughout the world' might appear to contradict the stress on the imminence and certainty of the End that appears to have been a major part of Mark's faith. If he believed that the Gentile mission would lead to the persecution that marked the beginning of the events of the end-time, the proclamation need not have lasted very long. Certainly he is unlikely to have anticipated that after 2,000 years the End would still not have arrived.

14.10–11   Mark's narrative continues with the account of Judas's agreement with the high priests to 'hand over' (REB *betray*) Jesus to them. The word is the same as in the predictions of the suffering and death of the Son of Man (9.31; 10.33) and the arrest of John the Baptist (1.14), and perhaps reflects Mark's belief that God had predetermined both the death of John and the crucifixion of Jesus. There has been much imaginative speculation about Judas's motive – he felt isolated among the other disciples and thought he deserved a more important place – he was disillusioned when Jesus failed to raise a revolt against Rome – he hoped to force Jesus's hand – it was simply for financial gain. Mark is not interested in motives and tells us nothing. What is important to him is that the divine purpose is being worked out.

14.12–16   The marked similarities with the account of obtaining the donkey (11.1–6) suggest that Mark interpreted both the entry into Jerusalem and the meal with his disciples as deliberately planned by Jesus. Even if the earlier story is explained as supernatural knowledge on the part of Jesus, here the way the disciples are to find the room where they will prepare the Passover must have been arranged by Jesus beforehand. Mark depicts Jesus as being totally in control of events and making sure that nothing prevents them happening.

Commentators spend much time discussing whether the Last Supper was a Passover meal or John's Gospel is right in dating the crucifixion on the day that the Passover animals were sacrificed. Because our aim is to discover Mark's meaning, this is irrelevant. Mark states plainly that the meal is the Passover, and there is nothing anywhere else in his narrative that necessarily contradicts it. The dating in 14.1 is easily explained as agreeing with this dating and provides no support for the Johannine account, and those who regard John as historically correct have to assume that the present statement is a late addition. There is little to support this conjecture. It does not necessarily follow, however, that Mark's identification is historically correct. We do not know.

The dating is somewhat confused. The Jewish day began at sunset, so that the first day of Unleavened Bread lasted from the evening of what we call Thursday to sunset on Friday. The Passover began at the same time, and lambs for the Passover (in fact the yearlings of either sheep or goats, Exod. 12.5), were killed on the previous afternoon, in our reckoning the Thursday afternoon. Mark appears to have mixed Jewish and Roman ideas of the day, unless he is using the terms loosely.

It is slightly odd that the action is initiated by the disciples, since everything has been arranged by Jesus and Mark stresses that he is totally in control. It was normally women who carried water in jars, so that it would be unusual to see a man doing so. The element of secrecy is a feature of the story. REB misses a key word in the message Jesus gives to the disciples. Instead of *'Where is the room in which I am to eat the Passover with my disciples'* the Greek has 'Where is my room . . .' He may be called 'Teacher', but his words have authority. The *large* room will be *set out in readiness* (literally 'spread out', meaning 'paved' or 'furnished with carpets or couches', '[and] ready'), again emphasizing that Jesus has planned everything to the last detail. As in the earlier story of the donkey, the disciples *found everything just as he had told them*. Preparing the Passover would include setting out the unleavened bread, the wine and bitter herbs, and roasting the lamb killed in the Temple in the afternoon.

14.17–21   At the beginning of the Passover festival as *In the evening* indicates, Jesus comes with the Twelve (REB adds *to the house* for clarity). Mark does not describe the Passover meal, either because he assumed that his readers would know the ritual actions or because it had no meaning for Gentile Christians at the time he was writing. He says simply that *As they sat at supper* (literally, 'as they reclined and were eating') and in a solemn declaration preceded by *Truly* ('Amen'), Jesus predicts that one of them will 'deliver him up' (REB *betray*, the word that we have met several times before, in the predictions of the death of the Son of Man (9.31; 10.33), references to Judas (3.19; 14.10–11), the arrest of John the Baptist (1.14) and the persecution of Christians (13.9, 11–12); all of these carry overtones of a destiny predetermined by God). The charge is the graver because it is one of those in the very closest friendship with him: *'one who is eating with me – one of the Twelve, who is dipping into the bowl with me'*. The common dish was part of the Passover ritual. The lament, or threat, is therefore the more severe: *'It would be better for that man if he had never been born'*. The sorrowful question, *'Surely you do not mean me?'* asked by each of them, expresses their horror and disbelief that any of them could do such a thing. (REB's paraphrase exactly gets the sense of the Greek, 'It isn't me, is it?') We might suppose that 'Who is it?' would have been a more natural reaction, but perhaps Mark's narrative indicates that they have no choice, since Jesus's fate has been foreordained.

Mark emphasizes this in Jesus's next words. REB's translation, *'The Son of Man is going the way appointed for him in the scriptures'*, brings out the sense of predestination and the emphasis on the fulfilment of prophecy. The treachery of Judas is part of the divine plan. We may find a certain tension here. Although the 'handing over' and death of Jesus are predetermined by God, Judas is so responsible that it would have been better if he had not been born. Mark quotes no Old Testament passage, and it is not easy to decide what he thought Jesus was referring to. Psalm 41.9 speaks of the way the psalmist's friend *who ate at my table* (REB; literally in both Hebrew and Septuagint, 'who ate my bread', cf. John 13.18) has now turned against him. Christians today naturally think of the servant of Isaiah 53, but there is no evidence that Mark was referring to this. Perhaps he took the phrase 'as it is written concerning him' as a way of stressing the predetermined plan that underlies so much of his description of the death of Jesus. The execution of the messiah was so completely contrary to what was expected that it must have been part of God's purpose and therefore must have been predicted in the Scriptures. But those prophecies had not been recognized or understood.

14.22–5   The account of the Last Supper differs slightly in

Matthew 26.26–9 and 1 Corinthians 11.23–6, and more markedly in Luke 22.15–20 (cf. 1 Cor. 10.16–17), while it is completely absent from John (although in John 6.48–58 Jesus speaks of eating the flesh and drinking the blood of the Son of Man). The *Didache* has preserved a tradition which is so completely different that it deserves to be quoted.

> And concerning the Eucharist, hold Eucharist (or 'give thanks') thus: First concerning the cup, 'We give thanks to you, our Father, for the holy vine of David your son, which you made known to us through Jesus your son. Glory be to you for ever'. And concerning the broken bread: 'We give you thanks, our Father, for the life and knowledge which you made known to us through Jesus your child. Glory be to you for ever. As this broken bread was scattered upon the mountains, but was brought together and became one, so let your church be gathered together from the ends of the earth into your kingdom, for yours is the glory and the power through Jesus Christ for ever.' (*Didache* IX.1–4)

Clearly words were spoken and bread and wine consumed at the Christian meetings for worship, but there seems to have been a variety of practices in different churches. Moreover, it is not clear how far the Eucharist was part of a proper meal rather than a symbolic eating and drinking as in modern services. Liturgists make much of the four actions, taking, giving thanks, breaking and sharing, but these are what the head of the family did at everyday meals (cf. 6.41; 8.6–7).

Mark may have kept closely to the tradition in his own church in his description of the Last Supper, but we do not know. We are equally ignorant of the meaning he put on the words of Jesus. The interpretations 'This is (has become) my body' and 'This represents my body' split the Church at the time of the Reformation. Many Protestant churches are now moving closer to the Roman Catholic liturgy, and, while repudiating the medieval doctrine of transubstantiation, stress the real presence of Jesus in the service. Mark knew nothing of battles that lay in the distant future, a future he did not expect to happen.

14.22   *During supper* (literally, 'And while they were eating') *he took bread, and having said the blessing he broke it and gave it to them, with the words: 'Take this; this is my body'.* Mark does not say at which point in the meal Jesus did this, or whether saying the blessing was part of the Passover rites. Although he believed the meal was the Passover, he does not seem to find in these rites an interpretation of the actions and words of Jesus.

'My body' does not necessarily mean 'my flesh', and the meaning of the symbolism may be that the symbolic action of the disciples implies that they are to share his character, in much the same way as earlier they shared his authority (3.14–15).

14.23–4   *Then he took a cup, and having offered thanks to God he gave it to them; and they all drank from it. And he said to them, 'This is my blood, the blood of the covenant* (literally 'this is my blood of the covenant'), *shed* (literally 'poured out') *for many.* REB has correctly distinguished between the two verbs, 'having said the blessing' (v. 22, cf. 6.41; 8.7) and 'having offered thanks' (as in 8.6; 'to God' is an explanatory addition not in the Greek), but this carries no great significance. This was the normal 'grace' offered before food.

Probably many readers today are so accustomed to the liturgy of the Eucharist that they fail to notice that according to Mark's account the disciples drank the wine before Jesus spoke the words, 'This is my blood'. This made it clear that the wine was symbolic and that they were not drinking blood, one of the things that was strenuously forbidden in the Law (Lev. 17.13–14; Deut. 12.15–16, 20–5). Luke records (how historically correctly it is impossible to determine) that when a group of Church leaders assembled in Jerusalem to determine the relations between Jewish and Gentile Christians, they decreed that one of the few demands of the Law that Gentile Christians were still to observe was to abstain from blood (Acts 15.29). It is still a problem for sensitive Christians today.

Commentators are naturally eager to recover the actual words that Jesus spoke, especially as v. 24 is the only other saying by Jesus that offers an explanation of his death (cf. 10.45). They copy from one another in claiming that 'my blood of the covenant' cannot be translated into Aramaic, and argue that Paul's 'This cup is the new covenant in my blood' is closer to Jesus's words, but this assumes that the

Greek phrase must be an absolutely literal translation of an Aramaic one. All that is required is to produce an idiomatic Aramaic phrase that a bilingual translator would turn into the present Greek one. One scholar has suggested that such an Aramaic phrase would read literally, 'This (is) my blood, it (is) of the covenant' (it is fascinating that REB breaks up the Greek in a similar way in the translation it offers). There is no reason for the words not to have been spoken by Jesus. Our purpose, however, is to make sense of Mark's narrative.

Some manuscripts read, 'This is my blood of the new covenant', but it is very probable that 'new' has come into the text from Luke 22.20 and 1 Corinthians 11.25. Since Mark believed that the Last Supper was a Passover meal, it would be natural to think of the covenant between Yahweh and Israel, but because the covenant is not defined as 'new' he may not have had Jeremiah 31.31–4 in mind. At any rate he does not quote the passage. Neither does he make any specific reference to Exodus 24.8, where the Sinai covenant is ratified by sacrifice and the sprinkling of the people with the blood, described by Moses as 'the blood of the covenant'. This is the only place in his entire narrative where Mark uses the word 'covenant' and it is impossible to know how he understood it. It would, however, seem a rather violent change to move from the sprinkling of blood on the people to the drinking of wine as symbolizing Jesus's blood. The significance of the word 'many' has already been discussed (pp. 131–2). 'Poured out' also occurs only here in Mark. It may well carry sacrificial ideas, but Mark makes no reference to sin, and it is precarious to suppose that he had in mind later Christian ideas of Christ's death as an atonement for the sin of the individual.

In later Jewish celebration of the Passover four cups of wine were drunk, and some scholars place the bread at the beginning of the meal and identify the cup as the last of the four cups of wine. Mark, however, places the two sayings together.

14.25   The final words of Jesus are, *Truly* ('Amen') *I tell you: never again shall I drink from the fruit of the vine until that day when I drink it new in the kingdom of God.* Those familiar with modern liturgies may be surprised that he did not say, 'Do this in remembrance of me'. Luke places these words after Jesus broke the bread and gave it to his disciples (Luke 22.19, though there are textual problems), while Paul has, 'This cup is the new covenant sealed by my blood. Whenever you drink it, do this in memory of me' in his account of the tradition he says was handed on to him (1 Cor. 11.25). Mark, however, gives no indication that Jesus expected the meal to be repeated by his followers. He probably took Jesus's words to refer to the image of the kingdom as a messianic banquet. They fit in with his expectation of the coming of the kingdom of God in the near future. (Again we may notice that the phrase is '*in* the kingdom of God'. Even if the idea is that of God inaugurating his authoritative rule, this involves the creation of a new society, though whether on earth or in heaven is not made plain.) Some commentators suggest that Jesus expected the disciples to carry on his work during the period between the resurrection and his (second) coming, when he would be absent from the world. More probably the prediction expresses in picturesque and forceful language the central feature of the events described in chapter 13. This is the last meal that Jesus will have with his disciples before the coming of the kingdom, which will soon arrive. Moreover it fits the deterministic thrust of the entire narrative. From now on Jesus will act as God has predetermined. Before he drinks the cup in the kingdom he has another cup to drink. The delay of the End, however, largely drains the sentence of its practical meaning for readers today.

14.26   REB has imposed an interpretation upon the next sentence: *After singing the Passover hymn*. The Greek has simply 'having sung', but since Mark understood the meal to be a Passover, he may have thought of the singing that took place in the Passover rites. Those interested in what may have happened historically suggest that Psalms 114–18 were sung. Mark makes no reference to them.

14.27–31   Prediction presupposes predestination. Even if Jesus could have escaped, he chose not to do so, for God had decreed the sequence of events. Here is one of the rare direct quotations of Old Testament prophecy in Mark. Jesus predicts that the disciples will all '*lose faith* (the verb is 'stumble' as in 4.17 and 6.3); *for it is written: 'I will strike the shepherd and the sheep will be scattered'*. The text is from Zechariah 13.7. The Hebrew reads, 'Strike the shepherd that the sheep may be scattered'. Septuagint manuscripts vary, some being close to the Hebrew, others having 'I will strike', which in Mark's narrative further stresses the sense that everything is happening according to God's purpose. Mark continues with another prediction of the resurrection, this time with an important addition: '*I shall go ahead of you into Galilee*'. The verb can mean 'go in front' 'lead', as in 10.32, and some think that Jesus meant that he would gather the scattered sheep and lead them into Galilee. It is more natural, however, to take it as meaning that Jesus will be in Galilee before the disciples get there.

Peter reacts violently: '*Everyone else may lose faith, but I will not*'. Jesus replies with the prediction: '*before the cock crows twice, you yourself will disown me three times.*' Peter responds by declaring that he is prepared to die with Jesus. We recall that Jesus had said that his followers must be prepared to take up their cross and follow him (8.34). In the event they all fail, and none is required at this point to die with Jesus. That will come in the persecutions that lie ahead. Even though a large number of manuscripts omit 'twice', it is probably what Mark wrote. His emphasis is placed on the prediction and its subsequent exact fulfilment, showing that the divinely purposed plan marches inexorably on, and there is a hint that the fate that met John the Baptist and Jesus will be that of Christian disciples as well.

14.32–42   REB produces a vivid account of the events in *a place called Gethsemane*. Again Peter, James and John are singled out to be closest to Jesus and are told to 'be on the alert' (rather than the bland *stay awake*). The command was given twice in the account of the events leading up to the End (13.35, 37), and here it signals that some final event is approaching. *Horror and anguish overwhelmed him* hits the mood exactly, but '*My heart is ready to break with grief*' misses an allusion to death. The Greek is literally 'my soul is deeply grieved unto death.

Although he knows that his fate has been determined, Jesus still prays that he may escape. The *hour* is another of the words found in chapter 13, where it is the hour of persecution (13.11, REB 'when the time comes') and of the End (13.32). Yet again the events leading up to the crucifixion are tinged with the sense of finality. The part of the prayer that Mark quotes begins with the Aramaic word for Father. Aramaic was Jesus's mother tongue and he naturally used it in prayer to God. At one time scholars claimed that it was the equivalent of the way a child calls its father 'Daddy', but it has now been shown that, while it was a little unusual as a form of address to God, it was not unique, and certainly had a wider use than only by small children. The *cup* represents suffering, as in 10.38, but coming so soon after the account of the Last Supper it perhaps casts its shadow (or light) on the Eucharist.

When Jesus returns to the three disciples and finds them asleep, it is to Peter that he addresses his reproach, *'Could you not stay awake for one hour?'* The following imperatives are in the plural, indicated in REB by the addition of *all of you*. *'Pray that you may be spared the test'* is literally 'that you may not enter into temptation (or testing)'. The noun is found only here in Mark, but he used the verb of Jesus's being tempted by Satan (1.13), as well as of the way opponents came to 'test' Jesus (8.11; 10.2; 12.15, REB 'trying to catch me out'). To us the words recall a familiar petition in the Lord's Prayer, but Mark does not record that prayer in his narrative. He probably linked the 'testing' with the period of persecution that preceded the End. The excuse that Jesus makes for their failure, *'The spirit is willing but the flesh is weak'*, has become proverbial, but the exact meaning that it had for Mark is uncertain. It may have had the sense that it has for us, contrasting human frailty with what we truly desire to do and be. On the other hand, this seems somewhat feeble in the context of the struggles that precede the End, and Mark may have intended to show that in the persecution and other disasters more was needed than merely a determination to stand firm, contrasting Peter's bold assertion with his failure now (and later).

The scene is repeated twice more, but the last time Jesus makes it clear that the die is now cast. The meaning of his words, however, is very uncertain. REB's terse *'Still asleep? Still resting? Enough!'* represents two verbs that may be taken as questions, statements or commands, and a third verb of unknown meaning. Most translations translate the verbs as questions. As statements the sense would be similar. If they are commands the meaning would either be ironic or indicate that Mark supposed that Jesus had ended his struggle to accept the cup and no longer needed his disciples to keep awake and alert. In this case *Up, let us go!* means that Jesus suddenly spots the arrival of Judas and the armed band. 'Still' is a false rendering of a Greek phrase, which, however weakened its sense, always looks to the future rather than the past. The sense is probably, 'Are you going to continue sleeping?', when the last events are about to happen. The third verb must fit both this and the following *'The hour has come'.* Jerome took it to mean 'it is enough', and most translations follow him. Other suggestions are: 'it is paid up' (i.e. either Judas has received the money, or the time is up) and 'Is it far off?' (i.e. is the hour still a long way ahead?). Most commentators take the meaning of the 'hour' from the next statement, *'The Son of Man is betrayed* ('handed over') *into the hands of sinners'.* Jesus's prophecy of the death of the Son of Man is about to be fulfilled. To Mark, however, the hour has close associations with the end of the world and the coming of the kingdom, and he may have taken this to be the beginning of the final events. In any case the sense of the playing out of a predetermined plot is plain. The mention of 'sinners' may seem odd. In 2.15–17 'sinners' are linked with tax-collectors as those with whom Jesus has table fellowship. In 8.38, however, Jesus calls the present generation 'adulterous and sinful', and here the word indicates the sharp contrast Mark makes between good and evil, the kingdoms of God and of Satan.

14.43–6   The narrative proceeds so swiftly and is so straightforward that little comment is needed. It is usual to emphasize Judas's villainy – *one of the Twelve, the traitor,* who had *agreed on a signal,* and told the Jewish authorities to *seize* the man and *get him safely away,* a signal that involved addressing Jesus as *Rabbi* and giving him the common greeting, though the Greek makes it plain that he overdid the *kiss.*

14.47–50   Mark states that it was *one of the bystanders* who attacked the high priest's servant. The later Gospels embellish the incident (Matt. 26.51–4; Luke 22.49–51; John 18.10–11), but it has a very minor place in Mark's narrative, and he does not say that the bystander was one of the disciples. Since it has no significance in Mark's account it may be another sign that Mark put in his book all the traditions that he knew.

Jesus then addresses the crowd that had come to seize

him. *Robber* is the same word that Jesus used in his attack on those selling pigeons and changing money in the Temple (11.17), but there is no reason to suppose that Mark drew any connection between the two events, even though he quotes Jesus as referring to the time when he taught in the Temple. 'Robber' probably has overtones of violence, and the term came to be applied to terrorists. Possibly Jesus means that they have arrested him as if he were one of the Jewish freedom fighters engaged in terrorism against Rome.

For Mark the key statement is *'But let the scriptures be fulfilled'*. REB gives a slightly wrong feel to the words, which would be better translated as 'the scriptures must be fulfilled' (cf. CEV, 'But what the scriptures say must come true', and NJB, 'But this is to fulfil the scriptures'). Once again Mark emphasizes that everything that is happening is part of the divine purpose and has been foretold in Scripture.

Then the disciples all (Greek, 'And they all') *deserted him and ran away*. Jesus said that his arrest was to fulfil the Scriptures (v. 49; cf. v. 21), but Mark's account describes how it was the prediction of Jesus (v. 27, itself referring to Scripture) that was fulfilled.

14.51–2   These two verses have intrigued most readers of Mark's narrative, and attempts have been made to identify the *young man*. Mark tells us nothing. Often imagination has led to the idea that he was Mark himself, who slipped out of his family's house, where the Last Supper is supposed to have been held, and followed Jesus and his disciples. This, it is thought, would explain how he knew what happened in Gethsemane and what words Jesus used. Or it is supposed that he came to warn Jesus of the plot, but arrived too late. Others suggest that Mark contrasted the faithfulness of the young man in staying behind with the desertion of the disciples. Others again find parallels to the resurrection narrative, pointing out that the body of Jesus was wrapped in a 'linen cloth' (15.46, the same Greek term), which Jesus left in the tomb (but only Luke 21.12 and John 20.5–6 say this and both have a different Greek word for the grave clothes; in any case the other Gospels should not be used to interpret Mark) and that the 'young man' who spoke to the women in the tomb was wearing a 'white robe' (another different Greek word), or linked him with the young man (the same word) in the tomb (16.5). It has even been suggested that there is a hidden symbolism pointing to the way converts took off their old garments and put on new white ones when they were baptized. Perhaps it is another example of the way Mark included every bit of tradition, even if it had little meaning in the story he was narrating.

14.53–72   This long section needs to be read as a whole, even though it divides fairly easily into several incidents, since only in this way does its full meaning become apparent.

14.53–4   Jesus is taken to the *high priest's house*, but Mark's main interest at this point is fastened on the way Peter *followed him at a distance right into the high priest's courtyard*, and joined the servants around the fire.

14.55–9   There has been much debate about the legitimacy of summoning a meeting of the Sanhedrin, the Jewish supreme *Council*, in the middle of the night. Mark either knew nothing of the later rules recorded in the *Mishnah*, which declared that in capital cases the trial had to be conducted and the verdict reached in the daytime (m. Sanh. 4.1), or the legal rules did not concern him. Whether the Jews had authority to put anyone to death has also been debated by scholars, as has the part played by the Jewish leaders in securing the death of Jesus. Mark was not interested in these questions either. The tradition as he received it stated that the Sanhedrin met and examined Jesus. After *many* had given *false* and contradictory *evidence*, the charge is brought that he had said, *'I will pull down this temple* (not Mark's usual word for the Temple), *made with human hands, and in three days I will build another, not made with hands'*. The words are not found in any of the teaching that Mark records, although Jesus prophesies the total destruction of the Temple in 13.2 ('these great buildings'). Once more, commentators, intent on deciding historical probabilities, turn to the other Gospels and wonder what words spoken by Jesus might lie behind the charge. Mark simply adds that *their evidence did not agree* and passes on to the condemnation of Jesus for blasphemy. This perhaps implies that it also was a false charge. Since, however, the desecration of the Temple marked a major phase in the events of the End (13.14), and Jesus had predicted its total destruction, Mark certainly believed that the Temple would be 'pulled down' (the same word as 'thrown down' in 13.2), though he does not appear to envisage the building of a heavenly temple when the kingdom of God arrived.

14.60–4　　The high priest decides to bring matters to a head, first by attempting to get Jesus to reply to the accusations, and then by directly asking *'Are you the Messiah, the Son of the Blessed One?'* Commentators, focusing on historical issues, point out that to address such a question to the accused was contrary to the rules in the *Mishnah*, and also wonder if its form owes something to later Christian ideas. We continue to stay with Mark. Surprisingly Jesus not only declares that he is the messiah but also enlarges on his messiahship, substituting the title Son of Man as he had done after Peter declared that the disciples believed he was the messiah: *'I am, and you will see the Son of Man seated at the right hand of the Almighty and coming with the clouds of heaven.'* The reply echoes Psalm 110.1 and Daniel 7.13, but is not a direct quotation. Some scholars have argued that Jesus meant that the members of the Sanhedrin will come to realize that these prophecies have been fulfilled in him, and since Daniel 7.13 refers to the Son of Man coming to God rather than coming from heaven, Jesus was not referring to the (second) coming. Given his beliefs about the End, it seems certain that Mark understood the words as a prophecy of the (second) coming of Jesus. He identified the Son of Man with Jesus, and he included an elaborate picture of the events leading up to the end of the world in his narrative. It is as the Son of Man, the son of God, that Jesus is put to death, and at the crucial moment the secrecy is stripped away. His final vindication will be his being seated alongside God when the kingdom is finally established.

Wherein the blasphemy consists is also debated. According to the *Mishnah* only pronouncing the name of God constituted blasphemy. Probably Mark held that the high priest took the crime to be claiming to be the messiah. Less likely is the suggestion that the words 'I am' was taken to be an expression of the divine name. REB paraphrases the Greek but gives the sense. The high priest *tore his robes*, a sign of grief and a recognition of guilt, and, in response to his question, the *judgement* of the members of the Sanhedrin *was unanimous: that he was guilty and should be put to death.*

14.65   Mark continues 'And some began to spit at him'. This may imply that those who did this were members of the Sanhedrin, but not necessarily. Historically minded commentators wonder if the Jewish leaders would fall into such despicable conduct, and suggest that the *attendants* carried out the mocking (as in Luke 22.63), but Mark seems to distinguish between the two groups. Many manuscripts add varying phrases after '*Prophesy!*': ['now], [Christ], Who is it who hit you?' (cf. mg.), taken from Matthew 26.68 and Luke 22.64. This is a good example of the way the other Gospels influenced copyists and underlines the importance of reading Mark on its own. In Mark 'Prophesy' means 'Speak as a prophet now' (possibly the mockery looks back to the prophecy about the Temple), whereas in the other two Gospels it means 'Tell us who hit you'.

14.66–72   The Jews ask Jesus to prophesy: Mark continues his narrative by describing how his prophecy about Peter was exactly fulfilled, down to the double crowing of the cock. It is true that a large number of manuscripts omit *and a cock crowed* in v. 68 (cf. REB mg.), and a small number of manuscripts omit *for the second time* in v. 72. The other Gospels say nothing about the double crowing of the cock, but this is no reason for supposing that Mark did not mention it. Indeed, it would fit perfectly with Mark's ideas about prophecy and the unfolding of a predetermined plot. We need to be careful about describing Peter's bursting into tears as repentance, for this was not Mark's main concern.

15.1–5   Mark's narrative rushes on rapidly. 'And immediately early in the morning' the Jewish authorities either *made their plans* or, more probably, 'held a council'. Those commentators eager to grasp historical fact suggest that the meeting in the night was an informal preliminary hearing, but Mark appears to think of two meetings of the Sanhedrin. They *hand* Jesus *over* to Pilate, the Roman prefect. The verb is the one Mark has used of Jesus's predictions of his arrest – the predetermined plot proceeds relentlessly. Pilate first asks Jesus outright, '*Are you the king of the Jews?*' Jesus's words in reply, 'You say', may accept the title, but more probably evade giving an answer, as REB's '*The words are yours*' interprets them. In response to *many charges* brought by the Jews, Jesus remains completely silent (the Greek is emphatic).

15.6–15   It is difficult for us to avoid interpreting Mark in the light
of the other Gospels, and differences among the manuscripts at several points suggest that copyists had the same
problem. It is vital to look closely at what he actually says.
According to the narrative, Pilate has already decided that
Jesus is guilty, but offers the crowd an opportunity to
release him. Whether there was a custom of freeing a prisoner at the time of Jewish festivals is a historical question
that worries commentators, but it may be passed by.
Mark's story depends on there actually being such a custom. Mark does not say that Pilate offered the crowd a
choice between the two prisoners, Barabbas, one of the
group of terrorists who had committed murder, and Jesus.
Since he mentions Barabbas first and then says that the
crowd arrived asking to have a prisoner released, he probably intends his readers to suppose that they had come to
ask that Barabbas should be set free. Pilate, knowing that *it
was out of malice that Jesus had been handed over to him*, asks if
they would like him to release *the king of the Jews?* (The
Greek word that REB translates 'malice' is the normal
word for envy, and most modern translations have 'jealousy'. The envy would be because of Jesus's influence over
the crowd. There are variations between the manuscripts,
but REB is probably wrong to take 'had been handed over'
impersonally and omit the reference to the chief priests as
those responsible.) The chief priests incite the crowd to ask
for Barabbas, and Pilate, a little surprisingly, then asks
what they wish him to do to *the man you call king of the Jews*
(again there are differences between the manuscripts,
some omitting 'whom you call'). The crowd shouts back,
'Crucify him!' Pilate then asks *'What wrong has he done?'*,
implying that he regards him as innocent, but the crowd is
insistent that he should be crucified. *So Pilate, in his desire to
satisfy the mob* (there is no change of word in the Greek; it is
still 'the crowd'), *released Barabbas to them*. He then *had Jesus
flogged* and *handed him over* (that verb again) *to be crucified*.
It is an odd sequence of events.

Clearly this is an attempt to place all the blame on the
chief priests and other Jewish leaders, yet Mark does not
flinch from showing that the decision to crucify Jesus was
Pilate's alone. Pilate's actions, however, are also part of
the fulfilment of the events that had been foretold and are
part of God's purpose.

177

15.16–20   Mark is intent on showing that Jesus was crucified as king of the Jews. It was the name Pilate had used when he questioned Jesus and when he tried to get the crowd to ask for his release. Now the soldiers use it in mockery. The crown of thorns is perhaps an imitation of the crowns found depicted on coins from the time and may not have been intended as an additional torture. Mark presents Jesus as the king he truly was, dressed in royal purple and crowned.

15.21–7   REB makes a break in the middle of v. 20, but Mark's narrative moves swiftly on, almost every sentence beginning with 'and'. Prisoners had to carry the cross-beam of their cross. The soldiers compel a chance passer-by, *Simon from Cyrene, the father of Alexander and Rufus*, to do this. Commentators have speculated on why Mark has named him so elaborately and whether the man's sons were known to Mark's readers. Had they, indeed, become Christians? Does Mark find meaning in the fact that Simon 'takes up the cross' as Jesus told his followers they would have to (8.34)? He does not tell us. Some scholars find, underneath the anguish and humiliation, Jesus depicted as enthroned as king on the cross, but Mark does not make it explicit and it is yet another of the things we do not know about Mark and his book.

The crucifixion takes its normal course. Mark would almost certainly have witnessed Roman executions and knew the procedure. That Jesus rejected the drugged wine may be a sign that he accepted the divine cup of suffering in its place, but again Mark barely hints at it. Scholars have often linked the statement that the soldiers 'cast lots' for Jesus's clothes, with Psalm 22.18, suggesting either that the psalm influenced the way the death of Jesus was told, or that the crucifixion fulfilled the Old Testament prophecy. Several of the words are the same in the Septuagint, but Mark does not give any indication that he made the connection or wishes his readers to do so. He is more concerned to show that the prediction of Jesus was fulfilled, for this was the predestined divine purpose.

The time of the crucifixion is exactly noted. The *charge against him* was written on a board attached to the cross, and reiterated the fact that it was as *The King of the Jews* that he was put to death. The two *robbers* crucified with Jesus were almost certainly terrorists like Barabbas. Is there any significance that it was these two men who were placed at the right and left hand of Jesus, the seats of honour that James and John asked for (10.37)? Perhaps, but Mark again is silent. Since the Romans executed by crucifixion only rebels, slaves, and the very worst criminals, he may have meant to show that, by crucifying him as a messianic pretender, Pilate revealed, as the demons had done, who he really was.

15.28   Scholars are almost unanimous that this verse (relegated to the mg. by REB) is a later addition to Mark's original narrative, and comes from Luke 22.37. It is found in many manuscripts but is absent from those reckoned to be the earliest and best. The passage quoted is Isaiah 53.12. All the main modern translations, including even the conservative NIV, omit it from their main translation. Mark, in contrast to the other Gospels, includes hardly any references to Scripture in his narrative.

15.29–32   The mocking continues, now by *passers-by*. REB provides a vivid picture, but obscures some important features of the narrative. *Jeered at him* is 'blasphemed' or 'slandered' (cf. 3.28). Although 'jeered' is an adequate translation for what was in effect shouting insults, Mark's word carries overtones of Jesus's divinity. *'Bravo!'* represents an exclamation of indeterminate sense, often expressing amazement. The word occurs only here in the New Testament. The accusation that Jesus said that he would destroy the Temple and build it again in three days recurs (cf. 14.58). Many scholars think that this is further evidence that Jesus must have said something that led to this allegation. *'Save yourself and come down from the cross'*, would be a lesser miracle than destroying and rebuilding the Temple. If he could do the one, as it was alleged he claimed, he ought to be able to do the other.

The *chief priests and scribes joined in* (the verb represents an adverb, 'likewise', 'in the same way'), *jesting with one another* (the verb means 'to ridicule', 'to mock', as in 10.34 and 15.20; REB has been influenced by 'to one another' and 'with the scribes', and misses the exact fulfilment of Jesus's prophecy). *'He saved others, but he cannot save himself'* sounds like a theological statement and has often been taken to express the heart of the Christian message. Only by refusing to save himself and dying for others could Christ save them. Whether Mark was aware of the kind of irony that is found in John's Gospel is uncertain, but the following words, *'Let the Messiah, the king of Israel come down now from the cross. If we see that, we shall believe'*, emphasizes that it is as the messiah that Jesus was executed. *Even* (Mark has simply 'And') *those who were crucified with him taunted him.* Yet again Mark must be taken on his own and the embellishments in the other Gospels pushed from our minds. The Greek word means 'to revile', and Mark simply adds the statement, without explaining why they should insult Jesus. It has been suggested that they asked him where his God was now, but this is sheer imagination.

15.33–9 Mark's account of the death of Jesus is stark in the extreme.

He does not explain what meaning he attached to the three hours of darkness. To attempt to explore his mind is pointless, and to relate it to Old Testament prophecy such as Amos 8.9 and to see in it a symbol of judgement is speculative and probably alien to Mark's way of thinking.

The only words that Jesus speaks are in Aramaic, and Mark translates the prayer for his readers, *'My God, my God, why have you forsaken me?'* Much is usually made of the fact that these are the first words of Psalm 22, and Mark's translation follows the Septuagint apart from a slightly different form of 'why?', but Mark gives no indication that this had any special significance for him. Common interpretations follow one of two lines: some stress the depths to which Jesus went in order to save humankind and see in the words the cost of bearing sin; others suggest that the whole of the psalm was in his mind and note that the psalm ends in triumph and confidence. Both are beside the point when we are trying to interpret what Mark actually wrote. The only natural way of understanding the words is that Jesus believed himself abandoned by God, whom he no longer addresses as Abba.

The words are misunderstood by *some of the bystanders* as an appeal to *Elijah.* Presumably they did not have a firm grasp of Aramaic, even though Mark appears to have taken them to be Jews. Some think the mistake shows that Jesus quoted the psalm in Hebrew, in which 'My God' is closer in sound to 'Elijah', but this once again is to turn away from Mark and ask what actually happened. One of these bystanders *soaked a sponge in sour wine*, the common wine drunk by soldiers and other poor people, and offered it to Jesus, saying, *'Let us see if Elijah will come to take him down.'* This is the earliest evidence for the idea, attested in later writings, that Elijah would come to the help of those in need. Commentators troubled by historical difficulties suggest that two traditions may have been combined, one containing the reference to Elijah, the other describing how a Roman soldier offered Jesus wine, seen by Christians as the fulfilment of Psalm 69.21 (the word translated 'sour wine' is the same in the Septuagint). To Mark it is a continuous story and any symbolism is hidden. He may have expected his readers to remember that Jesus had earlier identified Elijah with John the Baptist and said that he had already come – and been killed (9.11–13).

Then Jesus gave a loud cry and died. Mark's Greek is as terse as REB's translation. Throughout this section of his narrative he hardly wastes a word but describes the death of Jesus in as succinct, almost brutal, a way as can be conceived, in spite of his euphemistic 'expired, breathed out his life or spirit', rather than the stark 'died'. Unlike the other Gospel writers, he depicts Jesus as abandoned by God and in utter anguish. Only now does he introduce two features that may possibly reveal something of the meaning it had for him.

The curtain of the temple was torn in two from top to bottom. Mark does not suggest that the statement is meant to be symbolic. He continues with his usual 'And', and describes the event as bald fact. The curtain is probably the one that separated the innermost sanctuary (the 'Holy of Holies') from the main Temple chamber ('the Holy Place'), although some commentators take it to be the one that covered the entrance of the Holy Place. Three types of interpretation are usually offered: it actually happened, it is a legend that became part of Mark's tradition at some point, and Mark intended the words as a theological comment without supposing that the curtain in the Temple was actually torn. Theologically it is seen either as opening the way into the inner sanctuary that previously only the high priest could enter, or as a sign of the destruction of the Temple that Jesus had foretold. The imagery lies behind such passages as Hebrews 9.11–12, 24–8 and Ephesians 2.14, but is hardly intended by Mark, who had referred to the destruction or desecration of the Temple (13.2, 14;

14.57–8; 15.24). As always he remains enigmatic and mysterious. The alleged prophecy in 14.57–8 is described as 'false evidence', and the prediction in 13.2 is linked to the events preceding the End. Elsewhere Mark expresses a more positive attitude towards the temple as 'a house of prayer for all nations' (11.17), which Jesus defends.

When the centurion who was standing opposite him saw how he died (some manuscripts have 'how he cried out and died'), *he said, 'This man must have been* (literally, 'was truly') *a son of God.'* This is the only place in this entire episode where Mark offers any explanation – and that comes from a Roman soldier!

Yet how extraordinary it is! We soften it by subconsciously substituting a harmony of the Gospels for Mark's stark narrative and hearing in our minds the other words spoken by Jesus on the cross: 'Father, forgive them' (Luke 23.34), 'Today you will be with me in Paradise' (Luke 23.43), 'Mother, there is your son' (John 19.26–7), 'I am thirsty' (John 19.28), 'It is accomplished' (John 19.30), 'Father, into your hands I commit my spirit' (Luke 23.46). Even in Matthew, who keeps closest to Mark's account, it is the earthquake and the raising of the saints from the dead (which Matthew alone describes) that fill the centurion with awe and provoke his words (Matt. 27.51–4). In Mark, Jesus speaks only one sentence from the cross and dies uttering a loud cry.

Without the words spoken or thought by the centurion the story would most naturally be read as a total discrediting of Jesus's messianic claims, and a refutation of the Christian message. What in all this grim scene could possibly induce a Roman soldier to see in this executed terrorist 'a son of God'? Imagination may offer suggestions – Jesus's failure to curse those nailing him to the cross and mocking him as he hung there, perhaps. Less likely is the supposition that he saw the splitting of the curtain. Mark says only, 'When the centurion . . . saw how he died'.

In the mouth of a pagan centurion 'son of God' would have meant a semi-divine man, a demi-god. There is no article in the Greek, but then there is no article in 1.1, though there is when an unclean spirit (3.11) and the chief priest (14.61) use the term. Perhaps, therefore, we should not place too much emphasis on the lack of the article here. For Mark these are possibly the most important words in his entire narrative. Without a doubt, he understood what the centurion said as a recognition that Jesus was the Son of Man, the son of God. Whether he read an even greater meaning into the words than this we cannot know. Some suggest that he saw the centurion as the representative of those Gentiles who would later acknowledge Jesus as the son of God. Some even think that Mark intended the words as a confession of the Christian faith in a semi-credal way. Today we might possibly think of the centurion in Karl Rahner's phrase as an 'anonymous Christian', a man of another faith who was a Christian at heart, but Mark could not have held this attitude to members of non-Christian religions.

15.40–1 The disciples were mentioned for the last time in Mark's narrative in 14.50 and Peter in 14.72. They do not appear again.

But there were women *watching* the crucifixion *from a distance*, among whom Mark names *Mary of Magdala, Mary the mother of James the younger and of Joses, and Salome*. This is the first time Mark speaks of any of them, and he gives no more information about them than this. It is useless to search in the other Gospels for further information, for Mark may well not have known it, although he expects his readers to recognize both the women and James and Joses. What he does confide is that these women were disciples (*followed him*) and provided for his needs (*looked after him*, literally, 'served him') in Galilee, and that there were many other women as well. Many recent writers point out that apart from this statement we would not have known that many of Jesus's disciples were women and that he depended on them for food and shelter.

15.42–7 By his statement that *evening had come* Mark appears to mean that it was drawing near, for he describes the burial of Jesus as taking place before the sabbath, and the sabbath began at sunset on the day we call Friday. Why Mark says that it was the *day of preparation* is not clear, especially as he has to explain the term for Gentile readers. Commentators concerned with historicity point out that Mark believed that the Passover was on the Friday, which was therefore a holy day, and suggest that this is further evidence that the crucifixion took place on the day before the Passover, and claim that Jesus would not have been buried during the Passover. Whatever the facts, Mark's narrative is consistent. Presumably he believed that burial of the dead was permitted during the feast. The Law required that dead bodies should not remain hanging overnight (Deut. 21.22–3) and this was especially important on the sabbath. Josephus says that 'Jews are so careful about funeral rites that even malefactors who have been sentenced to crucifixion are taken down and buried before sunset' (*War* IV.5.2 [317]). Joseph of Arimathaea may have acted out of piety. His actions do not necessarily imply that he was a disciple. Yet Mark's comment that he was waiting for the kingdom of God and the fact that he buried only Jesus, taking considerable care of his body, suggest that he was at least well disposed to his teaching. Mark points out that his action in asking Pilate for the body of Jesus was courageous. Criminals who had been crucified often took several days to die, and the Romans are unlikely to have been sympathetic to what they regarded as Jewish superstition. He also says that Pilate gave permission after ascertaining that Jesus was dead. It is possible that this was included in the tradition to make it clear that Jesus had actually died. He adds that *Mary of Magdala and Mary the mother of Joses were watching and saw where he was laid*, perhaps simply to prepare for the continuation of his narrative in the next chapter, but possibly to remove any suggestion that the women went to the wrong tomb on the day after the sabbath.

16.1–8   There is a pause for the sabbath, but Mark's narrative flows on: [And] *when the sabbath was over*. The three women who watched Jesus being crucified come to anoint his body. Two of them had seen the stone rolled to seal the rock-tomb and naturally are worried about getting it removed. They look up and see that it has been rolled back and they go *into the tomb*. There they *saw a young man sitting on the right-hand side, wearing a white robe*. Mark neither explains how he supposed the stone had been moved, nor offers any suggestion as to who the young man might be. On the face of it he is a human being, but the fact that the women were *dumbfounded* (the verb translated 'overcome with awe' in 9.15 and 'horror . . . overwhelmed him' in 14.33) suggests that they regarded his appearance as uncanny. To call him an angel, however, gives a wrong impression in our culture today. Mark thinks of him as a divine messenger. The young man's exhortation, '*Do not be alarmed'* (the same verb), is followed by two important statements, *'He has been raised'* and *'he is not here'*, and a command, *'But go and say to his disciples and to Peter: "He is going ahead of you into Galilee; there you will see him, as he told you."'* 'As he told you' looks back to 14.28 (cf. 8.31; 9.31; 10.33–4). Mark again emphasizes the fulfilment of Jesus's prediction, including the promise that he would 'go ahead' of them (or 'lead them') 'into Galilee', but the promise, 'There you will see him', is new. He is not troubled that, if only the Twelve were present at the Last Supper, the women must have found it a strange message.

They, however, *ran away from the tomb, trembling with amazement* (the word was used in the story of Jairus's daughter, 5.42), and, most strangely, *They said nothing to anyone, for they were afraid.* Although Mark occasionally uses the word of religious awe, usually it means ordinary fear, and that is the meaning here.

At this point Mark's narrative breaks off. REB conceals this by making no break before the next paragraph (but cf. mg.), and produces what is plainly nonsense, for *And they delivered all these instructions briefly to Peter and his companions* flatly contradicts the very strong statement that the women said nothing at all to anyone in the previous sentence.

Before discussing Mark's account of the resurrection it will be best to consider, very briefly, the various attempts that were made by early copyists to 'complete' Mark's book.

1a. The older English translations continued with what is numbered as vv. 9–20. The passage is not in Mark's style and seems to have been compiled on the basis of the other Gospels, though it has some unique features. It is found in most surviving Greek manuscripts, although both Eusebius and Jerome noted that it was absent from many Greek manuscripts known to them. It is omitted in the two best manuscripts that have survived, as well as in one Latin manuscript and the oldest manuscripts of the Syriac and Armenian translations. In some other manuscripts it is accompanied with various marks showing that the copyists were doubtful about parts or all of it. Because it does not follow naturally on v. 8, some scholars think that it was not written specifically to continue Mark's narrative but was originally an independent account of the resurrection appearances of Jesus. For the incidents taken from the other gospels see the following parallels: v. 9 (Matt. 28.9–10; John 20.11–18; Luke 8.2); v. 11 (Luke 24.11); vv. 12–13 (Luke 24.13–35); v. 14 (Luke 24.41–3); vv. 15–16 (Matt. 28.19; Luke 24.47; Acts 1.8); vv. 17–18 (for exorcisms cf. Acts 5.16; 16.17–18; 19.12; for speaking in strange tongues cf. Acts 2.4; 1 Cor. 14; for handling snakes cf. Acts 28.3–6; for healing cf. Acts 5.12–16; 9.12, 18; 28.8–9; early Christian writers give other accounts of these activities); v. 19 (Luke 24.50; Acts 1.2, 9–11); v. 20 (cf. Luke's account of the spread of the gospel in Acts).

1b.   Jerome says that some Greek manuscripts had an addition after v. 14, which he quotes in Latin. This has survived in one Greek manuscript, and may be translated as: 'And they defended themselves, saying, "This age of lawlessness and unbelief is under Satan, who by means of unclean spirits does not allow the true power of God to be understood; wherefore reveal your righteousness now". They were speaking to Christ; and Christ replied to them: "The limit of the years of Satan's authority has been fulfilled, but other dreadful things draw near, even for those for whom, because they had sinned, I was delivered up to death in order that they might return to the truth and sin no more, in order that they might inherit the spiritual and incorruptible glory of righteousness which is in heaven"'. The Greek is as awkward as the English, and is plainly corrupt in at least one place. It seems to have been added to soften the criticism of the disciples.

2a.   One Latin manuscript has just the two sentences that REB adds at the end of v. 8, without the present vv. 9–20.

2b.   A few Greek manuscripts add these two sentences before vv. 9–20, producing what is the REB text.

2c.   Three of these manuscripts add a note after the two sentences and before they continue with vv. 9–20: 'This also is current'.

In this short commentary there is no space to comment in detail on these passages. What they show is that later copyists were dissatisfied with a Gospel that ended with the women saying nothing to anyone, and believed that it was essential to include some account of the appearances of the risen Christ. Our intention is to try to understand Mark's own book.

The first problem is to decide whether Mark intended to end his narrative at this point. At one time most scholars thought that this was incredible. To end a book with 'They said nothing to anyone, for they were afraid' seemed impossibly abrupt, even more so in the Greek. They wondered how Mark could possibly have failed to give an account of the resurrection appearances of Jesus, especially as he emphasized on two occasions that Jesus would 'go ahead' of the disciples into Galilee (14.28; 16.7), for it would leave one important prediction unfulfilled. Moreover, they assumed, though not always explicitly, that Mark must have known some resurrection appearances of Jesus, for the other Gospels and Paul mention them – he was a Christian believer after all. So they suggested either that Mark was prevented from writing any more because he suffered the martyrdom that he had so often warned his readers about, or that the end of his manuscript has been lost through some mishap. Matthew and Luke differ markedly in their accounts of the resurrection after Mark 16.8, despite the claim made by some scholars that Matthew and Luke knew the continuation of Mark's narrative. It seems fairly certain that the version of Mark that these Gospel writers knew ended at this point, and it is not possible to reconstruct his 'lost ending' from the later Gospels.

More recently several scholars have argued that Mark deliberately ended his narrative with the silence of the women, and offer several suggestions as to what he meant. One is that Mark was telling his readers that they had now to 'go into Galilee' to meet Christ. Whether he appeared to Peter and the other disciples is irrelevant. They must meet Christ and become his disciples for themselves. This, it is claimed, is fully in accord with Mark's attitude throughout his book, where he stressed that only those who are willing to believe will understand. It has been pointed out that Mark ends his narrative with 'two pieces of non-evidence' – a message delivered to women, whose words would have no value within the ethos of their society and who in any case failed to pass it on, and Jesus's promise to his disciples that they would see him in Galilee, which is not fulfilled in Mark's Gospel. All the responsibility is placed on Mark's readers, who must accept the words of Jesus on trust and become Christians through faith. Another commentator emphasizes the fear that the women shared with all the disciples who deserted Jesus and fled, and relates this to the fears that were current in the Christian community for whom Mark was writing. Mark ended his narrative in this way to teach them that their community existed solely because of the initiative of God. The disciples failed, the women failed, all human beings fail. But God succeeds. Against such interpretations it has been argued that they are too sophisticated and 'modern', and are totally out of keeping with anything that Mark would have met in his own society.

It is impossible to know whether Mark ended his narrative with the silence and fear of the women, or continued it in some way – perhaps by recounting an appearance by Jesus himself to the women when he reiterated his command to them, though Mark implies that they never said anything to the disciples. Judging from what we have discovered about Mark's narrative, such a continuation would have had to get the disciples to Galilee in some way so that Jesus could appear to them there, for Mark believed that all of Jesus's predictions were fulfilled. Imagination can roam freely over our total ignorance but cannot dissipate it. We do not know whether Mark wrote (or intended to write) anything more, and we shall never know.

What has become clear as we have followed his narrative from the prophecy that predicted the coming of John the Baptist to the message that the young man gave to the women and their running away from the tomb in terror and silence is that for Mark the suffering and death of Jesus are part of the predestined events leading to the End, and the resurrection is only an anticipatory victory. The final victory is the coming of the kingdom of God and appearance of the Son of Man. And that, he believed, would come soon.

MARK'S PORTRAIT OF JESUS

The portrait of Jesus that Mark paints is puzzling. At least, it would be puzzling if we did not subconsciously touch it up with features drawn from the other Gospels. After reading Mark's narrative as a continuous story we are now ready to examine that portrait as Mark drew it.

No one can read the book without being struck by the emphasis that Mark places on the authority with which Jesus speaks and acts. He is a travelling exorcist and healer, but stands apart from other exorcists in his power to drive out demons from men and women. He also possesses the power to quell the storm demon, to walk on the lake, and to turn a few loaves into feasts for vast crowds. He has the authority to forgive sins. He is addressed as 'Teacher', and his teaching is said to be 'with authority'.

When the Jewish leaders asked Jesus by what authority he was acting he refused to give an answer. How did Mark envisage that authority?

In Mark's portrait, Jesus forbids the demons to speak because they know who he is, and what they declare when they do speak is 'You are the Son of God', or 'son of the Most High God'. In a slightly different way one of them says, 'I know who you are – the Holy One of God'. Whether Mark wrote 'the son of God' in the very first sentence of his narrative or not, it is what he believed. When Jesus was baptized a voice came from heaven and said to him, 'You are my beloved Son'. When Jesus's appearance was wondrously changed on the mountain, a voice spoke out of a cloud, telling the disciples, 'This is my beloved Son'. Mark probably interpreted the parable of the tenants as an allegory in which the owner of the vineyard represents God, and the son is set apart from the servants who are the Old Testament prophets. In his account of the events leading up to the end of the world, Jesus says that only the Father knows the precise time when it will happen, no one else does, not even 'the Son'. The high priest put the direct question to Jesus, 'Are you the Messiah, the Son of the Blessed One?', to which Jesus replied, 'I am'. Finally, when the centurion who was on duty at the crucifixion saw how Jesus died, he said, 'This man was truly a son of God'.

What did Mark understand by the term 'the son of God'? It is far from obvious, for 1,900 years of Christian dogma stand between us and Mark. In every communion service many Christians recite the Nicene Creed: 'We believe in one Lord, Jesus Christ, the only Son of God, eternally begotten of the Father, God from God, Light from Light, true God from true God, begotten, not made, of one Being with the Father . . . For us and for our salvation he came down from heaven, was incarnate of (or from, translations vary) the Holy Spirit and the Virgin Mary and became truly human.' The rolling phrases were put together to block off what the orthodox regarded as heresy. Mark did not know the Nicene Creed, and would not have understood it if it could have been shown to him. No less important for Christian doctrine is the Chalcedonian Definition: 'Jesus Christ is . . . One and the same Son, the Self-same Perfect in Godhead, the Self-same Perfect in Manhood; truly God and truly Man . . . acknowledged in Two Natures unconfusedly, unchangeably, indivisibly, inseparably'. For us the difficulty is to look at Mark's portrait without wearing the blinkers of later doctrinal debates and beliefs that we have learnt to regard as the foundation of the Christian religion.

It is difficult to trace the development of the understanding of Jesus within the New Testament, though some have tried. The words, 'the son of God', would certainly have had a very different meaning for Mark from what they have to us who live on the other side of the Nicene Creed. But how different? The translators of REB reveal the difficulty. They waver between a capital and small 's' for 'son', possibly in an attempt to distinguish different ways they think the speakers understood the word. Yet to use a capital at all gives the word the overtones of the later creeds.

In the Old Testament 'son of' had a range of meanings, from being the normal physical offspring of one's parents to belonging to a group or class of people, as in 'the sons of the prophets' (2 Kgs. 2.15 and elsewhere, REB has simply 'prophets'). 'Son of God' did not necessarily carry the sense of divinity. The king could be called God's son (2 Sam. 7.14; Ps. 2.7; cf. Ps. 89.27), and so could Israel (Exod. 4.22; Jer. 31.9; Hos. 11.1). In the Wisdom of Solomon in the Apocrypha the righteous man is counted among the sons of God (Wisd. 5.5; cf. Sir. 4.10; 51.10). In both the Old Testament and later writings 'sons of God' are heavenly beings (Gen. 6.2, 4, REB 'the sons of the gods'; Deut. 32.8; Job 1.6, 2.1, REB 'the members of the court of heaven'; Ps. 29.1, REB 'you angelic powers'). In rabbinic tradition Honi the circle-drawer (first century BC) was said to pray 'like a son of the house' (i.e. a son of God in heaven), and a heavenly voice addresses Hanina ben Dosa (late first century AD) as 'my son'. The fact that Mark uses 'Jesus Christ' as a proper name and speaks of him as 'the son of God' probably shows that Christians by his time no longer thought of Jesus as a travelling healer and teacher, but they were still far from thinking of him as the pre-existent 'Son' who is 'of one Being with the Father' and came down from heaven in an incarnation.

How does this relate to Peter's reply to Jesus's question, 'And you, who do you say I am?' Peter said, 'You are the Messiah'. Again we are faced with the difficulty of knowing what Mark supposed Peter meant. Judging from the writings that have survived from the time, 'messiah' was understood in several different ways. Drawn from the figure of the king in ancient Israel, who was sacrosanct as Yahweh's 'son', the idea of a future king who would rule over the Jews after defeating their enemies and giving them back their independence and freedom, grew up in the centuries before the coming of Jesus. Sometimes this messiah was pictured as a human military leader, sometimes as a heavenly being. Sometimes he was immortal, sometimes he died like any other man. He does not seem to have been thought of as divine in our sense. At the time of Jesus it was the idea of a military leader against the Romans that was dominant in most people's minds. The question then arises, did Mark believe that Jesus was the messiah? And if so, what kind of messiah?

What is striking about Mark's narrative is that Jesus never volunteers that he is the messiah. Usually it is spoken by other people, and often Jesus weakens and transforms it in some way. He responds to Peter's declaration, 'You are the Messiah', first by giving strict orders not to tell anyone about him, and then by substituting the term 'the Son of Man'. In a similar way he accepts the high priest's question but immediately replaces 'messiah' with 'the Son of Man'. He rejects the teaching of the scribes that the messiah is 'a son of David', but it is not clear if he also denies that he is the messiah. In his account of the events leading up to the End, he predicts that 'impostors will come claiming to be messiahs or prophets' (the Greek speaks of 'false christs' and 'false prophets'), so that if anyone says 'Look, here is the Messiah' do not believe it. It is in mockery that the chief priests and scribes declare, 'Let the Messiah, the king of Israel, come down now from the cross. If we see that, we shall believe'. Possibly Jesus deliberately claimed to be the messiah when he entered Jerusalem to the cries of the crowd, 'Blessed is the kingdom of our father David which is coming', but Mark does not mention the actual term. It seems that Mark felt that 'the messiah' did not properly explain who Jesus was.

According to Mark the term that Jesus accepted was 'the Son of Man'. Much of the scholarly debate about the term is concerned with its origins and the meaning it had for Jesus himself. The Aramaic behind the Greek would normally be taken as 'a human being', and specialists are able to offer hundreds of examples. It also appears to have been used idiomatically to refer to an individual or a group, or to the speaker himself. What is certain is that the phrase 'the Son of Man' is a literal translation – and literal translations usually fail to express the overtones and idiomatic uses of the original. Either Mark or an earlier translator must have taken a conscious decision to retain this literal translation where they thought it referred to Jesus. Mark himself almost certainly understood it as a title for Jesus, in much the same way that he took Jesus Christ as a proper name. He gives no hint that he knew any of the earlier ideas about the Son of Man that scholars are eager to trace. The only times he connects Old Testament prophecy with the Son of Man are 9.12–13 and 14.21, which speak of the suffering that the Son of Man is to endure, and the fact that he is 'going the way appointed for him in the scriptures'. There is no prophecy of the suffering of the Son of Man as an individual in the Old Testament or later Jewish writings, so that it is no wonder that Mark does not quote one. What is important in Mark's portrait of Jesus is what happened to the Son of Man.

Scholars usually divide the Son of Man sayings into three types according to whether they refer to: (a) his sufferings, death and resurrection (8.31; 9.9, 12, 31; 10.33–4, 45; 14.21, 41), (b) his future coming (8.38; 13.26–7; 14.62), and (c) his present activity (2.10, 28). The statements possess their own meaning and do not require the addition of any background ideas that the term might have carried. In the second group of sayings Jesus seems to make a distinction between himself and the Son of Man, but this is illusory. Mark believes that Jesus was the Son of Man. Historically minded commentators suggest that it may come from a wrong translation of Jesus's Aramaic. Whether the translator was mistaken in thinking that the reference was to Jesus in 2.10 and 28 has been discussed in the commentary.

In Mark, Jesus is addressed as 'Rabbi' by Peter (9.5; 11.21) and Judas (14.45), and as Rabbouni by Bartimaeus (10.51, REB 'Rabbi'). More frequently Mark uses the Greek translation, 'Teacher'. Usually it is a term of address – by John (9.38), the sons of Zebedee (10.35), 'the disciples' (4.38) and 'one of the disciples' (13.1), the father of the boy with an unclean spirit (9.17), the rich man (10.17, 20), the Pharisees (12.14), the Sadducees (12.19) and a scribe (12.32). Jairus's servants describe Jesus as 'the teacher' (5.35), and Jesus instructs the two disciples sent to prepare for the Passover to say to the householder, 'The Teacher says . . .'(14.14).

Rabbi may have had a wider meaning than it has today, and part of this honorific sense may have carried over to the Greek 'teacher'. Yet, sparse though it may appear in comparison with the other Gospels,

Jesus's teaching was important to Mark. He distinguished between the teaching addressed to the crowds – cryptic and in 'parables' – and that given to the disciples – plain and explanatory, even though they often failed to understand it. Besides this teaching Mark recorded a considerable number of aphorisms, set within short narratives, and he seems to have regarded these as examples of the authority with which Jesus taught and his ability to silence all his opponents and questioners. We may find it strange that Mark speaks of Jesus giving teaching on several occasions without stating what that teaching was, and it may be that the tradition that Mark knew contained so little teaching by Jesus that he had nothing to include on these occasions. He seems to have included every scrap of teaching that he knew, putting isolated sayings where he thought most suitable.

As we have seen, one of the most striking features of Mark's narrative is the large number of exorcisms and miracles he records. While they are found mainly in the first half of his book, they are not totally absent from the second part, and since much of that section is taken up with conflicts between Jesus and various opponents, leading to the lengthy account of his arrest, trial and death, it is not surprising that so few occur there. Mark, like his contemporaries, accepted that all the miracles happened exactly as he describes them, and he made no distinction between the exorcisms, healings, and 'nature miracles'. The Jesus he portrays has authority over the demons, over disease, and over wind and waves. He is aware that other exorcists and healers practised their art, but he makes it clear that Jesus stood out as possessing greater authority and power. Those who witnessed the miracles are amazed, even terrified. Mark regarded the reaction of the onlookers as emphasising this authority. The wandering exorcist and healer who possessed enormous authority is a major feature of his portrait of Jesus.

It has been suggested that Mark's purpose was to combat a theology that depicted Jesus as a 'divine man' and wonder-worker by setting against the picture of Jesus as the worker of miracles that of the one who suffered and died on the cross. This can hardly be right when so much of the narrative is taken up with exorcisms, healings and nature miracles. Nevertheless, even though Mark's narrative runs smoothly on, there seems to be a division into two parts at 8.27. After Peter has declared that the disciples believe that Jesus is the messiah, Mark includes a greater amount of teaching, much of it given privately to the disciples, and some limited to the inner circle of Peter, James and John (together with Andrew in ch. 13). The predictions of Jesus's death and resurrection all occur in this part of the book. The hostility of the Pharisees and other Jewish leaders increases, though it is foreshadowed as early as 2.6 – and more definitely in 3.6. The pattern of persecution – John the Baptist, Jesus, the later followers of Jesus – is made clear by Jesus's statement that Elijah had already come and suffered as the Scriptures foretold and Mark's account of John's death at the hands of Herod, and by the question to James and John, whether they can drink the cup that he had to drink and be baptized with his baptism. It underlies the whole narrative, which is shot through with a strong sense of divine predestination. This much is clear, but two questions still need to be considered.

The first concerns the purpose of Jesus's death. It is vitally important not to allow the teaching of other parts of the New Testament and later Christian doctrine to affect our understanding of Mark's narrative. Only two statements by Jesus make any reference to the reason why God's purpose predestined him to be crucified, the 'ransom' passage (10.45) and the words spoken at the final meal with his disciples (14.22–5). Both have been discussed in the commentary, and it is necessary only to repeat that neither teaches that Jesus's death was a sacrifice to atone for the sins of individual human beings. Whatever Mark thought the purpose of Jesus's death was, it was not an atoning sacrifice, a vicarious punishment, or a substitute for the death that sinners deserved. In view of the death of John the Baptist and Jesus and the future suffering of Christian followers of Jesus, which form a threefold pattern of suffering and death, it seems much more likely that Mark thought of it as a martyrdom, but a martyrdom that had an important effect on the coming of the kingdom, and perhaps on the relation between God and Israel, though how it achieved this is not explained.

How far, then, did Mark depict Jesus as a servant? This is the theme in 10.41–5, but does not appear plainly elsewhere. Jesus tells his disciples 'among you, whoever wants to be great must be your servant, and whoever wants to be first must be the slave of all', but there is no suggestion that in this they are directly imitating him. Those who receive a child receive both him and the One who sent him, but this does not imply that Jesus is humble like a child. Mark's Jesus is a powerful figure, and Mark lays great emphasis on his authority. He has not come as a servant. It is the strong who are able to submit to martyrdom, as Mark warns his readers. It is not sufficient to have a willing spirit. It is those who endure to the end who are saved. Those who wish to find a paradox of authority and servanthood in Mark do so only by treating martyrdom as embracing the role of a servant, and this is not Mark's view. Only in 10.45 does Jesus say that the Son of Man came to serve. So isolated is this saying that we must wonder if Mark included it because it was part of the tradition current in his church, although he did not fully hold to it himself.

The second question is how Mark understood the future coming of the Son of Man. We have seen the importance that Jesus's prediction of the events leading to the end of the world and the coming of the Son of Man had for Mark. In the longest continuous body of teaching (13.5–37) Jesus presents the framework within which the whole drama has to be played out. It does not stand alone. The coming of the Son of Man is the moment when the kingdom of God is realized, and it will be in the near future. Those who are ashamed of Jesus will discover that the Son of Man is ashamed of them 'when he comes in the glory of his Father with the holy angels' (8.38). After his final meal, Jesus will not drink wine again until he drinks it in the future kingdom (14.25).

It is also the only framework within which the rigorist ethic of Jesus is explicable. This strenuous ethic of the total denial of self and giving up everything for the sake of the kingdom of God is feasible only within the short period before the end of the world. Even if the teaching to the crowd and the aphorisms that Mark quotes as showing the authority of Jesus and the way he can overcome all his enemies are treated as ethical teaching, the picture is not greatly altered. The additions are few. The sabbath is made for human beings and the Son of Man has authority over it, so that necessary actions on the sabbath are defended (2.23–8). The distinction between clean and unclean animals is abolished (7.19). Divorce is absolutely prohibited (10.11–12). Caesar may be paid what is his, but God must be given what belongs to him (12.17). The two commandments are more important than offering sacrifice – and the *Shema'* comes first (12.29–31). Even though the ethical commandments within the Decalogue are to be kept, selling everything and giving to the poor are vital for the disciple (10.21). These all fit into that short period before the End comes.

It must be repeated that Mark takes the account of the final events literally. Jesus, as the Son of Man, will be put to death, will rise from the dead, will meet the disciples in Galilee and, after a short period in which the gospel is proclaimed to all the nations, will return, this time 'in the clouds with great power and glory' and gather those whom he has chosen. This is no idiosyncratic view of Mark's. Paul sets out a broadly similar scheme in 2 Thessalonians 4.13—5.11, which is also to be taken literally, as is 'the end' in 1 Cor. 15.24–8, 51–7 (cf. 2 Thess. 2.1–12).

Jesus Himself

Many readers of this commentary will doubtless have become increasingly irritated that I have insisted on attempting to understand what Mark wrote and fastened on the picture of Jesus that he painted. Should we not be focusing our attention on Jesus himself?

If only we could! The problem is that Mark's picture is all that we actually possess – alongside the pictures that Matthew, Luke and John give us, and a few sketches from what have come to be called apocryphal gospels. How, then, can we recover the man behind the portraits?

Traditionally, the way has been to harmonize the four Gospels. But this can do no more than produce a composite portrait, in which differences have been smoothed away, often by refusing to admit that they exist.

Some years ago the attempt was made to recover the genuine teaching of Jesus by applying a set of tests. It was argued that sayings which are found in more than one strand of tradition (Mark, the source claimed to lie behind the material common to Matthew and Luke, and the teaching recorded by only one of the Gospel writers) has a greater claim to authenticity than that found in just one strand. It was also argued that sayings found in more than one type of material (parables, sayings embedded in stories, isolated sayings) are more likely to go back to Jesus himself than that preserved in just one type. Most importantly, it was maintained that teaching which was unique to Jesus – which differed from contemporary Judaism and the beliefs and practice of the early Church – had a greater claim to come from Jesus himself. It is now realized that these tests fail. Genuine sayings may have survived in only one place and type of teaching, while the last test is too powerful. It assumes that Jesus was not a man of his time and implies that he exerted no influence on his followers.

More recently attention has been directed to the language in which Jesus almost certainly gave his teaching, Aramaic. The publication of most of the scrolls and fragments discovered in the caves by the Dead Sea has enabled scholars to come much closer to the dialect of Aramaic spoken in Palestine in the time of Jesus, and it is now realized that what needs to be done is not to translate Mark's Greek into Aramaic but to reconstruct Aramaic sayings that would lead a translator to produce the sentences that are found in the Greek Gospels. The result is to produce a much more 'Jewish' Jesus than has usually been accepted by Christians, and also to strip away much of the later doctrinal developments. Jewish writers have also been active in providing their own insights into the teaching of Jesus. Certainly by returning to Jesus's native language a firmer base for recovering the historical Jesus has been created.

This approach has been useful in interpreting individual pieces of teaching. It may well be that Jesus used the term 'the Son of Man' in a general sense, meaning 'man' (human being), an individual or a group, as well as referring to himself. Thus it has been plausibly proposed that in 9.11–13 the Son of Man was not a title for Jesus, as Mark took it to be, but referred to Elijah in the first place, yet included over-tones of the suffering and death of Jesus as well. In 10.45 Jesus is not marking off his own death sharply from that of his followers, and 'the Son of Man' referred to James and John, and less directly to the other disciples, as well as to Jesus. On this understanding, it has been claimed, the whole passage develops the idea of service not that of a substitutionary death for sinners. An Aramaic saying may well have lain behind Jesus's words during the last meal, probably a Passover, that Jesus held with his disciples.

One issue that is of considerable importance is whether Jesus him-self accepted the imminent end of the world, a theme that runs right through Mark's narrative. It seems that he did, despite the efforts of several scholars to limit the belief to later Christian thought. There seems no reason to question several of the prophecies of the coming of the kingdom of God in the near future that Mark records, such as 'There are some of those standing here who will not taste death before they have seen the kingdom of God come with power' (9.1) and 'Truly I tell you: never again shall I drink from the fruit of the vine until that day when I drink it new in the kingdom of God' (14.25). The second is especially important, for Jesus tells his disciples that they will not drink together again until the kingdom comes, which presupposes that God will establish his kingdom soon. It also implies that the death of Jesus will make this possible.

In the end, however, we have to be reconciled to the fact that all that we actually possess as direct evidence are four portraits of Jesus painted by the four Gospel writers, each different, and that a 'photo-graphic' picture of the man who walked the roads of Palestine cannot be recovered. I hope that this commentary will have revealed Mark's portrait a little more clearly.

Christianity Today

One last question remains. If we have recovered Mark's portrait of Jesus at all correctly, what is to be made of the Christ of the creeds and the Chalcedonian Definition? Put in another way, is the later doctrine false to the way Jesus was seen by his first portrait painter?

The answer to these questions goes beyond the scope of this short commentary, but they must be faced and an answer, however inadequate, attempted.

The problem is partly a matter of culture, partly philosophical and partly religious.

Culture

Mark's world was very different from ours. This is seen most obviously in his attitude to the miracles and in the predetermined scheme of history that he believed would end very soon with the coming of the Son of Man and the establishing of the kingdom of God (in the double sense of God's authoritative reign and the society over which he rules). While we may be prepared to accept a psychosomatic explanation of some of the healing miracles, we do not explain mental illness as possession by unclean spirits and we regard turning a few loaves and fish into a hearty meal for a large crowd and the ability of a human being to walk on the surface of a lake as impossible. Those Christians who accept all the miracles literally are in effect treating Jesus as a god come down to earth. As for the coming of Jesus in the near future, even if some claim to believe this, they do not conduct their affairs on this basis. Planning for the future is built into the way we run our lives, with our career ambitions and pension schemes. Moreover, we find ways of getting round the plain teaching of Jesus that following him is a matter of all or nothing, and when an enthusiast sells all his possessions and gives the money away, as a man I know did, we regard this as brave but irresponsible. In our more tolerant age with our concern for animal rights we are offended by Jesus's attitude to the Syro-Phoenician woman and the death of the pigs. Mark's portrait will not fit into the frame within which we live our lives.

Philosophy

Some seek to resolve the problems that the differences of culture create by fastening on the question that Professor L. Hodgson asked: 'What must the truth be, and have been, if it appeared like that to men who thought and wrote as they did?' It is a useful question to consider, but we must wonder how far it is possible to arrive at a satisfactory answer. We are less confident than Hodgson was that 'the truth', abstract, transcendent and absolute, exists, or how it can be discovered even if it does. And if we look to the fashionable hermeneutics to provide the way, we should heed Dennis Nineham's warning that all too often hermeneutics is little more than an attempt to make out of the biblical writings something that it is possible to believe within today's secular and scientific society. Some of us remain historians at heart, and cannot abandon the attempt to think back imaginatively to past ages, and even as we recognize that we are foreigners in that strange land, at least we make an effort to learn the language, believing that it is important to do so. This is why I have tried to recover the portrait that Mark has painted and the frame in which he put it.

Religion

The religious quest remains. Here the 'after-life' of the text comes into its own. The influence of Scripture – for evil as much as for good – has come almost entirely from the power of this after-life. The Bible has had an influence not because of what the words meant to the original writer, but from the way they were taken by Christians in later times. The medieval Church fastened on the cry of the Jews in Matthew's Gospel, 'his blood be on us and on our children' (Matt. 27.25), saw the whole Jewish race as 'God-killers', and embarked on the policy of persecution, only held back from time to time by economic necessity. Martin Luther read Paul's quotation from Habakkuk, 'the righteous shall live by faith' (Hab. 4.4; Rom. 1.17; REB takes it in a different way from Luther), found release from his fear of judgement, and broke away from a religion of penance and indulgences. The South American finds in the story of the Exodus inspiration for pursuing a fight for liberation. It is the after-life of the text that preachers seize on as they write their sermons and that individuals look for as they read their daily Bible passage.

It might appear, then, that this commentary is beside the point, and I can appreciate the disappointment of many readers who looked for the life-giving water of a spiritual commentary or a commentary for the oppressed and underprivileged and found only the dry sand of a historical search.

Yet surely what Jesus actually said and did matters supremely. The meaning and purpose of his life are of central importance if the Christian faith is to be believed and the Christian way followed. Recovering Mark's portrait is the necessary first step towards discovering the historical Jesus. Now we need to set alongside that portrait the portraits that Matthew and Luke painted. But that is beyond the scope of this commentary.